OCR GCSE

History A
Schools History Project

Medicine Through Time

Bill Marriott   Paul Shuter   Bob Rees

www.heinemann.co.uk
✓ Free online support
✓ Useful weblinks
✓ 24 hour online ordering

01865 888080

Official Publisher Partnership

OCR AND HEINEMANN ARE WORKING TOGETHER TO PROVIDE BETTER SUPPORT FOR YOU

Heinemann is an imprint of Pearson Education Limited, a company incorporated in England and Wales, having its registered office at Edinburgh Gate, Harlow, Essex, CM20 2JE. Registered company number: 872828

www.heinemann.co.uk

Heinemann is a registered trademark of Pearson Education Limited

Text © Pearson Education Limited 2009

First published 2009
Second edition © Nigel Kelly, Bob Rees, Paul Shuter 2002
New materials © Pearson Education Limited, Paul Shuter 2009

13 12 11 10 09
10 9 8 7 6 5 4 3 2 1

British Library Cataloguing in Publication Data
A catalogue record for this book is available from the British Library

ISBN 978 0 435501 40 2

Edited by Ruth Nason
Proofread by Soundproofs Freelance Proofreading
Designed by Pearson Education Limited
Typeset by Wearset Ltd, Boldon, Tyne and Wear
Produced by Wearset Ltd, Boldon, Tyne and Wear
Original illustrations © Pearson Education Limited 2009
Illustrated by Alasdair Bright, David Atkinson and Wearset Ltd
Cover design by Pearson Education Limited
Picture research by Q2AMedia
Cover photo © Phisick http://www.phisick.com
Printed in Italy by Rotolito Lombarda S.p.A.

Acknowledgements
We would like to thank Ronald Finucane, University Distinguished Professor of Oakland University, for his help with the illustrations of pilgrimage; Constantine K. Christakos for his help with photographs of Ephesus; Keith Davies of the Freud Museum for his help with Freud's Egyptian medical artefacts; Wilf Matos from Robert Harding World Imagery for his determination in tracking down Source A on page 52; and Simon Watts for his translations of classical inscriptions.

p20 Source S Extract from A.G. Dowell *Village Life in Ancient Egypt: Laundry Lists and Love Songs* 1999 Clarendon Press. By permission of Oxford University Press; **p24 Source A** Ray Porter *The Greatest Benefit to Mankind: A Medical History of Humanity* 1997 HarperCollins Publishers Ltd; **p30 Source H** From *Greek Medicine* by E.D. Phillips 1973 Thames and Hudson. Reprinted by kind permission of Thames and Hudson Ltd, London; **p37 Fact File** From Vivian Nutton 'Healers in the medical market place: towards a social history of Graeco-Roman medicine', in Andrew Wear (ed.) *Medicine in Society: Historical Essays* 1992 Cambridge University Press; **p51 Source A** M. Alexander *Earliest English Poems* 2006 Penguin; **p51 Source B** W.O. Hassall *They Saw it Happen 55 BC–1485* 1956 Blackwell; **p101 Source H** Reprinted with permission from *Chem. Eng. News*, June 20, 2005, 83(25), p116. Copyright 2005 American Chemical Society; **p103 Source J** From E. Grundmann *Gerard Domagk: The First Man to Triumph Over Infectious Diseases* Lit. Verlag, Germany 2006; **p107 Source N** Letter by Sir Almroth Wright, published by *The Times* 30 August 1942; **p107 Source O** The Royal Society, Ref HF/1/3/4/3/1; **p111 Source Q** N. Cecil 'MRSA: a bug's rife' in the *Sun* 25 June 2001; **p127 Source J** L.M. Zimmerman and I. Veith *Great Ideas in the History of Surgery* 1993 Jeremy Norman Co.; **p129 Source L** Rita Donovan *As for the Canadians: the Remarkable Story of the RCAF's 'Guinea Pigs' of World War II* 2000 Buschekbooks, pp18–19.

The author and publisher would like to thank the following individuals and organisations for permission to reproduce photographs:

p2L Russell Knightley/Science Photo Library; **p2R** The Natural History Museum/Alamy; **p3** Herbert Kraft/akg-images; **p4** Science Museum/Science & Society; **p5** BARC, Archaeological Sciences, University of Bradford; **p6** E.O. Hoppé/Corbis; **p7** TopFoto; **p9** Science Museum/Science & Society; **p10** SCPhotos/Alamy; **p11** Paul and Jane Shuter; **p12** Egyptian/Freud Museum, London, UK/The Bridgeman Art Library; **p13** Egyptian 18th Dynasty (c.1567–1320 BC)/University Library, Leipzig, Germany/Archives Charmet/ The Bridgeman Art Library; **p14** Roemer-- und Pelizaeus-Museum, Hildesheim; **p15** Paul and Jane Shuter; **p17L** Wellcome Images; **p17R** Werner Forman Archive; **p19** Science Museum/Science & Society; **p19** Paul and Jane Shuter; **p23** Greek School (4th century BC)/Private Collection/ Ancient Art and Architecture Collection Ltd./The Bridgeman Art Library; **p24** (2nd century AD)/British Museum, London, UK/The Bridgeman Art Library; **p26** bpk/Antikensammlung, Staatliche Museen zu Berlin; **p27** ACE STOCK LIMITED/Alamy; **p28** Musée du Louvre/Maurice and Pierre Chuzeville, courtesy of the Department of Antiquities Greek, Etruscan and Roman; **p33L** Late 1st century/early 2nd century (marble)/© Ashmolean Museum, University of Oxford, UK/The Bridgeman Art Library; **p33R** Paul and Jane Shuter; **p35T** Paul and Jane Shuter; **p35B** Paul and Jane Shuter; **p36T** Paul and Jane Shuter; **p36B** Paul and Jane Shuter; **p37L** Roman/ Rome, Italy/Ancient Art and Architecture Collection Ltd/The Bridgeman Art Library; **p37R** York Archaeological Trust; **p38T** Paul and Jane Shuter; **p38ML** Paul and Jane Shuter; **p38MR** Paul and Jane Shuter; **p38BL** Paul and Jane Shuter; **p38BR** Paul and Jane Shuter; **p39T** Roger Coulam/Alamy; **p39B** English Heritage Photo Library; **p40** Paul and Jane Shuter; **p41** Paul and Jane Shuter; **p42T** Paul and Jane Shuter; **p42B** Paul and Jane Shuter; **p49** St Edmundsbury Borough Council/West Stow Anglo-Saxon Village Trust; **p52** Robert Harding; **p54** Angelo Hornak/Corbis; **p56** Bodelain Library, University of Oxford aqi0002_25MB; **p57B** The Bridgeman Art Library; **p58R** Syndics of Cambridge University Library; **p58B** akg-images/Erich Lessing; **p59** The Bridgeman Art Library; **p61T** Trinity College, Cambridge; **p61B** French School (13th century)/Bibliotheque Nationale, Paris, France/The Bridgeman Art Library; **p63** INTERFOTO Pressebildagentur/Alamy; **p64** INTERFOTO Pressebildagentur/Alamy; **p66T** Bodelain Library, University of Oxford aes0213_25MB; **p66B** Bildagentur-online/Alamy; **p69** Glasgow University Library, Department of Special Collections; **p70** British Library; **p71** Bettmann/Corbis; **p72** Wechtlin, Hans or Johannes Ulrich (c.1480–c.1526)/Private Collection/Archives Charmet/The Bridgeman Art Library; **p75** CuboImages srl/Alamy; **p76** akg-images; **p77** Bettmann/ Corbis; **p79** German School (16th century)/Private Collection/The Stapleton Collection/The Bridgeman Art Library; **p81L** Wellcome Images; **p81R** The Bridgeman Art Library; **p83** Corbis; **p84** akg-images/Erich Lessing; **p90** Wellcome Images; **p91** Hulton Archive/Stringer/Getty Images; **p96** Medical-on-Line/Alamy; **p97T** Mary Evans Picture Library/Mary Evans ILN Pictures; **p97B** Stefano Bianchetti/Corbis; **p98** Mucha, Alphonse Marie (1860–1939)/Musee Pasteur, Institut Pasteur, Paris, France/Archives Charmet/The Bridgeman Art Library; **p100** Everett Collection/Rex Features; **p102** Private Collection/The Bridgeman Art Library; **p104** Martin Bond/ Science Photo Library; **p105** St Mary's Hospital Medical School/Science Photo Library; **p108** www.CartoonStock.com; **p110** Frederick (1846–1896)/ Private Collection/The Stapleton Collection/The Bridgeman Art Library; **p111T** National Army Museum, London/The Bridgeman Art Library; **p111B** English School (19th century)/Private Collection/The Bridgeman Art Library; **p118** Thomas (1756–1827)/Private Collection/The Bridgeman Art Library; **p119** Bettmann/Corbis; **p120** Wellcome Images; **p121T** John Greim/Science Photo Library; **p121BL** 81A Productions/Corbis; **p122** Bettmann/Corbis; **p123** Hulton-Deutsch Collection/Corbis; **p124** Wellcome Images; **p125** Bettmann/Corbis; **p126** National Library of Medicine/Science Photo Library; **p127T** Canadian War Museum; **p127BL** Francois Mori/ Associated Press; **p127BR** CHU Amiens/epa; **p128** Bettmann/Corbis; **p129** Bettmann/Corbis; **p130** Deep Light Productions/Science Photo Library; **p131** Cuishing/Whitney Mediac Historical Library; **p132** 2008 ACT Health, Australian Capital Territory; **p141T** Bettmann/Corbis; **p141B** Wellcome Images; **p142** Wellcome Images; **p145T** Science Photo Library; **p145B** Rischgitz/Stringer/Hulton Archive/Getty Images; **p146** www.punch.co.uk; **p147** Topical Press Agency/Stringer/Hulton Archive/Getty Images; **p148** Mary Evans Picture Library; **p150** Mary Evans Picture Library; **p151** www. punch.co.uk; **p152** K.J. Historical/Corbis; **p153** Illingworth, Leslie Gilbert/ National Library of Wales, Aberystwyth; **p154** www.punch.co.uk; **p161** Wellcome Images; **p172** Bettmann/Corbis; **p174** Bettmann/Corbis.

Every effort has been made to contact copyright holders of material reproduced in this book. Any omissions will be rectified in subsequent printings if notice is given to the publishers.

Websites
There are links to relevant websites in this book. In order to ensure that the links are up to date, that the links work, and that the sites are not inadvertently linked to sites that could be considered offensive, we have made the links available on the Heinemann website at www.heinemann.co.uk/hotlinks. When you access the site, the express code is 8949P

Contents

Welcome to OCR History A GCSE (Schools History Project) Medicine Through Time

This book has been written specifically to support you during your OCR GCSE A (SHP) study of the topic Medicine Through Time.

The course includes a Medicine Through Time student book with ActiveBook and an ActiveTeach CD-ROM.

HOW TO USE THIS BOOK

The OCR GCSE A (SHP) Medicine Through Time student book is divided into lessons. The first six chapters follow a mainly chronological path through the history of Medicine Through Time. Chapters 9 to 11 are structured more thematically – this is so you can approach your exam questions in the most suitable way for the topics.

There are many important historical debates that you need to be familiar with for your GCSE. We have flagged up some examples throughout the text for you to discuss and form an opinion on.

Lots of the lessons begin with a 'Getting Started' activity to encourage you to really think about the content right from the beginning of the lesson.

The logos represent the following additional resources which are available on the teachers' copy of the ActiveTeach CD-ROM.

Each lesson has objectives so you know what you will learn and which skills you will be developing in each lesson.

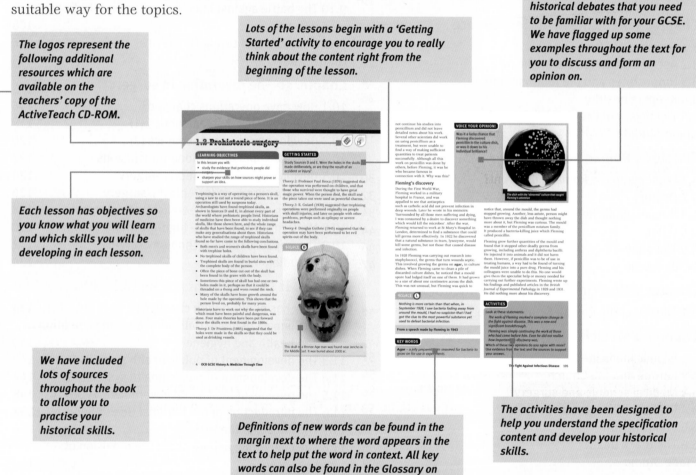

We have included lots of sources throughout the book to allow you to practise your historical skills.

Definitions of new words can be found in the margin next to where the word appears in the text to help put the word in context. All key words can also be found in the Glossary on pages 176–177.

The activities have been designed to help you understand the specification content and develop your historical skills.

Here you will find interactive activities that can be used as a whole-class teaching tool. Activities range from review triangles to interactive maps and decision-making activities. All activities are also accompanied by teacher notes with learning objectives and AfL opportunities.

From here you can launch video clips to support the student book and specification content. All video clips are accompanied by activity notes.

In addition to this, you will also find:

HISTORY DETECTIVE

There just is not enough room to include all of the facts in this book so you are going to have to be a detective and find out some for yourself! ————————

FACT FILE!

Fact File boxes contain a list of facts important to the historical context and will help you to develop your knowledge. ————————

BRAIN BOOST

Brain Boost sections have been designed to help with your revision and can be re-visited at any time during your course. ————————

GRADE STUDIO

Grade Studio is designed for you to improve your chances of achieving the best possible grades. You will find student focussed Grade Studio activities on the CD-ROM. Look for this logo to see where activities will be on the CD-ROM

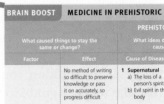

HISTORY DETECTIVE

In the rest of Chapter 4.3, you have the chance to work out which were the most important things in Roman public health – clean water, toilets and sewers, and baths. For each of these subjects, you will find a short introduction and a collection of sources. Complete a simple form for each source, answering these questions:

Location: Where the source is or where it refers to.
Date: When it was made and/or used.
Description: A brief description of what the source is
Conclusion: What you can learn from the source

Fact file

Cave paintings
In some parts of the world prehistoric paintings have survived. The paintings show things we think were important to prehistoric people – usually the animals they hunted, and sometimes a hunt itself. Some paintings, such as Source C, are of other things. Source C is one of several prehistoric paintings that show a man with antlers on his head. In some, the man is standing in a circle with 12 other men. Some historians think this shows a religious ritual. Others think that the paintings might be of a medicine man.

BRAIN BOOST   MEDICINE IN PREHISTORIC

	PREHISTO
What caused things to stay the same or change?	What ideas d caus
Factor	Effect	Cause of Disease
No method of writing so difficult to preserve knowledge or pass it on accurately, so progress difficult		1 **Supernatural** a) The loss of a person's spirit b) Evil spirit in th body

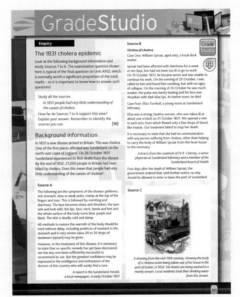

EXAM CAFÉ

The Exam Café is to be used when revising and preparing for exams. The Exam Café could be used in revision classes after school or in revision lessons.

The Exam Café will help you to prepare for the final exam. Like Grade Studio, the Exam Café has additional resources on the CD-ROM. From the CD-ROM you will be able to access a number of useful resources that will help you to organise your revision, practise exam questions, access sample mark schemes and locate extra resources to stretch yourself. Look for this logo to see where activities will be on the CD-ROM.

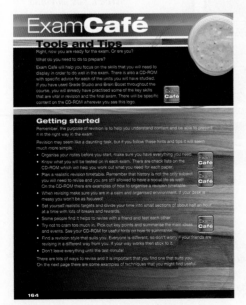

How to use this ActiveBook CD-ROM

In the back of your copy of the student book you will find an ActiveBook CD-ROM. This is for individual use and includes a copy of the book onscreen, Grade Studio activities that have been designed for individual student use and the whole Exam Café resource.

ACTIVETEACH CD-ROM FOR TEACHERS

To use the OCR GCSE A (SHP) Medicine Through Time ActiveBook CD-ROM in a whole-class environment, your school needs to purchase the ActiveTeach CD-ROM. The ActiveTeach CD-ROM provides the book onscreen to be used for whole-class teaching, allows you to add your own resources into the Resource Bank and use the annotation tools. The Zoom feature helps to examine sources in lots of detail. The CD-ROM also includes interactive activities to be used on the whiteboard as well as additional video resources to enhance your lessons.

You will see logos throughout the student book lessons to indicate where additional teaching resources appear on the ActiveTeach CD-ROM. There are 79 interactive activities, 6 video clips plus activity notes for all of these resources. In addition you will find all of the teaching notes and worksheets from the teacher guide to help your planning. As well as the interactive activities there are 16 Grade Studio activities and Exam Café resources for every chapter and specification point.

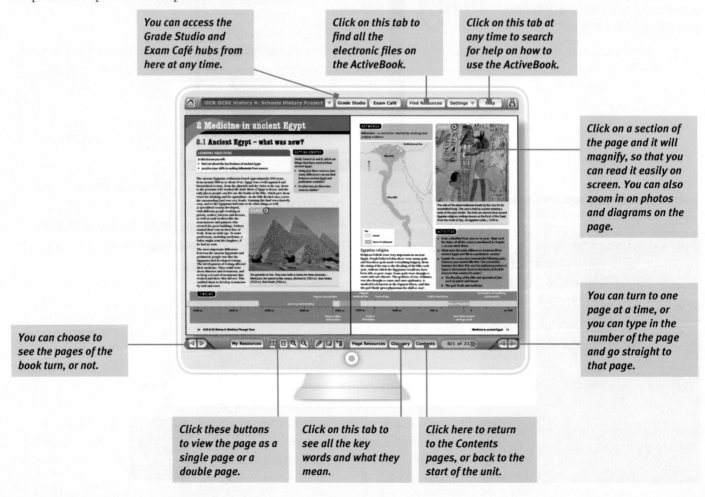

You can access the Grade Studio and Exam Café hubs from here at any time.

Click on this tab to find all the electronic files on the ActiveBook.

Click on this tab at any time to search for help on how to use the ActiveBook.

Click on a section of the page and it will magnify, so that you can read it easily on screen. You can also zoom in on photos and diagrams on the page.

You can turn to one page at a time, or you can type in the number of the page and go straight to that page.

You can choose to see the pages of the book turn, or not.

Click these buttons to view the page as a single page or a double page.

Click on this tab to see all the key words and what they mean.

Click here to return to the Contents pages, or back to the start of the unit.

BRAIN BOOST Introduction

To prepare for the exam you need to be able to answer the 'key questions' about each period in the history of medicine. They are:

- What caused people to be healthy or unhealthy?
- What ideas did people have about the causes and treatment of illness and injuries?
- Who provided medical care?
- What caused diagnoses and treatments to remain the same or to change?
- How far did new ideas and treatments affect the majority of the population?

One useful way of doing this is to use a chart which summarises the answers to these questions for each period. There is one of these charts for each chapter in the first half of the book. They can be found on the Active Book CD-ROM in the back of this book, or will be provided by your teacher. Completing the chart is a useful way to look back over the material you have just studied, to make sure you understand it, and correctly filled in charts will be useful for revision.

Notice how many of the sections of the chart have a place for Evidence. Good historians can always support what they say with evidence and so should you when you take exams. Filling in these sections of the chart will give you useful practice in selecting the facts which you can use to back up answers.

The chart is split into seven different sections:

What caused things to stay the same or change?
This is explained in more detail on the right.

Special reasons for health or disease?
In some places and times, for example towns in the Industrial Revolution, living conditions made people more likely to get certain diseases.

What ideas did people have about the causes of disease? What ideas did people have about treatments?
Where you can record some of the ways in which injury and diseases were treated.

Who provided medical care?
This is split into different Groups who provided care, e.g. Medicine Men, and Patients. This is because at some times the rich or the powerful were treated by different people than the poor.

New Features
Where you need to think about each period in relation to the ones which went before.

Did new ideas and treatments affect most people?
Again sometimes new ideas only helped the rich and powerful.

What caused things to stay the same or change?

This is about the factors that have influenced change and development. The most important factors are:

Science and/or Technology

For example, our highly developed science and technology, with x-rays and ultrasound helps medicine because it allows doctors to discover what is happening inside the body.

War

For example, plastic surgery was developed during the Second World War to help air crew with new and terrible burns.

Religion

For example, some religious groups today do not allow blood transfusions.

Government and the way society is organised and run

For example, the creation of the National Health Service and treatment that was free to the patient in Britain in 1948.

Communications

This can cover from the development of writing to air transport. For example, modern transplants are often only possible because organs can be flown from one hospital to another.

Chance

This looks at unplanned events. For example, penicillin was first found when Alexander Fleming was checking through the remains of old and failed experiments.

The OCR GCSE History A (SHP) course

The tables below show how 'Medicine Through Time' and 'Developments in British Medicine, 1200–1945' are part of your history course. Your teacher will have chosen which topics your class are going to study.

FULL COURSE

Unit A951 (Study in Development and Study in Depth)	
Study in Development: You will study *one* of the following:	
Medicine Through Time	Crime and Punishment Through Time
Depth Study: You will study *one* of the following:	
Elizabethan England	
Britain, 1815–1851	
The American West, 1840–1895	
Germany, c.1919–1945	

Unit A951 is worth 45 per cent of your final mark.

In the questions on the Study in Development, you will need to interpret and evaluate sources of evidence; demonstrate knowledge and understanding of the key individuals, events, developments and issues, and compare and explain the factors and processes involved in change and development over a long period of time.

In the questions on the Study in Depth, you will have to demonstrate your understanding of people and problems in the past through your study of the social, economic, political, cultural and religious aspects of a country over a short period of time. These questions will encourage an issues-based and investigative approach to the content.

Unit A952 (Historical Source Investigation)	
You will study *one* of the following:	
Developments in British Medicine, 1200–1945	Developments in Crime and Punishment in Britain, 1200–1945

Unit A952 is worth 30 per cent of your final mark.
It tests your ability to analyse and evaluate sources of evidence, using your knowledge of the topic to put the sources into their historical context

Unit A953 (Controlled Assessment)
You will study *one* of the following:
History Around Us: the investigation of a historical site and its historical context.
Modern World Study: the investigation of a current issue or problem from world events in the context of the past.

This unit of the course is worth 25 per cent of your final mark.

COURSE OBJECTIVES

As well as knowing which topics you are going to study, it is important to understand what skills you will be developing and assessed on.

- **AO1** – the ability to **recall, select and communicate** your knowledge and understanding of the historical topics you have studied.

- **AO2** – the ability to **explain and analyse**:
  a key concepts such as causation, consequence, change and significance
  b key features and characteristics of the periods studied and the relationship between them.

- **AO3** – the ability to understand, analyse and evaluate:
  a a range of sources as part of a historical enquiry
  b how aspects of the past have been interpreted and represented in different ways as part of a historical enquiry.

HOW SHOULD YOU ORGANISE YOUR NOTES?

It is important to remember that everyone learns in different ways. What might work for the person sitting next to you might not work for you. It is important that you find a style that suits you.

Research has shown that people learn in one of the following ways:

Visual learners	
What is a visual learner?	How do I know if I'm a visual learner?
Visual learners like to learn by looking and seeing.	You may be a visual learner if you: • have neat and organised work • are good at spelling and reading • imagine tasks • follow rules carefully • see things that others miss • remember information by using pictures • like to see instructions • like to use colours in your work.

Auditory learners	
What is an auditory learner?	How do I know if I'm an auditory learner?
Auditory learners like to learn by listening.	You may be an auditory learner if you: • can repeat word for word what has already been said • are easily distracted by noise • prefer to discuss ideas rather than writing them down • move your lips when reading • often sit with your head to one side when listening.

Kinaesthetic learners	
What is a kinaesthetic learner?	How do I know if I'm a kinaesthetic learner?
Kinaesthetic learners like to learn by doing things.	You may be a kinaesthetic learner if you: • use lots of hand movements when you talk • are tactile • need to use your hands when you are learning • move around the room a lot.

- What type of learner are you?
- How could you adapt your notes to make sure that you make the best use of the strengths of your personal learning style?
- Try to keep this in mind whenever you are making notes.

1 Medicine in prehistoric times

1.1 Did prehistoric people get ill?

What is prehistory?

For historians, a prehistoric society is one without writing. Although the prehistoric period does not have a definitive beginning and end, historians usually say that it started about 500,000 years ago. All of the evidence we are studying, however, comes from the last 20,000 years of the period.

Prehistoric people lived throughout the world. Not all peoples in the world left the prehistoric period at the same time. Once writing developed in a society, that society was no longer prehistoric. Britain remained prehistoric for longer than Egypt and the Middle East, where writing developed much earlier.

The earliest prehistoric peoples had the following features in common.

- They were nomads.
- They were hunter-gatherers, so they got all their food without farming.
- They lived in small groups without complicated political arrangements. There were no separate countries.
- They had a very simple level of technology. Spears, bows and arrows, axes, knives and scrapers were their main tools. All of these were made from wood, bone and stone.
- They had no system of writing.

Over thousands of years things changed slowly. The most important changes were the development of farming (which led people to stay in one place) and of metal tools.

GETTING STARTED

Compare Sources A and B.

- Is this all you need to answer the question whether prehistoric people got ill?

SOURCE **A**

A healthy human femur (thigh bone).

SOURCE **B**

A prehistoric human femur (thigh bone) with a growth on the bone.

ACTIVITIES

1. Explain which features of prehistoric peoples:
   a. might have affected their ability to develop a system of medicine
   b. might affect our ability to find out about their system of medicine.

TIMELINE

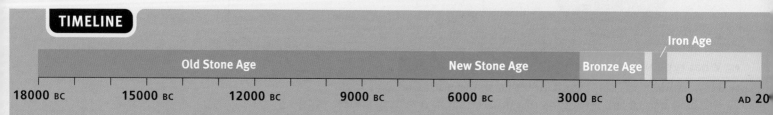

| 18000 BC | 15000 BC | 12000 BC | 9000 BC | 6000 BC | 3000 BC | 0 | AD 20 |

Old Stone Age   New Stone Age   Bronze Age   Iron Age

Did prehistoric people get diseases?

Because we don't have any writing from prehistoric times, the evidence we use presents special problems. There are two main sources of evidence: the remains of the people themselves, and the remains of things they made.

Prehistoric skeletons can tell us quite a lot. Archaeologists and doctors have studied them and found traces of diseases that still affect people today. Many diseases would only show in the body organs or flesh, which don't survive, but some diseases can be seen in the bones. For example, Source B shows a bone cancer. Other prehistoric bones show evidence of diseases that are caused by poor nutrition, such as anaemia. Also, prehistoric skeletons show evidence of injuries familiar to us now – broken bones and damaged joints and backs.

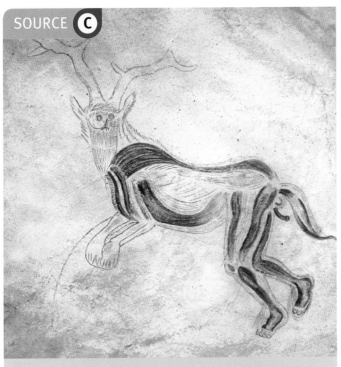

SOURCE **C**

Prehistoric people in France made this cave painting about 15,000 years ago. We cannot be sure what the painting shows. It is hard to see, and has deteriorated since it was found in 1914. This modern drawing done soon after it was found, makes clear the outline of a man with antlers, possibly wearing a mask.

GradeStudio

Analysis of Sources

Using the evidence in part 1.1 of this chapter, say whether each of the following statements is *definitely true*, *possibly true* or *definitely not true*, and give reasons for your answer.

1 Some prehistoric people suffered from disease.

2 All prehistoric people suffered from disease.

3 Prehistoric people who got diseases were treated by a medicine man who wore an antler mask.

Examiner's tip

This activity is about the way sources can be used as evidence to back up a statement. There are three main possibilities:

- The source does not back up the statement.
- The source *supports* the statement, but is not enough to *prove* it.
- The source *proves* that the statement must be true.

It is always important to be clear whether a source *supports* or *proves* an idea.

1.2 Prehistoric surgery

LEARNING OBJECTIVES

In this lesson you will:

- study the evidence that prehistoric people did surgery
- sharpen your skills on how sources might prove or support an idea.

Trephining is a way of operating on a person's skull, using a saw to cut out a round piece of bone. It is an operation still used by surgeons today. Archaeologists have found trephined skulls, as shown in Sources D and E, in almost every part of the world where prehistoric people lived. Historians of medicine have then been able to study individual skulls, like those shown here, and the whole range of skulls that have been found, to see if they can make any generalisations about them. Historians who have studied the range of trephined skulls found so far have come to the following conclusions.

- Both men's and women's skulls have been found with trephine holes.
- No trephined skulls of children have been found.
- Trephined skulls are found in burial sites with the complete body of the person.
- Often the piece of bone cut out of the skull has been found in the grave with the body.
- Sometimes this piece of skull has had one or two holes made in it, perhaps so that it could be threaded on a thong and worn round the neck.
- Many of the skulls have bone growth around the hole made by the operation. This shows that the person lived on, probably for many years.

Historians have to work out why the operation, which must have been painful and dangerous, was done. Four main theories have been put forward since the skulls were first found in the 1860s.

Theory 1: Dr Prunières (1865) suggested that the holes were made in the skulls so that they could be used as drinking vessels.

GETTING STARTED

Study Sources D and E. Were the holes in the skulls made deliberately, or are they the result of an accident or injury?

Theory 2: Professor Paul Broca (1876) suggested that the operation was performed on children, and that those who survived were thought to have great magic power. When the person died, the skull and the piece taken out were used as powerful charms.

Theory 3: E. Guiard (1930) suggested that trephining operations were performed originally on people with skull injuries, and later on people with other problems, perhaps such as epilepsy or severe headaches.

Theory 4: Douglas Guthrie (1945) suggested that the operation may have been performed to let evil spirits out of the body.

SOURCE D

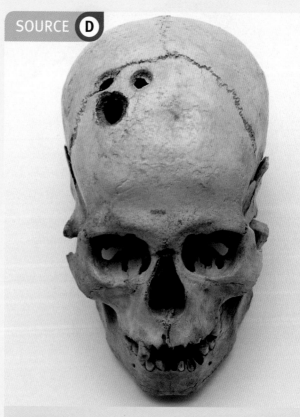

This skull of a Bronze Age man was found near Jericho in the Middle East. It was buried about 2000 BC.

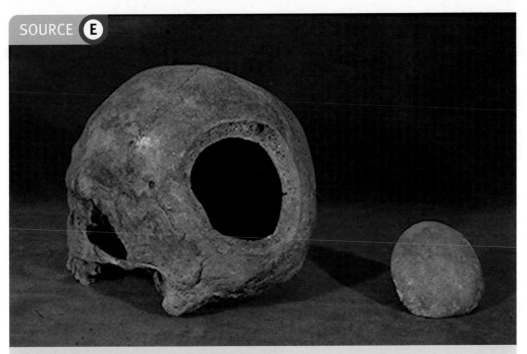

This skull of a prehistoric adult was found in 1938, at Crichel Down in Dorset. The piece of removed skull was buried with the body.

GradeStudio

Enquiry

1 a What was Dr Prunières' theory about the trephined skulls?

   b From the evidence here, do you think this theory was *definitely right, possibly right, probably wrong* or *definitely wrong*? Give reasons for your answer.

2 a What was Professor Broca's theory about the trephined skulls?

   b From the evidence here, do you think this theory was *definitely right, possibly right, probably wrong* or *definitely wrong*? Give reasons for your answer.

3 a What was Guiard's theory about the trephined skulls?

   b From the evidence here, do you think this *theory* was *definitely right, possibly right, probably wrong* or *definitely wrong*? Give reasons for your answer.

4 a What was Douglas Guthrie's theory about the trephined skulls?

   b From the evidence here, do you think this theory was *definitely right, possibly right, probably wrong* or *definitely wrong*? Give reasons for your answer.

5 a Which has been more useful in answering questions 1–4: Sources D and E, or the historians' conclusions from the range of skulls found?

   b Looking back over parts 1.1 and 1.2 of this chapter, what problems do sources such as B, C, D and E give historians?

Fact file

The prehistoric period

Historians divide the prehistoric period into four eras:

- Old Stone Age (Palæolithic) when people were nomadic hunter-gatherers.
- New Stone Age (Neolithic) when farming and living in one place became common.
- Bronze Age when metal tools were first used.
- Iron Age when the new metal (iron) greatly improved the tools and weapons that could be made.

The prehistoric period overlapped with some other historical periods, described in Chapters 2–4. During the height of the ancient Egyptian civilisation, most of Europe was in the New Stone Age. The Minoan civilisation flourished at the same time as the Bronze Age in other places, and during the Greek and early Roman periods Britain was in the Iron Age.

1.3 A clue: Aboriginal medicine

LEARNING OBJECTIVES

In this lesson you will:

- learn about the medicine of the Aborigines
- practise **empathy** – in this case understanding that people try to cure a disease according to what they believe was its cause.

KEY WORDS

Empathy – *the skill of looking at something from another person's point of view. It is important in history because we need to understand why people did things, and to properly understand we need to know what their beliefs and values were.*

Historians and evidence

Historians have a real problem interpreting the evidence about prehistoric medicine. We know some facts. There was illness. Some people's skulls were trephined. But we do not know what people thought about illness, and we do not know why trephining was done. To help provide explanations, historians have looked at the medical beliefs of various groups around the world whose technology and lifestyle are similar to those of prehistoric people.

The Australian Aborigines

Until the late 19th century, Aborigines in South and Central Australia lived in very similar ways to prehistoric people.

- They got their food by hunting and gathering. They did not farm.
- They had no domesticated animals, apart from dogs.
- All their weapons and tools were made from wood and stone.
- They did not have permanent homes. They moved from one place with water to another.
- They had many spoken languages but no written language. They made paintings of the animals they hunted and of their ideas about the spirit world.

This Aborigine way of life disappeared as contact increased with white settlers in Australia. However, anthropologists who visited the Aborigines in the 19th century wrote down what they learned about the people's ideas and beliefs at that time.

Aborigines believed that Spirit Ancestors made the world in 'the Dreamtime'. This explained many things for them. For example, why was a water hole in a certain place? Because the Spirit Ancestors put it there in the Dreamtime. Spirits were also thought to be the cause of new life, both human and animal. Anything that had no obvious physical explanation was explained as the work of spirits.

SOURCE F

An Aborigine medicine man blowing a special horn to scare away evil spirits.

ACTIVITIES

1   In what ways were 19th-century Aborigines like prehistoric people?

SOURCE **G**

An Aborigine medicine man with a 'pointing bone'. This is a poor-quality photograph because it was taken early in the 20th century.

Aboriginal medicine

Aborigines made a distinction between two types of medical problems. Some, mainly physical, problems had obvious causes and could be cured in practical, common-sense ways. So, for example, a broken arm was covered in clay. This set hard in the sun, like a modern plaster cast. Cuts were covered with clay or animal fat and bandaged with bark or animal skin.

On the other hand there were medical problems with no obvious cause. Aborigines explained an illness like this in two ways connected with the person's spirit.

1   The person was sick because their spirit had left their body. This might be because an enemy had captured the spirit with a special 'pointing bone' with gum on the end. The spirit got stuck on the gum, and the enemy hid or buried the bone. In this case, a medicine man asked the sick person and their friends and family if they knew of any enemies who might have done this. The cure was to find the pointing bone and free the sick person's spirit.

2   The person was sick because an evil spirit had entered their body. A medicine man was needed to drive the spirit out.

This gives us an important insight into the history of medicine. The cures that people used were related to what they thought had caused the disease. If the disease was thought to have a spiritual cause, then only a spiritual cure would make sense. It would also make sense to use charms to help healing, or to keep away evil spirits.

Conclusions

The 19th-century Aboriginal way of life was very similar to what we know about the way of life of prehistoric people. The ideas of the Aborigines may therefore help us to understand the ideas of prehistoric people. So, like the Aborigines, prehistoric people might have used both common sense and a belief in spirits in their medicine. The man shown in Source C (page 3) may have been a medicine man. The medicine man's (or woman's) explanation for many illnesses may have been that they were caused by evil spirits. Trephining may have been performed to let out evil spirits through the hole in the skull. The pieces of skull removed in the operation may have been worn as a charm to keep evil spirits away. This is the view of prehistoric medicine that historians think is most likely. However, it is only a theory. Because we have no written records from prehistoric times, we cannot be sure what people really thought.

ACTIVITIES

2   **a**   Describe an Aboriginal common-sense treatment.

　 b   Why do you think the Aborigines did not use a spirit cure in place of this treatment?

3   **a**   Describe an Aboriginal spiritual treatment.

　 b   Why do you think the Aborigines did not use a common-sense treatment instead of this?

4   Do you think Aborigines would use spiritual or common-sense treatments for the following problems? Explain the reasons for your answer in each case.

　 a   A sprained wrist caused in a fall.

　 b   A heart attack.

　 c   An epileptic fit.

　 d   A spear wound.

BRAIN BOOST — MEDICINE IN PREHISTORIC TIMES

What caused things to stay the same or change?

Factor	Effect
1	No method of writing so difficult to preserve knowledge or pass it on accurately, so progress difficult
2	An unstable society, large scale projects and long-term planning almost impossible so progress difficult
3	No understanding of how the body worked, so progress difficult

Special reasons for health or disease

Reason	Effect
	Moved around so probably did not build up sanitation problems which would cause disease

What ideas did people have about causes of disease?

Cause of Disease	Evidence
1 **Supernatural** a) The loss of a person's spirit b) Evil spirit in the body	
2 **Physical** Simple injuries like a broken arm or leg	

What ideas did people have about treatments?

Treatment	Illness	Evidence
	Cannot be sure	Skulls (Sources D E)
Encased in clay		Aborigines
Covered with clay or fat and bound with bark or animal skin		Aborigines
	Any disease without an obvious physical cause	

Who provided medical care?

Group	Patients	Evidence
Medicine men and women	Perhaps everyone	a) b)

New Features

Feature	Evidence
1 Spirits thought to cause disease	
2 Medicine men or women – special people to treat the sick	a) b)
3 Magical cures	a) b)
4 Common sense cures	

Did new ideas and treatments affect most people?

No evidence, but probably

For details on how to use this Brain Boost grid, and the others throughout the book, see page viii of the Introduction.

Grade Studio

The first question in Unit A951 includes sources. They will come from more than one period in the history of medicine, and some questions will need answers that cover more than one period. You may also find a question like this one, which just concentrates on the period the source comes from.

Which of these answers is best, and why?

Study Source A
Is this evidence that prehistoric people performed surgery? Use the source and your knowledge to explain your answer.

Source A

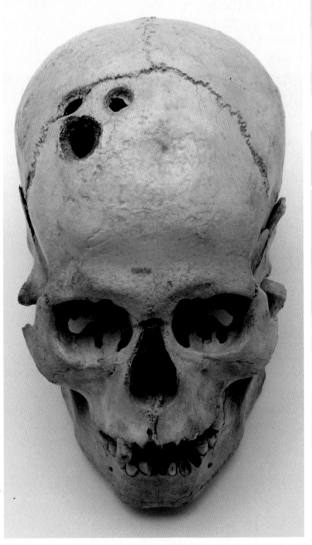

The skull of a Bronze Age man, found near Jericho in the Middle East. It was buried about 2000 BC

Answer A

Yes because you can see the holes that have been cut in the skull.

Answer B

Yes, this is one of many skulls that have been found like this from all round the world. They have holes cut in them like this one. The skulls aren't broken, so it isn't an injury. The bone grew again as you can see here, which shows they lived after the operation.

Answer C

The aborigines believed they got sick because evil spirits got into their bodies so they used to do things like use a bone to get them out, then they would be well again

2 Medicine in ancient Egypt

2.1 Ancient Egypt – what was new?

The ancient Egyptian civilisation lasted approximately 3000 years, from around 3000 BC to about 30 BC. Egypt was a well-organised and hierarchical society, from the pharaoh and the vizier at the top, down to the peasants who worked the land. Most of Egypt is desert, and the only places people can live are the banks of the Nile, which gave them water for drinking and for agriculture. As the Nile flooded once a year, the surrounding land was very fertile. Farming this land was relatively easy, and so the Egyptians had time to do other things as well.

A specialised society developed, with different people working as priests, scribes, lawyers and doctors, as well as craft workers like the stonemasons and painters who created the great buildings. Fathers trained their sons in their line of work, from an early age. In some professions, including medicine, a father might train his daughter, if he had no sons.

The most important difference between the ancient Egyptians and prehistoric people was that the Egyptians had developed writing. The development of writing affected their medicine. They could write about illnesses and treatments, and so keep a record of treatments that worked and those that did not. This enabled them to develop treatments by trial and error.

SOURCE A

The pyramids at Giza. They were built as tombs for three pharaohs – Menkaura, the nearest to the camera, (finished in 2503 BC), then Khafra (2532 BC), then Khufu (2566 BC).

TIMELINE

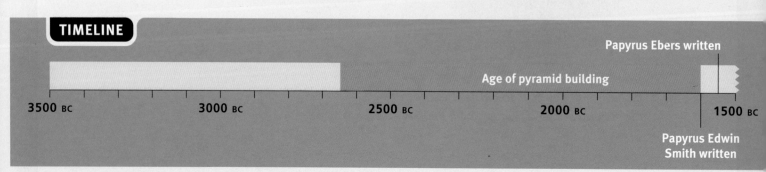

Papyrus Ebers written

Age of pyramid building

3500 BC   3000 BC   2500 BC   2000 BC   1500 BC

Papyrus Edwin Smith written

Inference – *a conclusion reached by studying and judging evidence.*

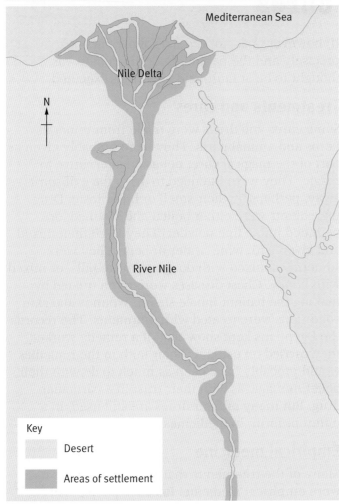

Egyptian religion

Religious beliefs were very important in ancient Egypt. People believed that there were many gods and that these gods made everything happen, from the rising of the sun to the flooding of the Nile each year, without which the Egyptians would not have been able to grow crops. Some gods were thought to cause and cure disease. The goddess of war, Sekhmet, was also thought to cause and cure epidemics. A medical book known as the Papyrus Ebers, said that the god Thoth 'gives physicians the skill to cure'.

SOURCE B

The wife of the dead nobleman kneels by the case for his mummified body. The case is held by a priest wearing a mask of the god Anubis. The texts are extracts from ancient Egyptian religious writings known as the Book of the Dead. From the tomb of Roy, an Egyptian noble, c.1290 BC.

ACTIVITIES

1 Draw a timeline from 3000 BC to 30 BC. Mark on it the dates of all the sources mentioned in Chapter 2, as you meet them.

2 What were the main differences between life in ancient Egypt and life in a prehistoric society?

3 Explain the connection between the following pairs. (Express your answer like this: *The connection between the River Nile and the settlement pattern in Egypt is that people lived on the banks of the Nile because they needed its water.*)

a The flooding of the Nile and specialised jobs such as priest and lawyer.

b The god Thoth and medicine.

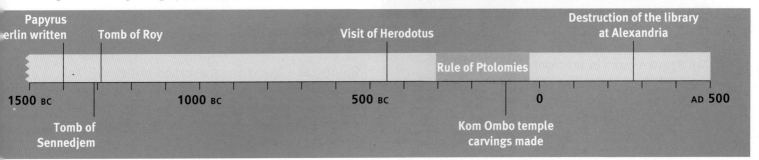

2.2 Spiritual causes and cures

LEARNING OBJECTIVES

In this lesson you will:

- study the evidence for spiritual causes and cures
- practise your ability to use evidence to support conclusions.

Written records left by the ancient Egyptians tell us what they thought caused illnesses and how they treated them. The Egyptians believed that many diseases were caused by an evil spirit entering the body. People often wore charms to keep such evil spirits away. If they became ill despite the charms, they turned to magic and the gods to make them well.

Egyptian medical books

The most important early Egyptian medical books were the Books of Thoth. They were kept in the temple of Thoth, god of writing and wisdom, by his priests. None of the Books of Thoth have survived, but a medical book from about 1550 BC which has survived – the Papyrus Ebers – was probably based on them. Books of this kind give clear instructions about how to treat illness. The instructions include the exact words to speak as a spell or prayer to the gods, as well as any medicine or other treatment to give. Doctors were supposed to follow the instructions precisely. If a doctor did so and the patient still died, then the doctor was not blamed.

SOURCE C

An amulet of the goddess Taweret, c. 900 BC. Taweret, shown as a pregnant hippopotamus, was the goddess of childbirth. Her face is shown looking fierce, to drive away evil spirits which might affect either the mother or the baby. Amulets like this were worn by pregnant women to keep themselves safe during pregnancy and childbirth. In those days, childbirth was a dangerous time.

If, however, a doctor did not follow the book precisely and the patient died, the doctor was thought to be at fault, and was often executed.

Treatments and cures

Some cures and drugs were made from minerals, herbs and animal parts. They were probably given as part of the magical cure, not as an alternative to magic. They were intended to drive the evil spirit away, perhaps by their smell or bitter taste. Drug ingredients were either boiled and strained, or pounded into a fine powder. They were then mixed and given with wine, water or beer. They were sometimes mixed with dough to make pills, or mixed with honey. Chest diseases were often treated by making the patient inhale steam. Wounds and skin conditions were treated with ointments. The records the Egyptians kept show that, if a remedy worked, they carried on using it. Their faith in the remedies would probably have been as much to do with their belief in magic as with their trust in a particular drug. But many of their drugs are still used, in a different form, in medicines today.

Empirical medicine

Many of the treatments that Egyptian doctors used were empirical medicine. Because people had written down symptoms and treatments over hundreds of years, there was good empirical evidence that some treatments worked, although the Egyptians did not have our modern scientific knowledge of how and why they worked. For example, the Egyptians thought that workers on big projects like building the pyramids could be kept healthy if they were given radishes to eat, to scare away evil spirits. Doctors now know that some elements of radishes help prevent dysentery, which is easily caught and passed on when many people live and work close together.

KEY WORDS

Empirical – *based on observation not theory. For example, you can have empirical knowledge that cars need petrol to go, but not have the theoretical understanding of how petrol is used in the engine to make the car go.*

Fact file

Egyptian medical books

Only a few medical books have survived from ancient Egypt. They were written on papyrus, a kind of paper made from reeds. The books we know about have been found by archaeologists, and are known by the name of the modern owner, or the museum where they are kept. The Papyrus Edwin Smith was bought by Smith, an American Egyptologist, in 1862. It was written about 1600 BC and considers wounds and the work of surgeons, as well as treatments and drugs. The Papyrus Ebers, written about 1550 BC, contains over 700 remedies. It is named after a German Egyptologist, Maurice Ebers, who acquired it in 1873. The Papyrus Berlin, owned by the Berlin Museum, was written about 1450 BC, and concentrates on the treatment and protection of mothers and babies.

SOURCE

A page from the *Papyrus Ebers*, in hieratic writing, an Egyptian form of writing which was quicker than hieroglyphs. Made about 1550 BC, this papyrus was probably a copy of much older books. It has 110 pages, including over 700 treatments, and covers intestinal disease, ophthalmology, dermatology, gynaecology, obstetrics, pregnancy, contraception, dentistry, and the surgical treatment of abscesses, tumours, fractures and burns.

ACTIVITIES

1 What does Source C tell us about what the Egyptians thought caused medical problems?

2 Why are ancient Egyptian medical books important to historians of medicine?

3 What do the *Books of Thoth* and the *Papyrus Ebers* tell us about what the Egyptians thought caused disease?

4 Why can some aspects of Egyptian medicine be described as 'empirical'? Explain your answer.

5 Where there was no obvious physical cause for disease, some Egyptian doctors thought disease was caused by spirits and gods.

   Copy this statement and underline it.

   a Give some evidence to support the statement and explain why this evidence supports it.

   b Explain whether the statement describes a new or an old idea in the history of medicine.

SOURCE

Here is the great remedy. Come! You who drive evil things from my stomach and my limbs. He who drinks this shall be cured just as the gods above were cured.

This spell was for a doctor to chant while giving medicine to a patient. An Egyptian doctor who used the papyrus had written next to the spell, 'This spell is really excellent – successful many times.'

A spell from the *Papyrus Ebers*

SOURCE F

If you examine someone mortally ill, his body shrunken with disease, and you do not find disease in his body except for the surface of the ribs, the members of which protrude like pills, you should then recite a spell against this disease in your house. You should then prepare for him these ingredients for treating it: ground blood stone of Elephantine; red grain; carob; cook in oil (and) honey. This should be eaten by him over four mornings for the suppression of his thirst and for curing his mortal illness.

A treatment from the *Papyrus Ebers*

2.3 Religion, anatomy and surgery

LEARNING OBJECTIVES

In this lesson you will:

- find out about the effect of religion on ancient Egyptian medicine
- practise your ability to use evidence to support conclusions.

Anatomy is the study of the structure of the body. Knowing how the human body is made up, and how it works, is an important part of medicine. The Egyptians learned some human anatomy as an unintended consequence of their religious beliefs. They believed that after a person died, his or her soul left the body. Later the soul returned to the body and the person began an afterlife, very like the life they had led before they died. It was important, therefore, to keep dead bodies in good condition for their souls to use when they returned.

The Egyptians devoted much time to finding ways of preserving dead bodies. They soaked the bodies in various liquids, including salts and bitumen. They covered them in oils and wrapped them in bandages. This process was called embalming, and the embalmed bodies were called mummies. Embalming included cutting open the body to take out some of the main organs (the lungs, liver, stomach and intestines), because these would rot inside the dead body.

SOURCE G

In the best treatment, first of all they draw out the brains through the nostrils with an iron hook. When they have removed what they can in this way they flush out the remainder with drugs. Next they make a cut in the side, with an obsidian knife, through which they take out all the internal organs. They clean out the body cavity, rinsing it with palm wine and powdered spices, and then they stitch it up again. When they have done this, they cover the corpse in natron for 70 days and so mummify it. Then they wash the corpse and wrap it from head to toe in linen bandages smeared with the finest gum. Finally the relatives put it in a man-shaped wooden coffin and store it in a burial chamber, where it is propped upright against the wall. This is the most costly method of preparing the dead.

A description of one method of mummification from *The Histories*, a book by Herodotus, a Greek traveller and historian who visited Egypt about 450 BC

SOURCE H

Parts of the mummification process are shown in this painting on a coffin from around 600 BC. The lower section shows the body (darker than the living people) being washed in a solution of natron (sodium chloride). The middle section shows the body covered with natron crystals during the 40-day drying-out stage. At the top, on the left, the mummy has been placed in its tomb with the canopic jars underneath. These held the liver, lungs, stomach and intestines. On the right the god Anubis is attending to the mummy.

The organs were left whole and stored in canopic jars, which were kept with the mummy.

The process of embalming gave the Egyptians a good understanding of some parts of human anatomy. Removing the major organs meant that they knew where these were in the body. However, their belief in the afterlife, which led them to finding out this much, also prevented them from doing any further research into the structure of the body. Because they believed that bodies were needed for the afterlife, they would not dissect them any further – but dissection of human bodies is essential to gain a full knowledge of human anatomy.

Surgery

As for all crafts in Egypt, the skill of surgery was passed from father to son (or sometimes daughter). The Papyrus Edwin Smith, written in about 1600 BC, describes some simple surgical procedures, including ways of treating dislocated arms and legs. None of the existing written records discuss major operations, and the mummies that have been examined so far do not show any signs of major surgery.

On the other hand, as we have seen, the Egyptians had a reasonable grasp of human anatomy. The written evidence shows that they performed minor surgery, like the removal of cysts and tumours. Because so much surgery was done, it is likely that it was one of the medical skills in which people specialised. The minor operations probably had quite a good recovery rate, because the wounds that were left after operating were treated with willow. We now know that willow leaves and bark produce a form of antiseptic, which would have protected the wound against infection.

ACTIVITY

1 Egyptian doctors knew something about anatomy. They were aware of the heart, lungs and brain.
2 Egyptian doctors did surgical operations.

Copy the two statements above, about Egyptian medicine, and underline them. Underneath each statement:

a Give some evidence to support it and explain why the evidence supports it.
b Explain whether it is a new or an old idea in the history of medicine.

VOICE YOUR OPINION!

In what ways did religion help or hinder Egyptian medicine? Try to think of examples for each.

SOURCE I

Forty-six vessels go from the heart to every limb. If a doctor, surgeon or exorcist places his hands or fingers on the back of the head, hands, stomach, arms or feet, then he hears the heart. The heart speaks out of every limb.

From the *Papyrus Ebers*, about 1550 BC

SOURCE J

If you examine a man with a dislocation of his jaw where his mouth is open and he cannot close it, you should put your two thumbs on the ends of the two rami of the mandible [lower jawbone] inside the mouth. Put your fingers under his chin and make them fall back into the correct position.

From the Papyrus Edwin Smith, about 1600 BC

SOURCE K

A carving of Egyptian surgical instruments from the temple of Kom Ombo, made c.100 BC. The instruments include probes, saws, forceps, flasks, scalpels, scissors and even plants (presumably medicinal herbs to put on the wound after surgery to help it heal). Surgical instruments were mostly made from bronze, and some have been found looking just like these.

2.4 Natural causes of disease

LEARNING OBJECTIVES

In this lesson you will:
- study the evidence for a belief in natural causes of disease in ancient Egyptian medicine
- practise your ability to use evidence to support conclusions.

The River Nile was vital to Egyptian life. Every year the river flooded. The Egyptians dammed and channelled its waters into irrigation ditches to keep their crops growing. This control of the flood waters by damming gave some doctors an **analogy** which helped them to think about the body and disease. They thought the human body might be full of channels, rather like the irrigation system. They knew that there were many vessels inside the body, through which blood and other fluids flowed. If an irrigation channel was blocked, the life-giving water would not flow into the fields. Perhaps the same thing happened inside the human body? If one of the vessels became blocked, would the person become ill?

This was a very different idea about the causes of disease from those held earlier. Now the disease was believed to have a physical as well as a spiritual cause. Therefore part of the treatment should be physical as well. Egyptian doctors who thought in this way used a variety of treatments:

- Vomiting was thought to be good for some patients. It might clear blockages in some parts of the body.

KEY WORDS

Analogy – *a comparison of one thing to another, which helps people to understand the first thing. Analogies have been important in the history of medicine. The ancient Egyptians made an analogy between the vessels that carry liquid around the human body and the irrigation channels from the River Nile. They knew that good, working irrigation channels carried water to the fields so that healthy crops would grow. This helped them to understand, by analogy, that vessels carried liquid around the body, keeping it healthy.*

ACTIVITIES

1 Study Source N.
   a Describe the irrigation system.
   b How is it similar to the human body?
2 What was the connection between irrigation in Egyptian farming and the idea that blockages in the body might cause disease?
3 Which three types of treatment did Egyptian doctors use to cure diseases they thought were caused by blockages?
4 Look back at Sources C, D, J and L. For each source say whether you think the cause of disease was thought to be a blockage or not, and give reasons for your answer.

- Purges (medicines that worked as laxatives) were often used. They might clear some blockages from the stomach and bowel.
- Bleeding was also used. A doctor would deliberately cut a vein so that the patient would lose a certain amount of blood. It was thought that this might clear any blockages in the blood vessels.

These methods were not accepted by everyone, and the doctors who used them did not reject spiritual explanations for disease. The treatments mentioned in the Papyrus Ebers show both natural and supernatural theories about the causes of disease.

Egyptian public health

The ancient Egyptians believed in keeping clean. It seems that their concern with cleanliness (see Source O) was more to do with religion and comfort

SOURCE

Another remedy for the belly: colocynth 8 ro, senna 8 ro, s'm 8 ro, sweet beer 15 to, are mixed together, boiled, strained and taken in 1 day. It causes the man to evacuate all accumulations that are in his belly.

Ro and to were units of measurement. Senna is still used in laxatives today.

Treatment from the *Papyrus Ebers*, about 1550 BC

An Egyptian toilet seat, made from limestone. Underneath it there would have been a pot which could be emptied.

A wall painting showing irrigation and farming scenes from the tomb of Sennedjem, c. 1310 BC.

than with health. The fact that priests washed more often than other people suggests a religious connection to their washing practices. The Egyptian development of mosquito nets was more to do with comfort than the knowledge of the illnesses that mosquitoes can carry. But, whatever their reasons, their attitude to cleanliness helped them to keep healthy. Shaven heads were normal, for both men and women. Clothes were changed regularly.

Despite their sophisticated water drainage system for growing crops, the Egyptians do not seem to have developed a drainage system for their toilets. Only well-off people had bathrooms and the baths were just shallow troughs with a drainage pipe leading to a large jar. Toilets were more common, but these were just stone seats over a large removable jar. Perhaps this shows that water was too valuable to be wasted in deep baths or in sluicing away sewage, which could be carried to the fields by slaves and used as manure.

The Egyptians drink from cups of bronze which they clean daily – everyone, without exception. They wear linen clothes which they make a special point of continually washing. Their priests shave their whole bodies every third day, to guard against lice, or anything else equally unpleasant while they do their religious duties. Twice a day and every night these priests wash in cold water.

From *The Histories* by the Greek historian Herodotus, about 450 BC

ACTIVITIES

For this activity you will need to look back over the whole chapter on ancient Egypt.

5   Copy each of the statements below, about Egyptian medicine, and underline it. Underneath each statement:

   a Give some evidence to support it and explain why the evidence supports it.

   b Explain whether it is a new or an old idea in the history of medicine.

- Egyptian doctors used treatments based on herbs, plants and animal parts.
- Some Egyptian doctors thought the body was like the River Nile, with channels running through it. If the channels got blocked, a person would become ill.
- Many Egyptians thought the best way to stay healthy was to scare away the evil spirits that might cause disease, and so they wore charms to help them do this.
- Egyptians were very concerned about their personal hygiene and this helped to protect their health.
- Some Egyptian doctors gave their patients careful physical examinations.
- Egyptian doctors treated wounds, dislocations and tumours.

2.5 Medicine in a workmen's village

Although a lot survives from ancient Egypt, it is mainly from the lives of rich and powerful people. An exception is the village of Deir el-Medina, which was home to the workmen who built the royal tombs. What does Deir tell us about medicine for people who were not rich?

SOURCE P

Year 29, Month 4 of the inundation [1155 BC]

Total given to the Doctor by Weser-hat [a workman]:

bronze jug worth 4 deben; fine basket worth 5 deben; sandals, two pairs worth 4 deben; …

total 22 deben

A deben was a weight of copper which was used to fix value when goods were used to pay for services.

From a papyrus which records details of life in the village of Deir el-Medina

SOURCE Q

In this source some words in the original were unreadable and they are shown as xxx.

Work given to the washerman Baki:

House of xxx: kilts, 2; underpants, 2; tunics, xxx; sleeve, 1; xxx; bands, 3.

House of Iny: kilts, xxx; loincloth, 1;

House of Amen: kilt, 1; loincloth, 2; sleeve, 1; handkerchiefs, xxx

House of Khonsu: kilt, 1; loincloth, 1; shawl, 1; underpants, 1; sleeve, 1; rags, xxx

House of Pen-dua: kilts, 2; loincloths, xxx

From a list found in Deir el-Medina

ACTIVITIES

1 What does the evidence from Deir el-Medina tell you about health and hygiene for workmen?

BRAIN BOOST — MEDICINE IN ANCIENT EGYPT

What caused things to stay the same or change?		What ideas did people have about causes of disease?		New Features	
Factor	Effect	Cause of Disease	Evidence	Feature	Evidence
1	Efficient farming meant some people had spare time, and some could specialise in Medicine for most of their lives	1	a) Amulet of the goddess Taweret to drive evil spirits away from pregnant women and babies (Source C) b) *Papyrus Ebers* (Source D)	1 Doctors	a) b)
2	Helped knowledge of anatomy through things leant during mummification	2	a) Vomiting, Papyrus Ebers (Source M) b) laxative, Papyrus Ebers (Source L)	2 Some knowledge of anatomy – heart, lungs, liver	a) b)
3	Hindered knowledge of anatomy because bodies could not be dissected further because of the belief in the use of the body in the afterlife			3 Physical causes of disease	

		What ideas did people have about treatments?				New Features

Treatment	Illness	Evidence	Feature	Evidence
1 Medicine and spells		*Papyrus Ebers* (Source D)	4 Hygiene	a) b)
2 Vomiting Purging Bleeding		*Papyrus Ebers* (Source L)	5 Toilets	
3 Surgery: cautery and cutting out tumours	Dislocations, swellings and tumours	a) b)		

Factor	Effect
4	Understanding of the River Nile helped doctors think of the body as a series of channels

Special reasons for health or disease	
Reason	Evidence
Health The Egyptians had many cures that were based on empirical reasoning, they had recorded cures which worked, which they used, even if they were wrong about why they worked	

Who provided medical care?		
Group	Patients	Evidence
Trained doctors	Probably most people in Egypt, certainly the rich and workmen	a) b)

Did new ideas and treatments affect most people?
The evidence of Deir el-Medina suggests they did

GradeStudio

Examiner's tip

Some questions require you to use sources. In these questions you will need to use your knowledge of the topic to interpret and evaluate the sources. When you are asked to use specific sources you must do so, but you may also use any other sources within the question if they are relevant.

Source R

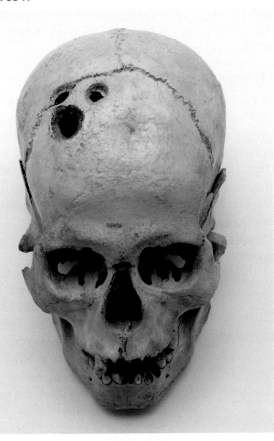

The skull of a Bronze Age man, found near Jericho in the Middle East. It was buried about 2000 BC

Source S

A carving from the temple of Kom Ombo in Egypt, made about 100 BC

a Study Source R. Why is Source R evidence of surgery during prehistoric times? Use the source and your knowledge to explain your answer.

[5 marks]

b Study Source S. What sorts of illnesses would ancient Egyptian doctors have treated with the instruments shown in Source S? Use the source and your knowledge to explain your answer.

[5 marks]

c Study both sources. Do these sources prove that surgery improved between the prehistoric period and the ancient Egyptian period? Use the sources and your knowledge to explain your answer.

[5 marks]

3 Medicine in ancient Greece

3.1 Greece, c.1000 BC – c.150 BC

In the ancient world Greece was a culture, not a country. The people we call the ancient Greeks lived not only in modern Greece and the Greek islands, but also in cities built on the shores of the Mediterranean, in modern Albania, Turkey, Italy, Spain and Africa. They shared a language and religious beliefs.

The Greeks started building their first cities, in mainland Greece, from about 1000 BC. By about 750 BC these cities had developed into city-states, which ruled over the surrounding countryside and began to colonise land around the shores of the Mediterranean.

At this time the Greeks explained many of the mysteries of nature by the actions of their gods. So, for example, volcanoes were caused by Hephaestos, the god of fire. He was a blacksmith. The smoke and flames of a volcano were said to be created by him as he worked at his forge. The changes in the seasons were explained by the myth of the goddess Demeter and her daughter Persephone. For six months of every year Persephone was forced to live in Hades, the world of the dead. This made Demeter so angry that, during this time, she would not allow plants to grow. Every spring, however, Persephone was released from Hades and Demeter, happy again, allowed the plants to grow.

The Greek world around 450 BC

Greek civilisation was at its height between 600 BC and 300 BC. The individual city-states developed and became more powerful. This was very different from Egypt, where there was a strong central state. While the Greek city-states were all different, each had a leisured upper class or classes who had plenty of time to spend on their interests. Science, **philosophy** and mathematics were important to many Greeks.

The Greek world, c. 450 BC

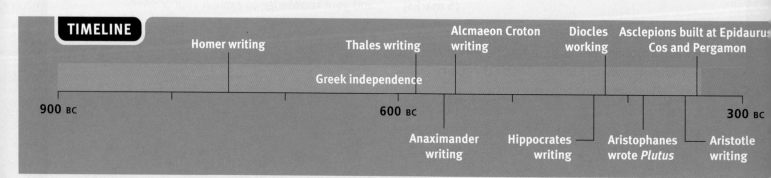

TIMELINE

Homer writing

Thales writing

Alcmaeon Croton writing

Diocles working

Asclepions built at Epidaurus Cos and Pergamon

Greek independence

900 BC   600 BC   300 BC

Anaximander writing

Hippocrates writing

Aristophanes wrote *Plutus*

Aristotle writing

They replaced the old supernatural explanations for events with new rational ones produced by philosophers. One philosopher, Thales of Miletus, predicted an eclipse of the Sun in 585 BC because he understood some of the movements of the Sun, Moon and planets. He also thought that water was the basis of all life. In about 560 BC Anaximander developed a theory that all things were made of four elements – earth, fire, air and water. Pythagoras, who died about 500 BC, was fascinated by mathematics. He put forward the idea that life was concerned with the balance between opposites.

Medicine developed too. Our first knowledge of Greek medicine comes from the poems of Homer. Historians believe that these were written about 750 BC, and based on earlier poems that had been passed down by word of mouth. They tell of the siege of Troy, and of the soldiers who fought in the Trojan war. Doctors are described giving common-sense treatment to wounded warriors, while treating other illnesses and diseases as having supernatural causes. It is the gods who send plagues, in Homer's work called the *Illiad*.

Two different medical traditions developed – rational and supernatural. The rational tradition was associated with Hippocrates, who was born about 460 BC. The medical books linked with him were written from about 430 BC onwards. The supernatural tradition was associated with the cult of the god Asclepios. It was said that Asclepios' sons had fought in the siege of Troy, and stories about him were common in Homer's time. However, the real growth of the cult of Asclepios came much later and the great temples that were the home of the cult were built after 400 BC. It is important to keep these dates in mind. What happened in Greece was not that a primitive supernatural system of medicine was replaced by a more advanced natural or rational medicine. Both traditions developed and flourished at the same time.

ACTIVITIES

1. Was the Greeks' explanation for the changes in the seasons *rational* or *supernatural*? Give reasons for your answer.
2. Was the Greeks' explanation for volcanoes *natural* or *supernatural*? Give reasons for your answer.
3. Describe a **change** in ideas in the Greek period.
4. Describe a **development** in ideas in the Greek period.
5. Was Hippocratic medicine a development from the work of the philosophers?
6. Was Hippocratic medicine a development from the supernatural medicine of the cult of Asclepius?
7. Was it possible for the Greeks to have any contact with the civilisation of Egypt?
8. How was the political organisation of Greece different from the political organisation of Egypt?

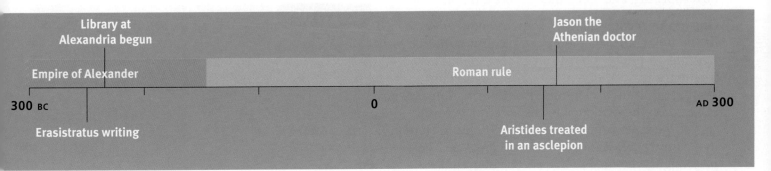

Library at Alexandria begun

Jason the Athenian doctor

Empire of Alexander

Roman rule

300 BC   0   AD 300

Erasistratus writing

Aristides treated in an asclepion

3.2 Asclepius and temple medicine

In this lesson you will:
- work out what happened in asclepions
- make inferences from, and evaluate evidence.

Asclepius was the Greek god of healing. The temples built for his worship, called 'asclepions', were used for treating the sick. The cult of Asclepius became more important during the 5th century BC and the three most important asclepions – in Epidaurus, Pergamum and Cos – were all built or rebuilt around 350 BC. Asclepius had two daughters, Panacea and Hygieia.

As you can see from Source C, the asclepions were large and complicated sites. People who were ill would go to an asclepion and spend at least one night there, praying to Asclepius and being treated. They would usually go through the following processes:
- make an offering or sacrifice to Asclepius
- bathe in the sea to cleanse and purify themselves
- sleep for at least one night in the abaton, a long, narrow building open to the air on each side. While sleeping in the abaton, patients expected to be visited by the god. Some had dreams. Others were probably treated by the priests. The snake was Asclepius' sacred animal. In Greek carvings, he is usually shown holding a staff with a snake wound round it. The priests used snakes as part of the treatment in the abaton. Ointments were often rubbed into the part of the body where symptoms occurred. Sometimes the snakes licked the sick part as well.

The patients were supposed to wake up cured the next morning, and some did. Others did not.

One of our most important sources about what happened in an asclepion is an account written by Aristides, a philosopher from Athens, about his treatment in AD 150. Aristides had spent years visiting different asclepions. The information above is based on the evidence in his account. Another source we have is the story of a visit to an asclepion in a comic play, *Plutus*, by Aristophanes, a Greek playwright who died in 388 BC. See Source B.

SOURCE B

First we had to bathe Plutus in the sea. Then we entered the temple where we placed our offerings to the gods on the altar. There were many sick people present, with many kinds of illnesses. Soon the temple priest put out the light and told us all to go to sleep and not to speak, no matter what noises we heard. The god sat down by Plutus. First he wiped the patient's head, then with a cloth of clean linen he wiped Plutus' eyelids a number of times. Next Panacea [the god's daughter] covered his face and head with a scarlet drape. The god whistled and two huge snakes appeared. They crept under the cloth and licked his eyelids. Then Plutus sat up and could see again, but the god, his helpers and the serpents had vanished.

In the play, Plutus had gone to the asclepion to be cured of blindness.

From *Plutus*, a play by Aristophanes

SOURCE C

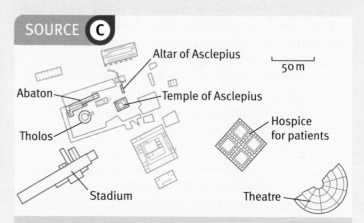

The main buildings of the asclepion at Epidaurus, c.350 BC.

ACTIVITIES

1 a How large is the site at Epidaurus compared with your school?

  b Does this tell you anything about the cult of Asclepius?

The cult of Asclepius flourished until the end of the Roman period (about AD 400). The practice of taking sick people to a religious site, in the hope that they would be cured, lasted even longer. This is what happened in many medieval pilgrimages. Until the middle of the 20th century, in some Greek islands, and in parts of southern Italy and Sicily, sick people spent the night in church hoping to be cured. Cures were regularly reported. This is an example of continuity (an idea or practice that stays the same for a long time). When studying the history of medicine we tend to concentrate on change, but continuity is also an important part of the overall picture.

SOURCE **D**

A carving made about 350 BC, showing Asclepius treating a boy called Archinos.

SOURCE **E**

Ambrosia of Athens became blind in one eye. She had laughed at being told of cures to the lame and the blind. But she dreamed that Asclepius was standing beside her, saying he would cure her if she would dedicate a silver pig as a memorial to her ignorance. He seemed to cut into her diseased eyeball and pour in medicine. When she woke in the morning she was cured.

Euhippus had had a spear point fixed in his jaw for 6 years. As he was sleeping in the temple Asclepius pulled out the spear point and gave it to him. When day came he left, cured and holding the spear point.

A man had his toe healed by a serpent. While he slept a snake crawled out of the shrine and licked his diseased toe. He woke cured, saying he had dreamed that a beautiful young man had put a drug on his toe.

Inscriptions like these, called **iamata**, recorded cures that were said to have happened in the temple.

A small selection from the stone inscriptions set into a wall of the asclepion at Epidaurus

ACTIVITIES

2 We have a number of sources of evidence about the cult of Asclepius. For each of Sources B, C, D and E, study the source and answer the following questions about it.

   a When was it made?
   b How useful is it? (What does it tell us?)
   c How reliable is it? (Should we believe it?)

3 Asclepions were both popular and successful. What evidence can you find to support this statement?

GradeStudio

Examiner's tip

Being able to distinguish how **useful** a source can be, and whether it is **reliable** or not, is very important, especially in Unit A952. It is a good habit always to ask yourself both questions about any source you use.

3.3 Hippocrates and the four humours

LEARNING OBJECTIVES

In this lesson you will:

- find out about the new medical ideas associated with Hippocrates
- practise describing and explaining.

We know very little about Hippocrates, who probably lived from about 460 BC to about 375 BC. He is associated with a collection of medical books known as the 'Hippocratic books'. The books were either written by him or his followers. The books show a new type of Greek medicine, concentrating not on the illness but on the patient. Hippocrates insisted that all diseases had physical causes. He firmly rejected magical and supernatural cures. He wanted doctors to observe each patient and the progress of their illness carefully. This system of observing the patient, which the Egyptians had also adopted, has developed into what we now call 'clinical observation'.

The Hippocratic books benefited from the ideas of two earlier Greek thinkers. Pythagoras (c. 580–500 BC) had taught that a healthy body was one in perfect balance. Alcmaeon of Croton (about 500 BC), a pupil of Pythagoras, had argued that a healthy body had the right balance of hot and cold, and wet and dry, within it. Any obvious imbalance (a high temperature or shivering) was a sign of ill health. The correct treatment would put the body back in balance.

Hippocrates emphasised the careful noting of symptoms. This was to help predict what would happen if another patient had the same disease. If there was a pattern in the development of a disease, the doctor would know what would happen next. Hippocrates believed it was important to let illness follow its natural course and to provide the patient with a clean and calm environment. A doctor could use natural, herbal remedies, but only once he was sure what was going on. Complete rest was the usual Hippocratic treatment.

Hippocratic medicine tried to avoid surgery, but sometimes surgery was the only option. Surgery in Greek times was dangerous because dissection was not allowed and doctors had only a vague idea about

Fact file

Clinical observation

Clinical observation is the careful noting of all the symptoms of a disease and of the changes in the patient's condition during the course of an illness. A doctor was supposed to follow four steps:

- **Diagnosis.** Study the symptoms of the patient. In what ways is the patient different from normal?
- **Prognosis.** Try to predict the course the illness will follow, by thinking about previous patients with the same symptoms.
- **Observation.** Continue to observe the patient, noting changes in their condition and comparing these to the prognosis.
- **Treatment.** Treat the patient, but only when observations have confirmed the prognosis and previous experience has shown the treatment to succeed.

anatomy. The Hippocratic books about surgery dealt mainly with the type of procedures that had the highest success rate – the setting of fractures and the resetting of dislocated bones.

The four humours

The Hippocratic books sometimes talked about the body being made of different elements, which needed to be in balance for a person to be healthy. Some years later, the Greek thinker Aristotle

SOURCE F

The tombstone of Jason, an Athenian doctor, who died in the 2nd century AD. Jason is examining a patient. To the right (shown much larger than life-size) is a bronze bleeding cup. It was heated, placed over a small cut, and then cooled. This created a small vacuum, which drew out some blood.

(384–322 BC) put forward a clear theory about this, and the cause and treatment of disease.

He suggested that the body was made up of four liquids or 'humours' – blood, phlegm, yellow bile and black bile. He connected these with the four seasons – yellow bile with summer, black bile with autumn, phlegm with winter, blood with spring – and said that there could therefore be too much of the connected humour in the body in a particular season. This would be a problem because, according to Aristotle, a person needed to keep the humours in perfect balance in order to be healthy.

The careful observations of Greek doctors must have helped to shape the theory. Some illnesses, such as colds and bronchial problems, are more common in winter than summer. These illnesses are likely to produce lots of phlegm. In the theory of the four humours, the presence of too much phlegm was seen as a cause of disease, not a symptom. To treat a patient, doctors sought to restore the balance of humours. If a patient was feverish and hot, it was thought that they probably had too much blood in their body. The solution was to 'bleed' the patient – cutting into a vein to take out some blood.

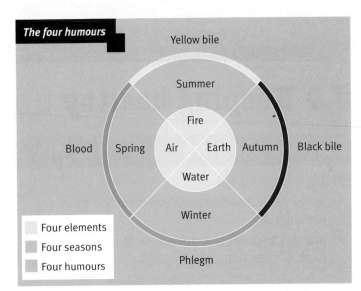
The four humours

Four elements
Four seasons
Four humours

SOURCE **G**

Quinsey has the symptoms of shivering, headache, swelling under the jaw, dry mouth. The patient found it hard to spit, or breathe lying down. He was bled from the first vertebra of the spine. He had to breathe a mixture of vinegar, soda, organy and watercress pounded together then mixed with oil and water and heated. He breathed it through a hollow reed, while hot sponges were applied to his jaw and neck. He gargled with herbs and had his throat cleaned out with a ball of wool on the end of a twig of myrtle.

A description of symptoms and treatment given in a book in the Hippocratic collection, called *On Diseases*

ACTIVITIES

1 What was Pythagoras' idea about health?
2 Alcmaeon of Croton developed Pythagoras' idea.
   a What was Alcmaeon's development?
   b Explain why it was a development.
3 What was new about Hippocrates' ideas?
4 Describe the four stages of 'clinical observation'.
5 a What were the four humours?
   b How were they connected to the seasons of the year?
   c According to the theory of the four humours, what caused disease?
   d What treatments were associated with the theory of the four humours?
6 Compare Source D on page 23 with Source F.
   a What clues are there in Source D that this is supernatural medicine?
   b What clues are there in Source F that this is rational medicine?
7 A doctor who accepted the theory of the four humours might bleed a patient. What would this doctor see as the cause of the problem, and in which season of the year would the doctor be happiest doing this treatment?

GradeStudio

Understanding

Briefly describe Hippocratic medicine.   **[5 marks]**

Examiner's tip

This is like the first part of questions 2–4 in Unit A951.

The whole of each question is worth 20 marks, and this part is worth just 5 of those 20, so don't spend too much time on it. Make sure you do two things:
• give examples
• describe and explain your examples.

3.4 Keeping healthy

LEARNING OBJECTIVES

In this lesson you will:

- study public health and Greek medicine from Alexandria
- practise your skills in answering 'describe and explain' questions.

'Regimen' was a word the Greeks used a lot when they discussed health. It covered all aspects of people's lives – what they ate or drank, how much they slept, how much exercise they took, what they did as a job, and so on. Everything was taken into account. The modern word is 'lifestyle'.

Healthy habits

The idea of a regimen for a healthy life was not new. The Greeks had always believed that eating and drinking well helped people to keep healthy. Exercise and keeping clean were also important parts of Greek life. Many of the Hippocratic books set out exactly what should be eaten, drunk or avoided for perfect health, and when meals should be taken. They also outlined the best forms and amount of exercise to take. Following all the books' advice about hygiene, eating and exercise would have filled a normal day! Doctors seem to have realised that these were ideal measures which only the rich would be able to take, and they gave more general advice for ordinary working people who had limited time and money to spend on their regimen.

Advising people to follow a healthy regimen helped to prevent disease. However, the Greeks did not take more public measures to prevent disease in their populations, such as building sewers or creating clean water supplies for their cities.

ACTIVITIES

1 **a** What was the Greek idea of a healthy lifestyle?

   b In some ways modern ideas about a healthy lifestyle are similar to those of the ancient Greeks. Does this mean that there has been no progress in our understanding of how to keep healthy since that time? Explain your answer.

SOURCE

After waking, a man should not get up at once but should wait until the heaviness of sleep has gone. After rising, he should rub his body with oil. He should then wash his hands, face and eyes with pure water. He should rub his teeth inside and out with his fingers, using fine peppermint powder to clean the teeth and remove the remains of food. He should oil his nose and ears, preferably with perfumed oil and rub oil into his hair every day, washing and combing it only at intervals.

After such a morning toilet, people who have to work, or choose to work will do so, but people of leisure will first take a walk. Long walks before meals clear out the body, prepare it for receiving food, and give it more power for digesting.

From a book by Diocles, a Greek doctor of the 4th century BC

SOURCE I

A vase painting from about 550 BC, showing women washing.

GradeStudio

Understanding

Briefly describe public health in ancient Greece.

[5 marks]

Alexandria – a great medical centre

Between 334 and 326 BC, Alexander the Great conquered a vast empire which stretched from Greece as far as India. In 332 BC he founded a new capital city, Alexandria, in Egypt, and soon after this, the great library of Alexandria was built. The intention was that all the knowledge of the world should be collected there. The library was stacked with the works of famous doctors, writers and philosophers. The greatest thinkers of the Greek world gathered there to work.

Knowledge of anatomy could only progress when human dissection became acceptable. Philosophers like Plato and Aristotle argued that, once the soul of a person had left the body after death, it was acceptable to cut the body up. Being able to dissect human bodies meant that people could gain a more accurate knowledge of the position of the organs and could examine the veins and arteries, muscles and bones.

Dissection was allowed in Alexandria. For a short time even dissection of the living was carried out. Criminals who had been condemned to die were dissected and consequently the movement of blood around the veins was discovered. The practice of dissecting living bodies was soon stopped, but dissection of the dead was still allowed and advances in anatomy were made. The work carried out at Alexandria stressed accurate observation of what was actually there.

Herophilus (c. 335–280 BC) worked in Alexandria on the comparative anatomy of humans and animals. He also studied the nervous system, and worked out how this connects to the brain. However, he saw the nerves as channels carrying pneuma (the life force), rather than nervous impulses, which we now know to be the case. Erasistratus (c. 250 BC) wrote about anatomy and health. He was a methodical anatomist, noticing the differences between arteries, veins and nerves. He thought at first, like Herophilus, that the nerves carried pneuma, but then rejected this idea when he found that nerves were solid, not hollow.

Because of the advances in anatomy, surgeons had a better idea of how the human body functioned, but this did not make surgery a great deal safer. There were still no anaesthetics or antiseptics, and hygiene was very poor. Unless their problem was simple, patients undergoing surgery were more likely to die than not.

Alexandria was famous for its study of surgery and medicine. Doctors who had studied there went to practise all over the world. But after the first few years, teachers and students split into various groups supporting the theories of the earlier writers. They developed competing theories of medicine and were more concerned with finding evidence to support their favourite theories than with studying what was actually there.

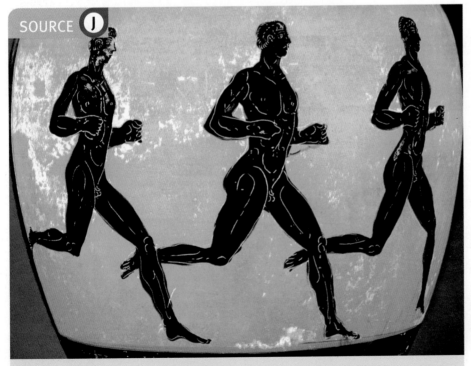

SOURCE J

A vase painting from 333 BC, showing young men racing.

VOICE YOUR OPINION!

Were Herophilus and Erasistratus scientists?

ACTIVITIES

2 What is the connection between Sources I and J?

3 What are the links between the power of the state, the library in Alexandria, and developments in medicine?

4 How did religious theories about the soul help medicine?

5 What advances in anatomy were made in Alexandria?

6 How did competition and jealousy affect the work done in Alexandria?

3.5 The legacy of Greek medicine

GETTING STARTED

Study Source K. How can you be sure whether this is rational or supernatural medicine?

Greek doctors practised all over the Mediterranean world. Some elements of Greek medicine had a significant impact on later cultures, both on the kinds of medicine they practised and on their ideas about how illness should be treated. Some of these ideas and practices were passed down, lost, then rediscovered.

A code of conduct and practice

One of the most significant legacies handed down by the Greeks was the idea that doctors should follow a set of rules of behaviour. Hippocrates set out the 'Hippocratic Oath' for doctors to take, which outlined the way they should behave.

Clinical observation is used in all hospitals and medical centres today. Doctors always want to see a patient before they prescribe treatment for his or her illness. Records are kept of all the illnesses and treatments that a patient has had. When a patient is in hospital, charts are kept to record progress.

HISTORY DETECTIVE

What did the Hippocratic Oath say? What are the Declaration of Geneva (1948) and the Oath of Lasagna (1964)?

SOURCE K

A Greek vase from about 400 BC, showing a doctor treating a patient.

BRAIN BOOST — MEDICINE IN ANCIENT GREECE

What caused things to stay the same or change?		What ideas did people have about causes of disease?			New Features		
Factor	**Effect**	**Cause of Disease**		**Evidence**	**Feature**		**Evidence**
1	a) A settled society – the study of medicine could develop b) No strong central control so different ideas could flourish c) The great library at Alexandria founded – medical ideas spread and develop faster	1 Supernatural		a) b) c)	1 Asclepions (special places for treatment of the sick)		a) b) c)
		2		a) b) Aristotle	2 Trained doctors who examined their patients and had a moral code		a) b)
		What ideas did people have about treatments?					
2	a) Cult of Asclepios develops centres of medicine and treatment b) Stops human dissection for most of Greek civilisation, but allows it for a time in Alexandria	**Treatment**	**Illness**	**Evidence**	3 Clinical observation – diagnosis by observation and forecasting		
		1	Any	a) play Plutus (Source B) b)	4 Theory of the Four Humours		
3	New ideas about the natural world encouraged doctors to look for new and better explanations for disease in medicine	2 Bleeding		a) Vase painting (Source K) b)	5 The idea of a regimen for health – a mixture of exercise and hygiene		
Special reasons for health or disease		**Who provided medical care?**			**Did new ideas and treatments affect most people?**		
Reason	**Evidence**	**Group**	**Patients**	**Evidence**			
		1	Probably most people	a) Hippocratic books b) Jason's grave			
		2 Priests in the Asclepions	Probably all who went to the Asclepion				

GradeStudio

In Unit A951, question 1 part (a) requires you to use sources. You will need to use your knowledge of the topic to interpret and evaluate the sources. When you are asked to use specific sources you must do so, but you may also use any of the other sources within the question if they are relevant.

You are advised to spend about 8 minutes on this question.

Source A
Here is the great remedy. Come! You who drive evil things from my stomach and my limbs. He who drinks this shall be cured just as the gods above were cured.

A spell from the Papyrus Ebers. The doctor was to chant this spell while giving the patient the medicine. The Egyptian doctor who used the papyrus had written next to the spell, 'This spell is really excellent – successful many times.'

a Would Hippocrates have approved of the treatment used in Source A? Use the source and your own knowledge to explain the answer.

[5 marks]

Which of these two answers is better, and why?

Answer 1

Hippocrates would not have approved because he believed that all diseases only had natural causes, but this treatment is a supernatural treatment because it is a spell as well as a medicine. So Hippocrates would have thought this was wrong.

Answer 2

I think he would have approved because the doctor who used the source had written down that it was really excellent and had been successful many times.

Examiner's tip

- This is just the first part of a typical question 1 from A951. In the real paper there will be three sources and part questions.
- You should spend about 25 minutes on the whole of question 1, and each part is worth 5 marks, so you should split the time evenly between the three parts of the question.
- Although you are using only one source for part question (a), you have to think about two historical periods – ancient Egypt (where the source comes from) and ancient Greece (Hippocrates).
- In order to answer the question you need to remember what Hippocrates thought about the causes of disease, and to work out (or remember) what the source tells you about Egyptian beliefs about causes of disease.

4 Roman medicine

4.1 What made the Romans different?

Rome started as a small state in Italy. It was determined to expand, conquering first the other states in Italy and then, by 275 BC, the Greek cities in Italy. Next Rome began to conquer the Greek cities around the Mediterranean, and won a long war against Carthage, to take control of the north African coast. In 146 BC the cities of mainland Greece fell.

Rome ruled a growing empire, in an efficient and centralised way. Decisions were made in Rome, or referred to Rome for approval. Once made, they were carried out by governors of the provinces and civil servants, backed by a powerful army. It was vital to keep this army healthy, and so the Romans developed **public health** projects – providing sewers and clean water for their towns and cities. Like the Greeks and the Egyptians, the Romans were great builders, but their work was more practical. Roman building achievements included aqueducts, sewers, roads and bridges, rather than temples and monuments to the dead.

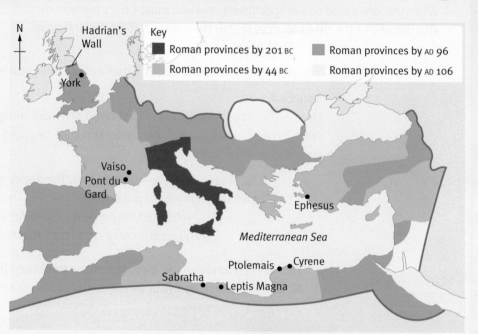

Key
- Roman provinces by 201 BC
- Roman provinces by 44 BC
- Roman provinces by AD 96
- Roman provinces by AD 106

Hadrian's Wall
York
Vaiso
Pont du Gard
Ephesus
Mediterranean Sea
Ptolemais
Cyrene
Sabratha
Leptis Magna

KEY WORDS

Public health – *health measures that affect the whole community, not just a few people. In Roman times this meant clean water, sewers and toilets. Today, as well as these three, public health includes things like vaccination against diseases.*

ACTIVITIES

1 Study the timelines for Prehistory, Egypt, Greece and Rome. How does the Roman period compare in length with the others?
2 Study the maps of Egypt, Greece and the Roman Empire. How is Rome different from the other two?
3 List three characteristics of Roman civilisation.
4 Are these characteristics similar to, or different from, the main characteristics of Greek civilisation?

TIMELINE

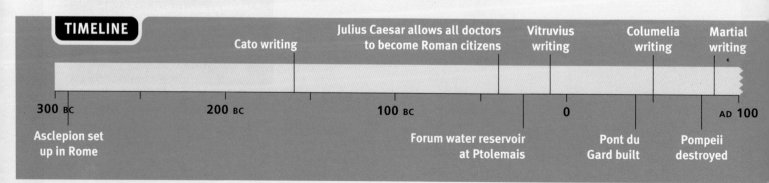

Cato writing | Julius Caesar allows all doctors to become Roman citizens | Vitruvius writing | Columelia writing | Martial writing

300 BC — 200 BC — 100 BC — 0 — AD 100

Asclepion set up in Rome | Forum water reservoir at Ptolemais | Pont du Gard built | Pompeii destroyed

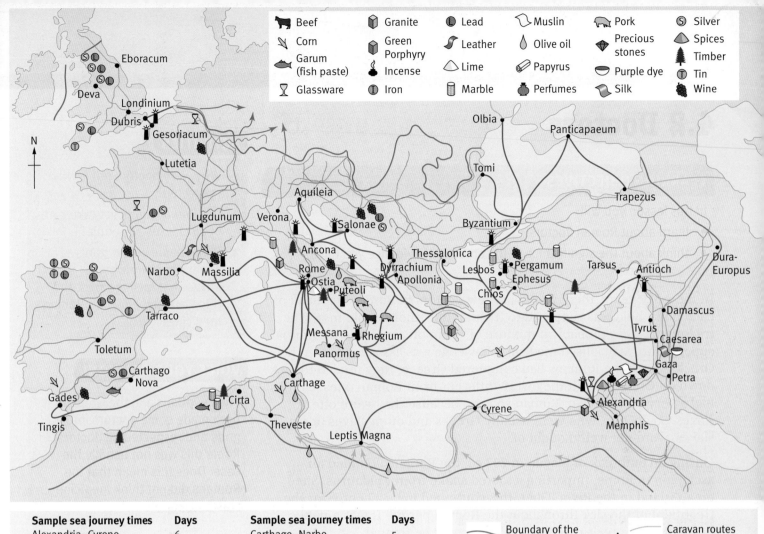

Sample sea journey times

Sample sea journey times	Days	Sample sea journey times	Days
Alexandria–Cyrene	6	Carthage–Narbo	5
Alexandria–Ephesus	4–5	Gades–Ostia	9
Alexandria–Massilia	30	Ostia–Carthage	3–5
Alexandria–Puteoli	15–20	Ostia–Narbo	3
Alexandria–Antioch	8–10	Ostia–Tarraco	6
Byzantium–Caesarea	20	Rome–Caesarea	20
Byzantium–Gaza	10–12		

Boundary of the Roman Empire c. AD 200 — Caravan routes — Sea routes — Lighthouse — Land trade routes in Germany — Roads — Rivers

Communications

The Roman Empire depended on good communications. There were good roads, harbours and ports, and the seas and land were kept clear of pirates and robbers. Roman troops could be moved quickly to any part of the empire. Trade was vital and widespread, as the map below shows. Rome itself depended on grain from Egypt. The combination of peace (it was called the *Pax Romana*) and good communications meant that ideas could move quickly, as well as goods.

ACTIVITIES

5 Where did Rome get most of the following? (There may be more than one answer.)
  a Wine   b Pork   c Beef

6 Cyrene was the source for important medical herbs. How would they reach Hadrian's Wall?

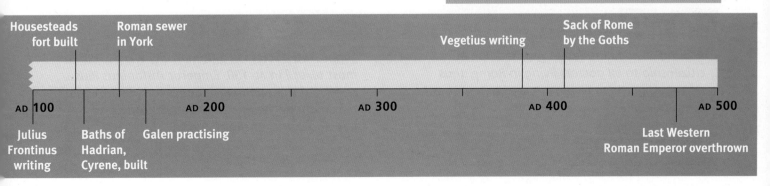

Housesteads fort built — Roman sewer in York — Vegetius writing — Sack of Rome by the Goths

AD 100 — AD 200 — AD 300 — AD 400 — AD 500

Julius Frontinus writing — Baths of Hadrian, Cyrene, built — Galen practising — Last Western Roman Emperor overthrown

4.2 Doctors

ACTIVITIES

1 Why were doctors not highly respected?

2 Did Roman medicine take care of all classes of people?

3 Rome had a well-organised government which was efficient at raising taxes. Did this have any effect on Roman medicine?

LEARNING OBJECTIVES

In this lesson you will:

- learn about Roman doctors
- think about the significance of the amount of evidence you have.

In the early years, there were very few doctors in Rome. The head of each household was supposed to treat all the other people in it. The treatments were probably a mixture of common sense and traditional superstition. Specialised medical knowledge was associated with the Greeks. Since the Romans had conquered Greece, they tended to look down on Greek ideas if they were different from Roman ones. Greeks had a very low status in Roman society, because they were often slaves. So doctors, who were usually Greeks and often slaves or ex-slaves, were not well thought of.

During an outbreak of plague in 293 BC, the Romans founded an asclepion in Rome, importing a sacred snake from Epidaurus. Sited on an island in the River Tiber, this continued to be a centre for the treatment of the sick throughout the Roman period. It was a public hospital where poor people and slaves could be treated.

The Roman rulers wanted their whole population to be healthy. Apart from anything else, they needed to be able to recruit healthy soldiers. They appointed public doctors in Rome, and all over the empire. These men were paid by the state, and treated the poor. As the army spread out to garrison the growing empire, hospitals were set up for wounded soldiers. They were called *valetudinaria*. Because these were popular, others were set up for the civil servants who governed the empire, and then still more to treat the poor.

Doctors were still seen as having low social status. However, in 46 BC Julius Caesar passed a decree allowing them to become Roman citizens, and after this, those who successfully treated the wealthy and powerful could become famous and wealthy themselves. Greeks continued to dominate the medical profession throughout the Roman period.

VOICE YOUR OPINION!

The Egyptians and the Greeks both made some doctors into gods and respected all doctors; in Rome this was not usually the case. Does this mean that the Romans did not think medicine was very important?

SOURCE A

They have sworn to kill all barbarians with their drugs, and they call us barbarians. Remember that I forbid you to use doctors.

Cato treated his own family with cabbage, either externally, eaten, or mixed with wine.

The Roman writer Cato, who died in 149 BC, warning his son against Greek doctors

SOURCE B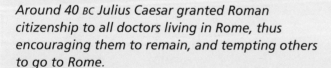

Around 40 BC Julius Caesar granted Roman citizenship to all doctors living in Rome, thus encouraging them to remain, and tempting others to go to Rome.

Caesar also excused doctors from many taxes.

The Roman historian Suetonius, writing about AD 100

SOURCE C

[Approved doctors in a Roman city were excused most taxes.] In AD 150, Emperor Antoninus Pius restricted the number of 'approved' doctors to a maximum of five, seven or ten, according to the size and status of their towns.

Audrey Cruse, *Roman Medicine*, 2004

Fact file

Doctors' tombstones

An important source of information about Roman doctors is their tombstones. Here you can see two examples, and a table that summarises what we can learn from all the tombstones that have been discovered so far.

The social and ethnic status of doctors in Rome from the 1st to the 3rd century AD

	Total	Greek	% Greek
Citizens	186	118	63
Freedmen	170	158	93
Slaves	55	54	98
Foreign, non-citizens	31	23	74
Total	442	353	80

These figures represent doctors for whom tombstones have been found. They can only be a small fraction of the total number of doctors in those 300 years. Freedmen were ex-slaves.

A tombstone of a Roman doctor, from Leptis Magna, a Roman city in modern Libya

The tombstone of a doctor found in Rome. The inscription reads:

Claudius Agathembus a doctor I lie here
Knowledgeable in swift remedies for all kinds of illness
I have set up this common memorial for myself and my wife Myrtale
We are together with the blessed in Eleusis.
He was originally from Sparta.

ACTIVITIES

4 How do attitudes to doctors change between Source A and Source B?

5 What might have happened between Sources B and C to produce the new policy about tax?

6 How does the Leptis Magna tombstone show continuity with Greek medicine?

7 From what you know about doctors, would you expect the tombstone from Rome to come from the early Roman period or later? Give reasons for your answer.

8 What can you learn from the table?

9 Why is any statement about doctors based on this table likely to be more reliable than a statement based on either of the two photos?

4.3 Roman public health

LEARNING OBJECTIVES

In this lesson you will:
- study a range of evidence about Roman public health
- practise your skills of inference and using evidence to reach your own conclusions.

a Introduction

For the Romans, prevention was better than cure. However, before they could prevent illness, they had to decide what caused it. The Romans were a practical people and they learnt much from observation. One of the things they observed was that people who lived near marshes and swamps tended to get ill, and often die, from the disease we now call malaria. Was there a connection between the swamps and the illness? The first solution was to build a temple to Febris, the goddess of fever, in the largest swamp near Rome. If you believe in supernatural causes and cures for disease, this is an obvious thing to do. However, over time, the Romans must have noticed that just as many people were dying as before. The next measure they took to try to solve the problem was to drain the swamps. The fewer swamps there were near Rome, the less malaria there would be. It worked.

This shows two important things about the Roman system of public health.

- It could only work within the Romans' understanding of the causes of disease. However, sharp observation and common sense got them a long way. They realised that the swamp was part of the problem, and took action, while not knowing the way in which malaria is spread by mosquitoes. The Romans often solved problems in this empirical way, acting on what they knew was happening rather than waiting to know exactly why it was happening.
- The Romans were willing to tackle large engineering projects in order to solve problems. Draining the swamps around Rome cannot have been cheap or easy, but the Romans had the willpower, resources and technology to do it.

Their empirical observations suggested to the Romans that a number of things were likely to cause disease:
- bad smells or 'bad air'
- bad water
- swamps and marshes
- being near sewage
- not keeping clean.

They therefore took all these things into account when choosing a site for a new house, town, or military camp. They also worked hard to get rid of these problems in the great towns and cities they had already built.

These ideas about preventing disease were tied to another Roman concern, always to have a strong army. Two things followed from this. The first was that army camps and barracks must always follow the ideas, to keep their soldiers healthy. The second was that, as the army depended on being able to recruit healthy new soldiers, disease should be prevented in the whole population. The government paid for public doctors and hospitals where the poor were treated. Measures like this, for the whole community, not just a few people, are called 'public health'.

ACTIVITIES

1 What was the Romans' main aim about disease?
2 Why was a temple to the goddess Febris built in the swamps near Rome?
3 What did the Romans do when this did not work?
4 What two things does the story of the marshes near Rome tell us about Roman public health?
5 What is public health?
6 What five things were Roman public health measures designed to avoid?

In the rest of Chapter 4.3, you have the chance to work out which were the most important things in Roman public health – clean water, toilets and sewers, and baths. For each of these subjects, you will find a short introduction and a collection of sources. Complete a simple form for each source, answering these questions:

Location: Where the source is or where it refers to.
Date: When it was made and/or used.
Description: A brief description of what the source is.
Conclusion: What you can learn from the source about Roman public health.

Mark the site of each source on a map, and its date on a timeline.

The activities for each subject will help you to reach a conclusion about it.

b Clean water

The Romans used their engineering skills to bring pure water into their towns. There were 14 aqueducts, bringing 1350 million litres of fresh water per day into Rome. The water ran through brick and stone channels. The Romans had no system for pumping water, so the whole course of the channel had to run gently downwards. This meant that most channels started in the nearest hills or mountains. Aqueducts were built to carry the channels across valleys, while sometimes tunnels had to be cut through hills. When the water reached the city, it was used for many purposes.

It was not only Rome that had a complicated and expensive water system. Rome's system was copied in all the main towns of the empire.

Grade Studio

Examiner's tip

Unit A952 tests your ability to use sources. This exercise is designed to help you practise two skills in using sources:

Inference – working things out from the source which must be the case, but which the source does not tell you.
Utility – working out what a source can be useful for.

SOURCE **D**

The Roman forum at Ptolemais (Tolmeita in modern Libya), built in the late 1st century BC. The forum was an open square, of 4200 square metres, around which were the most important buildings of the town. What appears to be the ground level of the forum is really the top of a roof covering 14 large reservoirs, which were fed by an aqueduct. The top photo shows part of the forum today. The square hole in the middle was for a grille, which allowed light and air to pass into the reservoir below. The lower photo shows one of the reservoir chambers, with light coming from the grille holes in the forum. The chamber has not been fully excavated, and was much deeper in Roman times.

SOURCE E

We must take great care in searching for springs and, in selecting them, keep in mind the health of the people. If a spring runs free and open, look carefully at the people who live nearby before beginning to pipe the water. If their bodies are strong, their complexions fresh, their legs sound and eyes clear, then the water is good. If this water is boiled in a bronze cauldron without any sand or mud left in the bottom of the cauldron, then the water will be excellent.

Vitruvius, a Roman writer and architect in the 1st century BC

SOURCE F

The new Anio aqueduct is taken from the river, which is muddy and discoloured because of the ploughed fields on either side. Because of this, a special filter tank was placed at the start of the aqueduct, where soil could settle and the water clarify before going along the channel.

Julius Frontinus, the curator of Rome's water supply, writing in about AD **100**

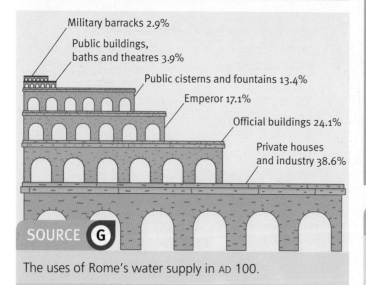

Military barracks 2.9%
Public buildings, baths and theatres 3.9%
Public cisterns and fountains 13.4%
Emperor 17.1%
Official buildings 24.1%
Private houses and industry 38.6%

SOURCE G

The uses of Rome's water supply in AD 100.

SOURCE I

A lead water pipe found in the Roman city of Vaiso (modern Vaison-la-Romaine, in southern France). It was probably made in the 1st century AD. Pipes like this were used to take water from the settling tanks, where water entered the town, to the different areas of the town.

ACTIVITIES

Use these questions to help you use the sources to consider the importance the Romans placed on clean water.

7   Is there any evidence to suggest that the Romans had worked out a system for water supply?
8   Does the evidence show that the Romans spent considerable time and money on water supply?
9   Does the evidence show that the Romans only cared about water supply in Rome?
10 Does the evidence of water supply suggest that Rome had a strong government?
11 How did the Romans use aqueducts and reservoirs to supply their towns with clean water?

SOURCE H

The Pont du Gard aqueduct, which carried water to the Roman town at Nîmes in southern France. Built in the middle of the 1st century AD, the aqueduct could carry more than 22 million litres of water per day, and the full route is 31 kilometres.

c Toilets and sewers

Public toilets were a common feature in Roman towns and cities. The toilet seats were like stone benches with holes in, around the edge of the room. Underneath was a channel where water was constantly running, to wash the waste out of the building. Instead of toilet paper, people used a sponge on a stick, which could be cleaned in another channel of clean water running in the floor in front of the benches. There were no separate cubicles, as in modern toilets, and people could sit and chat; it was a social time.

A Roman sewer at York, 2nd century AD. Made from millstone grit, this sewer took waste from the legionary fortress to the River Foss. Cleaning and maintenance could be carried out through a series of manholes which gave access to the channel.

The smaller, inner arch is the original outlet of Rome's main sewer, the Cloaca Maxima, into the River Tiber. The distance from the water to the top of the arch is more than 2 metres. The sewer was flushed by the poorest-quality water that the aqueducts brought into Rome. We don't know when the sewer was built, but major repairs were carried out in 33 BC.

Old men still admire the city sewers, the greatest achievement of all. They were built 700 years ago, and they are still undamaged. It is said the tunnels are large enough for a wagon load of hay to pass through.

When Marcus Agrippa became aedile [the official in charge of the water and supply and the sewers] in 33 BC he travelled on a tour of inspection under the city in a boat. There are seven rivers made to flow in seven tunnels under the city, these finally flow into one great sewer. These rivers rush through like mountain streams, and, swollen by all the rainwater, they sweep away all the sewage.

Pliny the elder, a Roman author, writing in *The Natural History*, AD 77

The toilets at one of the public baths (the Seaward Baths) in Sabratha, a Roman town in modern Libya. The baths were built in the 1st century AD, and were luxurious. Originally the floor and walls, as well as the seats, were covered with marble. The roof extended to the pillars, and there was an open courtyard.

Mi

Mii

Miii

Miv

Mv

Key

Stone walls

Clear water

Waste channel

The remains of the toilets at Housesteads fort on Hadrian's Wall, built about 125 AD.

SOURCE O

A modern artist's reconstruction of the toilets at Housesteads.

SOURCE P

For hours, for a whole day he'll sit
On every public lavatory seat.
It's not because he needs a sh*t:
He wants to be asked out to eat.

A poem by the comic poet Martial, written about 86 AD

VOICE YOUR OPINION!

Some seats in public toilets were more popular than others. Look back at the evidence about the toilets in Sabratha and suggest which seats there were the most popular, and why.

ACTIVITIES

Use these questions to help you use the sources to consider the importance the Romans placed on providing public toilets and sewers.

12 Is there any evidence to suggest that the Romans had worked out a system for toilets and sewers?

13 Does the evidence show that the Romans spent considerable time and money on toilets and sewers?

14 Does the evidence show that the Romans only cared about toilets and sewers in Rome?

15 Does the evidence of toilets and sewers suggest that Rome had a strong government?

16 Describe the common features of a Roman public toilet, and how it worked.

A Roman toilet from Ephesus, built during the 1st century AD.

GradeStudio

Unit A952 has questions about a set of sources, which you have to interpret and evaluate. This whole section on Roman public health is designed to give you practice working with collections of sources.

You will often find a question that asks how useful a source is. For example:

Study Source P. How useful is this source to a historian studying the Roman public health system?

Opposite are summaries of different answers to this question. Work out a hierarchy, from worst to best.

a Useful because we can see that the seats were over the large channel that took out the waste, and we can also see the small channel of fresh water they washed the sponges in, and that they all sat together.

b Useful because it is a primary source. It comes from the Roman time.

c This is useful because it shows typical features of Roman toilets. In other ones, from Hadrian's Wall to Africa, you see the same things: the seats built up which had a waste channel running underneath, and the fresh water channel to wash the sponges in.

d Useful because it shows us what their toilet seats were like and that they were made from stone.

e A bit useful, but we can't tell whether they were mixed or had a roof.

d Public baths

Taking a bath was a social occasion too. A visit to the public baths could include a warm bath, a hot bath, time in a steam room, a swim, time in the exercise yard or the gymnasium, a massage, resting and chatting to friends, and a cold bath; and all this at a very low cost. The actual cleaning of the body was done by scraping sweat and dirt off the skin with a strigil. At some times bathing was mixed, but usually men and women either had separate public bath houses to go to or they went at separate opening times to the one public bath house. Many rich people had their own private bath complexes. The prices at the public baths were kept very low, so that the poor could afford to use them.

SOURCE R

Nuts, drinks	14
Pig's fat	2
Bread	3
3 chops	12
4 Sausages	8

A price list for snacks, found written on the wall of the Suburban Baths in Herculaneum, which were destroyed in AD 79. The prices are in 'asses', a Roman coin of low value.

SOURCE S

The bather entered the public baths through a courtyard of stylish design. From here the bather entered the changing room, where he could leave his clothes in a locker, and proceed to the baths proper. There were a great number of variations on the basic pattern of cold room, tepid room, hot room, sweating room, and cold plunge. There were also rooms where the natural oils the body had lost through perspiration could be restored by a rub down with olive oil, which was then scraped off with a metal flesh-scraper called a strigil. Here the pummelling by a masseur might go on as well. Ball games and other exercise might take place in the courtyard. The less active would settle for a game of dice and a drink

Anthony Birley, *Life in Roman Britain*, 1964

SOURCE T

I am surrounded here by every type of noise (my apartment overlooks the baths). I hear the groans as the he-men pump iron and throw those heavy weights all over the place. They are either really putting their backs into it, or just shamming. If there is a lazy chap who is just satisfied with a massage, I can hear the slap of the hand on his shoulder. If a ball-player comes up and starts yelling his score, I can't concentrate. Pile on top of that the row of some so-and-so, a thief being caught, and one of those blokes who likes singing in the bath, as well as those who dive into the pool with giant splashes of water. That's as well as those with loud voices. Think about the skinny plucker of arm-pit hair, whose yells are so loud everybody notices him, except when he is working and he makes somebody else yell for him. Now add on the medley of noise from drink sellers, sausage, pastry and hot food vendors, each hawking his goods with his own individual cry.

From a letter written by Seneca in about AD 50

SOURCE U

A mosaic from the doorway to the changing room in the Roman baths in Sabratha, in modern Libya. The text says 'Leave washed and healthy'. The curved implements are strigils, tools used to scrape sweat and dirt off the body after exercise or sweating in the hot room.

The Baths of Hadrian at Cyrene, in modern Libya. They were built in the late AD 130s.

SOURCE **X**

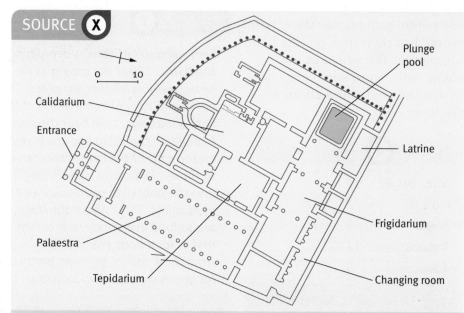

- Plunge pool
- Calidarium
- Entrance
- Latrine
- Frigidarium
- Palaestra
- Tepidarium
- Changing room

0   10

Modern archaeologist's plan of the baths of Hadrian at Cyrene.

SOURCE **W**

The walls of one of the hot rooms in the Seaward Baths at Sabratha. You can see the holes where the hot water pipes ran through the walls to make the room very hot.

ACTIVITIES

Use these questions to help you use the sources to consider the importance the Romans placed on public baths

17 Is there any evidence to suggest that the Romans had a consistent view about what was involved in taking a bath?

18 Does the evidence show that the Roman government spent considerable time and money on baths?

19 Does the evidence show that the Romans only cared about baths for the rich in Rome?

20 Does the evidence of public baths suggest that Rome had a strong government?

21 Does the evidence show that Romans only went to the baths to get clean?

22 Describe the different stages of a Roman bath, plotting a route through either the Baths of Hadrian at Cyrene or the Stabian Baths at Pompeii.

e The development of Roman public health

The graph below gives a fairly crude summary of the development of public health systems in Rome itself. The better the quality of the provision of clean water and sewage disposal, the higher the graph goes. The graph has been compiled from the table below, in which marks out of 5 are given for both sewage disposal and the provision of clean water.

None of the systems of public health that we have been looking at existed in Rome in 400 BC. So, in the table, both 'sewage disposal' and 'clean water' have been marked 0 out of 5. The systems for clean water and sewage disposal were developed over the next 300 years, and this development is reflected in the marks in the table. By about 100 BC the systems in Rome were very well developed, and so they are marked with 5s. From this time onwards the Romans didn't make any real developments in the quality of their systems. Rome grew bigger, and so there were more sewers and more aqueducts bringing in more water, but the increases were in quantity, not quality.

	400 BC	300 BC	200 BC	100 BC	AD 1	AD 100	AD 200	AD 300	AD 400	AD 500	AD 600
Sewage disposal	0	1	2	5	5	5	5	5	5	4	1
Clean water	0	1	2	5	5	5	5	5	5	4	1
Total	0	2	4	10	10	10	10	10	10	8	2

ACTIVITIES

23 Make your own table and graph for the standard of public health in Britain for these years. Don't worry about making rough and ready judgements about what marks to give. Being consistent is the most important thing.

24 Compare your graph for Britain with the one for Rome. What are the similarities and differences?

25 Why do you think the two graphs are different?

26 For each of the following statements, copy the statement into your book, say whether it is true or false, and support your answer with evidence from the course so far.
   a The rate of change in the history of medicine is constant.
   b In the history of medicine, change is always progress – things always get better.

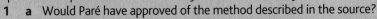

GradeStudio

Examiner's tip

This graph shows three important ideas in the history of medicine, which will often come up in the exam.

- **Progress**, when things get better. Between 400 BC and about 100 BC there was progress in the standard of Roman public health, but then it slowed down.
- **Regress**, when things that have improved become less good again. With the fall of the Roman Empire, the standard of public health in Rome became worse in AD 600 than it had been in AD 400.
- **The rate of change**, which is not steady. Sometimes change happens quickly. The fastest rate of change shown on the graph is between 200 and 100 BC. On this graph, the steeper the line, the faster the rate of change. At other times, change may happen very slowly, or not at all. For 500 years, from 100 BC to AD 400, the graph shows that the rate of change in Roman public health stalled completely. Throughout the course, you will see periods of fast change and periods of slow change.

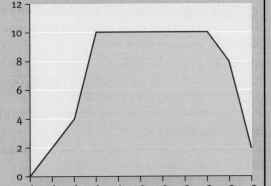

Keep these three ideas in mind when you answer questions in the exam.

Look at the exam questions below. For which questions are these ideas important? You will be able to work this out even for questions on parts of the course that you haven't studied yet.

1 a Would Paré have approved of the method described in the source?
   b What dangers faced patients during and after operations at the beginning of the 19th century?
   c Do these sources prove that by the 1870s surgery had improved little since the time of Paré?
2 a Briefly describe the medical progress made by the ancient Egyptians.
   b Explain why bloodletting was widely used in the Middle Ages.
   c Why did the ancient Greeks make more progress in medicine than people in the Middle Ages?

4.4 Galen

LEARNING OBJECTIVES

In this lesson you will:
- learn about the career and ideas of Galen
- improve your skills in 'Explain why …' questions.

Galen's life

Galen was born around AD 129 in Pergamum, one of the three great centres of the cult of Asclepios. He first trained as a doctor at the asclepion there, and later continued his studies in Alexandria. In AD 157 he returned to Pergamum as a doctor to the gladiators. Presumably this work gave him plenty of opportunity to study the inside of the human body – through the fighters' wounds. He went to Rome in AD 161 and became famous there, both for his success and for his boasting and showmanship. In AD 169 he was appointed doctor to the emperor's son, Commodus. This gave Galen a secure place in the Roman hierarchy and allowed him more time to concentrate on writing. He wrote more than 100 medical books.

Galen as a doctor

Standards had slipped since the time of Hippocrates, but Galen restored them – especially the idea of very close observation of a patient's symptoms. He believed in the theory of the four humours and developed many treatments based on the 'theory of opposites'. For example, if a woman came to him with a cold, he might prescribe pepper. Vigorous exercise or gymnastics would be the best treatment for a man who was weak or recovering from a serious illness. We know about Galen's work as a doctor from his own writings about treatments that worked and patients who survived.

Galen as an anatomist

When he was in Alexandria, Galen was able to study a human skeleton, but human dissection was no longer allowed there, for religious reasons. In Rome and Pergamum it was not even permitted to study a human skeleton, still less dissect a human body. Galen knew this was a problem. He encouraged young doctors to go to Alexandria so that they could at least study skeletons. If this was not possible, he recommended that they should always be on the lookout for a chance to see human bones. Galen told of seeing the bones of a robber by the side of a road through the mountains – presumably the body had been displayed on a gibbet as a warning to others – and a time when a flood had washed away part of a cemetery and human bones could be seen when the flood subsided. However, Galen could not base his study of anatomy on chances like these. He dissected animals instead. For many purposes, he recommended barbary apes as the most human-like animal available. For other experiments, he felt able to use pigs and other domestic animals.

Galen was a close and accurate observer of anatomy through his dissections. However, animal bodies are not like human bodies in all respects. Galen's theories of human anatomy were based on some key errors. Galen's study of the brain was undermined by his use of animals. He described a network of small blood vessels on the under-surface of the brain, called the *rete mirabile* (the wonderful network). He gave this a very important place in his theory of how the body works. Unfortunately, it is found only in certain animals and not in humans. Galen's observation also let him down. He was convinced that there were minute holes in the septum dividing the two chambers of the heart. These holes play an important part in Galen's physiology – but there are, in fact, no such holes.

Galen's importance

Galen was a great influence on Arab and Christian doctors in the Middle Ages. There are a number of reasons for this. Galen drew on the work and ideas of all the great doctors since Hippocrates. He wrote many books, most of which survived. He wrote powerfully, always dealing with possible objections to his theories. In many ways, his writing was like a speech in a debate. Also, he provided a complete theory of medicine; his books dealt with diagnosis and treatment, surgery, anatomy and physiology. Perhaps even more important, although he wrote in the 2nd century AD, when the Romans worshipped many gods, Galen's theories were acceptable to Christians and Muslims who worshipped only one god. Galen often talked about 'the creator' in his writing. He thought of the body as the work of a great architect or designer. This fitted in well with the religious beliefs that were to dominate Europe over the next 1300 years.

- **Pneuma** (life-giving spirit) was breathed in, went from the lungs to the heart and mixed with the blood.

- **Chyle** (the goodness from food) went from the intestines to the liver where it was made into blood with Natural Spirit.

- **Blood with Natural Spirit** went through the body nourishing and enabling growth. From the heart some went to the lungs, and some passed through the septum where it mixed with the pneuma to form blood with Vital Spirit.

- **Blood with Vital Spirit** went into the arteries giving power to the body. When this blood reached the brain it was changed into blood with Animal Spirit.

- **Blood with Animal Spirit** went through the nerves (which Galen believed were hollow) to give the body sensation and motion.

The animal which you vivisect should not be old – so that it will be easy for you to cut through the vertebrae.

...Now assume that you have already done what is here described, so that the spinal marrow lies exposed ... If you wish to paralyse all the parts of the body below this section and stop any movement ... then sever the spinal marrow with a cut running completely through so that no parts remain joined together ... If you cut by the thoracic vertebrae then the first thing that happens is that you see the animal's breathing and voice have been damaged. If you cut through between the fifth vertebra of the head, then both arms are paralysed.

Part of Galen's description of an experiment on a pig, to show the importance and function of the spinal cord.

From *On Anatomical Procedures*, written in the late 2nd century AD

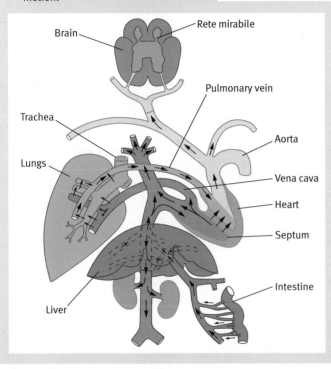

Brain — Rete mirabile — Pulmonary vein — Trachea — Aorta — Lungs — Vena cava — Heart — Septum — Intestine — Liver

 GradeStudio

Explain

In Unit A951 you have a choice of one question from three for your second question. This question will be in three parts and the second part will be an 'Explain' question. For example, a question of this type could be:

> Explain why Galen's ideas were so important for over a thousand years after he died. **[7 marks]**

To get the best mark you need to *explain*, not just mention, more than one reason. For example:

> ...Galen's books gave a summary of all the ideas of Roman medicine and were very well written, with lots of 'proof'. Also he talked about a creator who had made the body, and this fitted in with the ideas of Christianity and Islam that there was only one God.

ACTIVITIES

1 Galen trained as a doctor in Pergamum and Alexandria. What is the significance of these two cities in the development of medicine in the ancient world?
2 How might Galen's books have helped him to become an influential doctor, even after his death?
3 Galen's first job was as a doctor to gladiators. Why might this have given him some special advantages?
4 Explain, according to Galen's physiology, what happened to:
   a pneuma
   b food
   c blood with natural spirit
   d blood with vital spirit
   e blood with animal spirit.
5 Should historians of medicine see Galen's work as a development or a change?
6 What effect did religious beliefs have on Galen's work?
7 Galen's ideas of anatomy and physiology were wrong. Does this mean they are not important in the history of medicine?

4.5 The army

It was very important to keep the army healthy, and to keep the population healthy so that healthy soldiers could be recruited. Rome depended on its armies to conquer and then hold on to its great empire. There were special medical troops to treat the wounded on the battlefield and a number of military hospitals were built. Good water, sewage disposal and healthy sites were provided for military bases whenever possible. Permanent military bases, such as those along Hadrian's Wall, often had bath houses as well. Overall, health standards were very high in the army.

BRAIN BOOST — ROMAN MEDICINE

What caused things to stay the same or change?

	Factor	Effect
1		Large projects requiring complex organisation and a lot of money could be undertaken, like public baths, sewers and aqueducts
2		Rome's interest in Public Health was partly because it wanted a healthy army
3		Beliefs did not allow human dissection, which held back understanding of anatomy

Special reasons for health or disease

Reason	Evidence
	The spread of sewers, toilets, clean water supplies, toilets and sewers throughout the Roman Empire

What ideas did people have about causes of disease?

	Cause of Disease		Evidence
1	Spiritual	a)	
		b)	Building a temple to Febris to stop fever in Rome
2	Bad air, especially associated with bad smells or marshes	a) b) c)	
3	Bad water	a) b) c) d)	
4		a)	Bath mosaic (U) says 'leave washed and healthy'
		b)	Public baths including exercise facilities, e.g. Cyrene

What ideas did people have about treatments?

	Treatment	Illness	Evidence
1	Pepper		
2		General weakness; recovering from a major illness.	Galen

Who provided medical care?

Group	Patients	Evidence
Asclepions		
Public doctors paid by the state		
	The poor	

New Features

	Feature		Evidence
1	Well developed public health system concentrating on preventing disease	a) b) c) d) e)	Sewerage systems e.g. Rome, York — Public baths which included exercise facilities, e.g. Cyrene
2	New ideas about anatomy based on the dissection of animals		

Did new ideas and treatments affect most people?

Unit A951, second question, part (c)

For the second question on Unit A951 you will be asked to answer *one* of three questions. Each of the questions will have three parts and the last part, part (c), will need an answer that covers more than one period in the history of medicine.

Make sure you are clear what time period the question covers. This one is calling for examples from the end of the Roman Empire to the present day.

The question has a statement that you are asked to judge. Make sure you are clear what the statement says.

c 'Since Roman times chance has hindered rather than helped, medical progress.' Explain how far you agree with this statement.

When you see 'explain' in a question like this, make sure you include facts or examples in your answer, and explain *why* they support your answer.

Look for the key instruction words in the question – not just 'explain', but 'explain **how far**'. This is a sign that there is not a simple 'yes' or 'no' answer. The question asks you to decide whether the statement is a little bit true, or very true – is it 10 per cent right or 90 per cent right?

5.1 The fall of the Roman Empire in the West

GETTING STARTED

- Is technology better now than when your grandparents went to school?
- Is travel faster than when your grandparents went to school?
- Are doctors able to cure more illnesses than when your grandparents went to school?
- Imagine a world where the answer to all those questions was 'No'.

In the late 4th century AD the Roman Empire was in decline. Tribes of Huns, Goths and Vandals were threatening the empire. The Roman state seemed to have lost the power and drive it would need to reform itself. In AD 395 the empire split into two – an Eastern Empire, ruled from Byzantium, and a Western Empire, ruled from Rome. The Western Empire was soon in trouble. In AD 410, the Goths invaded Italy and sacked Rome itself. In AD 476 the last Roman emperor in the West was deposed by a Germanic chieftain.

One way to see what the fall of the Roman Empire meant for ordinary people, and for medicine, is to focus on the Roman province of Britain. The last Roman troops probably left Britain around AD 410, leaving it to the mercy of the invading Saxons. The link with Rome was broken, and features of life in Roman Britain that depended on a strong central government quickly fell into disrepair. Within one hundred years, many Roman towns had either been abandoned or become Saxon settlements. The water supply stopped working. The sewage system no longer worked. Houses no longer had sophisticated heating systems – a fire in the middle of the floor was more common. There were no more public or private baths. The strong and stable Roman rule – known as the *Pax Romana* – degenerated into something close to anarchy. In England, several small British kingdoms were all fighting for survival against bands of Saxon invaders.

As a result of this upheaval, knowledge was lost. Roman and Greek manuscripts were neglected and destroyed. Hardly anybody could read anyway. People with the engineering skills to build, or repair, the Roman public works died, and no new people were trained to take their place. People were living in a country where technology was much less advanced than in their grandparents' time. Only the rich could afford the best doctors, because there was no state to pay doctors to look after the poor. The poor often had to rely on local wise women (and sometimes men).

SOURCE A

Well-wrought this wall: Wierds broke it
The stronghold burst...
Snapped rooftrees, towers fallen,
the work of Giants, the stonesmiths,
mouldereth.
...
And the wielders and wrights?
Earthgrip holds them – gone, long gone,
fast in gravesgrasp while fifty fathers
and sons have passed

Part of an Anglo-Saxon poem, 'The Ruin', written in AD 700. It describes a ruined Roman city – probably Bath.

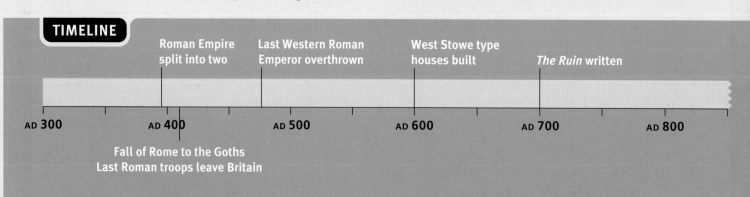

TIMELINE

	Roman Empire split into two	Last Western Roman Emperor overthrown	West Stowe type houses built	*The Ruin* written	
AD 300	AD 400	AD 500	AD 600	AD 700	AD 800
	Fall of Rome to the Goths / Last Roman troops leave Britain				

SOURCE B

Catch a frog when neither moon nor sun is shining. Cut off the hind legs and wrap them in deerskin. Apply the frog's right leg to the right foot and the left leg to the left foot of the gouty patient and he will certainly be cured.

A cure used by 'Gilbert', a doctor in the early 11th century

SOURCE C

A reconstruction of a Saxon house from about AD 600, based on an archaeological excavation at West Stowe, a Saxon village in Suffolk.

GradeStudio

Enquiry and interpretation

In the first question in Unit A951, the one that has sources, you might find a question like this:

Study Source B. Would Hippocrates have approved of the method described in Source B? Use the source and your knowledge to explain your answer.

> **Answer 1**
> I don't think he would have done because it sounds pretty stupid.

> **Answer 2**
> Hippocrates would not have approved. He did not believe in any spiritual cures. He thought everything was physical, and to do with the body getting out of balance. But Source B has gone back to some magical ideas – the stuff about catching it without moon or sun is pure magic, so Hippocrates would have thought this was nonsense.

a Which of these is the better answer?

b What makes the better answer good?

ACTIVITIES

1 Who were the 'Giants' in Source A?

2 How would you describe the belief about the causes of disease shown in Source B?

3 Study Source C and compare it to the evidence about Roman buildings in Chapter 4. Had building techniques got better or worse? Explain your answer.

4 Historians have sometimes called the period between AD 476 and about 850 the Dark Ages. Why do you think this is?

5 Did medicine in Britain progress or regress between about AD 400 and 800? Support your answer with reference both to sources and to other facts about the history of medicine.

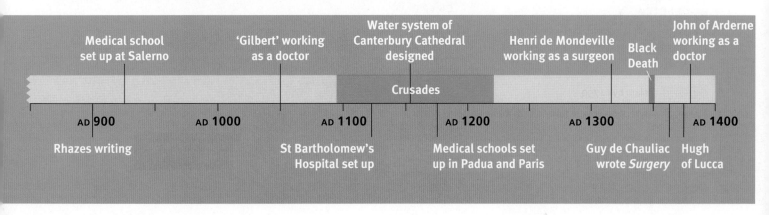

Timeline:

- Medical school set up at Salerno
- 'Gilbert' working as a doctor
- Water system of Canterbury Cathedral designed
- Henri de Mondeville working as a surgeon
- Black Death
- John of Arderne working as a doctor
- Crusades

AD 900 — AD 1000 — AD 1100 — AD 1200 — AD 1300 — AD 1400

- Rhazes writing
- St Bartholomew's Hospital set up
- Medical schools set up in Padua and Paris
- Guy de Chauliac wrote *Surgery*
- Hugh of Lucca

BRAIN BOOST   MEDICINE IN THE DARK AGES

What caused things to stay the same or change?	
Factor	**Effect**
1	a) Public works, like aqueducts, sewers and baths, could not be kept going b) Government could no longer pay for free doctors for poor people
2	Ideas could not spread easily from place to place
3 Loss of manuscripts due to fighting and disorder	
4	a) Fewer people could read b) Doctors not trained in the old ways
5 Loss of technological knowledge	

Special reasons for health or disease	
Reason	**Evidence**
	Roman towns and buildings falling into disrepair and out of use (Source A)

What ideas did people have about causes of disease?	
Cause of Disease	**Evidence**
	Gilbert's frog cure (Source B)

What ideas did people have about treatments?		
Treatment	**Illness**	**Evidence**
	Gout	

Who provided medical care?		
Group	**Patients**	**Evidence**
	The rich	
	The poor	

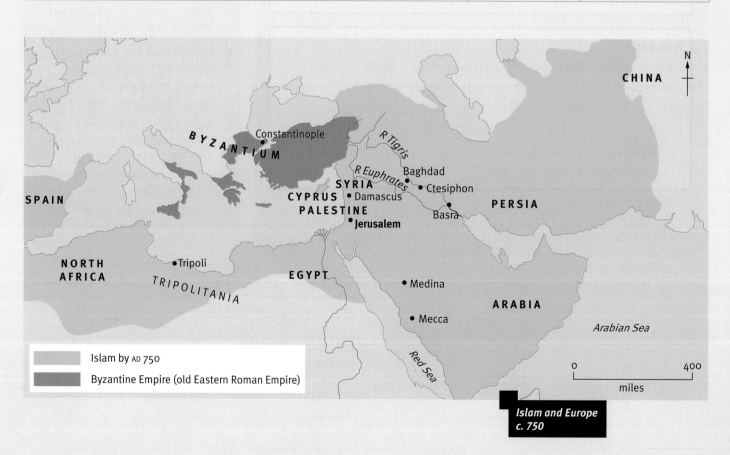

Islam and Europe c. 750

Islam by AD 750
Byzantine Empire (old Eastern Roman Empire)

6 Medicine in the Middle Ages

6.1 Islamic medicine

LEARNING OBJECTIVES

In this lesson you will:

- see how Greek and Roman medical knowledge came back to the West via Islam
- look at the best way to answer AO3 questions about reliability of sources.

GETTING STARTED

Compare the map on page 50 with the map of the Roman Empire on page 30. Which was the real successor to the Roman Empire: Christian Western Europe, the Byzantine Empire, or Islam?

The Western Roman Empire had collapsed by AD 500. The Eastern Empire survived and kept Greek and Roman learning, including medical ideas, alive. Some of these ideas were taken to Arabia by Nestorians, Christians who fled persecution in the Eastern Empire.

ACTIVITIES

1. How did Greek and Roman learning survive the fall of Rome?
2. What part did chance play in this survival?
3. What is the Qur'an and what does it teach?
4. What united all the people who became part of the Islamic Empire?

Islam

A new civilisation grew up in the Middle East, based on the religious teachings of Muhammad. Muhammad was a prophet, passing on the words of Allah. These words were written down to form the Qur'an, the holy book of Islam. The followers of Islam were called Muslims. They were expected to follow the teachings of the Qur'an exactly. They also had to follow the 'wise sayings' of Muhammad, collected in the Hadith.

The Islamic Empire

After Muhammad died, in AD 632, Islam was led by a series of caliphs, who were supposed to carry on Muhammad's teachings. Muslims were told to spread Muhammad's teachings and the caliphs did – sometimes by force. By AD 1000 they ruled a huge empire that stretched from Spain in the west to the River Indus in the east. People in the Islamic Empire all spoke Arabic, and Islam was the most important religion.

The various caliphs were rich and powerful and built beautiful cities, such as Baghdad and Cairo. They grew richer through trade, as they began to control important trade routes. In the cities they set up schools and, later, universities, because learning was important to Muslims. They also built mosques in which to worship. They built public baths, because the Qur'an said that hygiene was important.

Religion and ideas

All religions influence the way people think, including their ideas about medicine. Religion affects how people behave, and both Christianity and Islam refused to allow dissection of human bodies. This prevented surgeons from studying the human body in order to improve their knowledge and skill. Islam affected medicine in other ways, too.

The importance of learning

Islam encouraged learning. Books were so important in the Arab world that by AD 794 Baghdad had its own paper factory. Arab doctors used the Greek medical texts that had been translated by the Nestorians, and collected and translated even more. They took forward the medical ideas in these books and wrote their own medical books. So they preserved the medical works of people such as Hippocrates and extended medical knowledge too.

Treating patients

Both Muslims and Christians thought that diseases could be sent by their God. Christians often encouraged prayer, the repenting of sins and fasting, rather than treatment. The Hadith told Muslim doctors to try to cure patients: 'Oh servant of Allah, use medicine. Allah has not created pain without a remedy for it.'

Other ideas

The Qur'an insisted on cleanliness. Arab doctors observed that hygiene was important for health. Charity and caring for others were also important in Islam. This meant that hospitals were set up to care for the sick. At the hospital that was set up in Cairo in AD 1283, patients were given money when they left, so that they did not have to go straight back to work.

Diagnosing and treating disease

Arab doctors accepted and used ideas about diagnosis that were set out in books by Hippocrates and Galen. They used the idea of keeping the four humours balanced in the body. More importantly, they accepted the Hippocratic idea of clinical observation. They carefully observed and recorded the symptoms of patients and the effects of various treatments, so that they could learn by experience.

Arab doctors used processes that they invented, such as distillation, to prepare drugs for treating diseases and for use as **anaesthetics**.

Hospitals and doctors

Islamic towns and cities often had several hospitals to care for the sick. Hospitals were also used to train doctors, and a doctor who passed his training was given a licence. He could then set up his own medical practice or work in a hospital. Rhazes, Avicenna and Abulcasis were three famous Arab doctors. There were still many people in the Islamic world who set themselves up as healers without a licence, and they were not stopped from working.

ACTIVITIES

5 How did the teachings of the Qur'an influence Islamic medicine?

6 What continuity was there between Greek and Islamic medicine?

7 How did Arab doctors learn their job?

KEY WORDS

Anaesthetic – *something used by doctors to reduce pain. It can be a general anaesthetic, which affects the whole body, or a* local anaesthetic, *which just affects part of the body.*

SOURCE B

All that is written in books is worth much less than the experience of a wise doctor.

Written by Rhazes in about AD 900

KEY PEOPLE

Rhazes AD 860–923

Rhazes was an Arab doctor. In about AD 900 he was asked to set up a new hospital in Baghdad. He ran the hospital and also wrote about 200 medical books – both translations and notes on Greek books and books about his own medical discoveries. The most famous was *On Smallpox and Measles*. He was the first to observe and describe the difference between these two diseases. He also wrote a huge encyclopedia of medicine that covered Greek and Arabic ideas. It was called *El Hawi*.

KEY PEOPLE

Avicenna AD 980–1037

Avicenna was an Arab doctor who wrote many medical books. His *Canon of Medicine* was an encyclopedia of medicine that was translated into Latin, and so brought Greek learning back into Western Europe. The *Canon* was used as a standard textbook until about AD 1700.

SOURCE A

Doctors in the Islamic Empire used many herbal remedies.
This is an illustration from an Arabic translation, made in about AD 1229, of a Greek herbal remedy book by Dioscorides.

SOURCE C

The main symptoms of smallpox are backache, fever, stinging pains, red cheeks and eyes and difficulty breathing.

Excitement, nausea and unrest are more pronounced in measles than in smallpox, while aching in the back is less.

From *On Smallpox and Measles*, written by Rhazes in about AD 900

Surgery and dentistry

Arab doctors saw surgery as a last resort, despite the fact that, unlike Western surgeons, they had invented a way to anaesthetise the patient. They soaked a sponge in a mixture of narcotics, such as hashish and opium. They kept a supply of these sponges, dried out. When they needed to use one, they dampened it and either put the whole sponge over the patient's face or inserted two pieces in the nostrils.

The greatest Arab surgeon was Abulcasis (AD 936–1013), who wrote a surgical textbook with careful explanations and diagrams. One of the first points he makes in his book is that surgeons should never operate before knowing exactly what is causing the pain. They should work out what they are going to do and have all their equipment and anaesthetics ready before they begin, so that they can work as quickly as possible.

Arab surgeons were more willing to do surgery that did not involve opening up the body. They were skilled at operating on the eyes, successfully removing cataracts and tumours. Abulcasis wrote about sewing up wounds, setting fractures and dealing with dislocations, and included illustrations showing doctors what to do.

Arab dentists were more careful and skilled than Western ones. They even made artificial teeth from bone.

SOURCE D

I saw an Arab doctor in the hospital who was treating a knight that had a boil on his leg and a woman whose wits were wandering. He applied a poultice to the leg and the boil began to heal. He ordered a fresh diet for the woman. Then a European doctor arrived. He said: 'This man has no idea how to cure people'. He sent for a strong man with an axe, put the leg on a wooden block and told the man with the axe, 'strike a mighty blow and cut cleanly'. The man did as he was told. The marrow spurted out and the patient died at once. He turned to the woman and said, 'the devil has got into her brain'. He shaved her head with a razor, then used the razor to expose her brain, which he then rubbed with salt. She died also.

Written in about AD 1150 by Usama Ibn Munqidh, who fought in the Crusades against European soldiers in the Middle East

Fact file

Why the Crusades were good for medicine

The Crusades were a series of bitter wars fought between Christians and Muslims for control of the Holy Land. There were nine Crusades between 1095 and 1302, and both sides committed some terrible atrocities. How can the Crusades have been good for medicine?

War is often good for the development of medicine, because it gives doctors lots of practice at dealing with wounds, and they tend to work out new and better methods to use.

The Crusades were good for Western medicine for a different reason though. They brought Christians from the West – from modern Britain, France, Germany and Italy – into closer contact with the Islamic world. So the Europeans got to know more about Islamic culture. This included the medical books and ideas of the Arab doctors, who were much more advanced than their Western counterparts, partly because they had not lost the knowledge of Hippocrates and Galen.

So, the Crusades helped medicine in the West by being part of the route by which many of the books of Hippocrates and Galen, which had been lost, became available again.

 Grade Studio

Examiner's tip

In Unit A952 you may be asked a question about the reliability of a source. For example:

> **Study Source H.**
> **How reliable is this source for a historian studying Islamic medicine? Use the source and your knowledge to explain the answer.**

The last part of the question is important.

What does the source tell you? That the treatment of the Christian doctor killed the patients. Who wrote the source? A Muslim who fought against the Crusaders. He might well be biased against the Christian doctor, and his writing that the Christian doctor killed both the patients could be an example of bias.

But what does 'your knowledge' tell you? That Islamic medicine was more advanced than Western medicine, and that Muslim doctors used surgery only as a last resort. This suggests that the source may well be reliable.

Use these hints to help you to write a good answer to the question.

6.2 Europe and the Church

LEARNING OBJECTIVES

In this lesson you will:
- find out how important the Church was in the Middle Ages
- practise spotting continuity in the history of medicine.

ACTIVITIES

1 What got worse and what got better between about 500 and 1000?
2 In what ways was the Church like the Roman Empire?

The collapse of the Roman Empire had been a disaster for civilisation in the West. A world of cities, law, safe travel and communication, and learning, including the study of medicine, had turned into one of subsistence farming and widespread ignorance, ruled by a small elite warrior class.

By about the year 1000 things had improved. Larger states were growing up, which could usually keep law and order. Still about 96 per cent of the population of Western Europe worked on the land. Learning was largely confined to the Church, and in particular to the monasteries, where monks preserved some libraries, and continued to read books and make new ones.

The Church was an international organisation. At its head was the Pope, and there were clashes between the Pope and the kings of various countries, about how much power each had over the Church and churchmen. In England this quarrel led to the murder of Archbishop Thomas Becket in his cathedral in Canterbury, on the orders of the king, Henry II.

How the Church affected medicine

- The Church preserved and passed on knowledge. The libraries of the monasteries held some copies of Greek and Roman and later Arab medical books.
- The Church helped to set up universities and medical schools. Doctors were trained and, by working together, their teachers developed new and better ideas.
- The Church insisted that spiritual things always outranked physical things. If a person was dangerously ill, it was more important to be blessed by a priest than to be treated by a doctor.
- The Church set up hospitals all over Western Europe, which treated the sick, including the poor.
- The Church limited, but did not usually forbid entirely, human dissection, which is vital for any real progress in anatomy.
- Monks and friars often acted as doctors, treating the sick.
- The Church tried to control knowledge and stopped some ideas from circulating. Roger Bacon, a lecturer at the Universities of Oxford and Paris, was arrested in the late 1270s to stop him teaching about the importance of astrology in medicine.
- The Church supported the idea of spiritual causes and cures for disease. It developed, and benefited from, the idea of pilgrimage.

SOURCE E

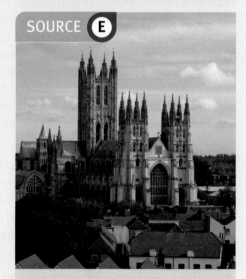

Canterbury Cathedral. First built soon after 600, it was rebuilt many times. The rebuilding of the 13th–15th centuries made it one of the grandest cathedrals in Europe.

SOURCE F

To consult doctors and to take medicine befits not religion and is contrary to purity.

St Bernard of Clairvaux (1090–1153). Not all churchmen felt as he did.

Pilgrimage

In the Middle Ages the Church taught that illness could be cured through the help of saints. Praying or making a promise to a particular saint, or, even better, going on a pilgrimage to the saint's shrine, might persuade that saint to help cure your disease. Making an offering to the saint was usually part of the process. The churches and cathedrals that housed the shrines of the most popular saints became very rich.

Wherever there was a major shrine, the Church collected records of the miracles that happened there. At Canterbury Cathedral, two monks, Benedict and William, sat by Becket's tomb for the first 10 years after his death, and collected 703 stories of miracle cures. At the start they recorded cures mainly amongst poor people from Canterbury or nearby. Quickly this began to change and by 1172 the records were of richer people, and people from all parts of England and from the rest of Western Europe. We can only tell where 531 of the 703 came from. Of this 531, about a third came from places outside Britain, a third came from south-east England, and a third came from the rest of Britain.

ACTIVITIES

3 Draw up a table like the one below. Fill it in, being sure to explain the reason why you have decided that something helped or hindered medicine.

How the Church helped the progress of medicine	How the Church hindered the progress of medicine

4 Overall, did the Church help or hinder progress in medicine?
5 What beliefs about the cure of disease can be seen in Sources K to N?
6 Is there any reason to suspect the reliability of any of these sources?

SOURCE G

Crippled pilgrims praying for a cure, taken from a 13th-century manuscript. Normally the body of the saint would not be removed from the shrine like this, but some shrines were built so as to display parts of the body.

SOURCE I

On 29 August 1307 papal commissioners examined the tomb of St Thomas Cantilupe in Hereford. They found:

170 silver ships, 41 wax ships, 129 silver images of human limbs, 1636 wax images of parts of the body, an uncountable quantity of wax eyes, breasts, teeth and ears; 108 walking sticks for cripples; 3 carts; many ladies' jewels including 450 gold rings and 70 silver rings.

When they left Hereford in November the commissioners checked again. There were one more wax and two more silver ships, another silver image of a man and 85 more wax images of parts of the body.

Ronald C. Finucane, *Miracles and Pilgrims*, 1977

SOURCE H

Robert, a priest, was near death, and some pious women made a vow to Becket; a cure followed. The saint later appeared to Robert to ask why the vow had not been kept. Robert protested that he had not made it. Becket replied, 'Certainly you did not vow; but since others made this vow on your behalf, payment lies upon you.'

From the Canterbury collection of Becket's miracles

SOURCE J

A girl from Eynsham, blind on one eye, wished to go to St Frideswide's for a cure. Taken to the shrine, she slept there. In the morning, after shedding many tears, bloody pus flowed from her eyes and she recovered her sight.

From the Oxford collection of miracles of St Frideswide

Grade Studio

Examiner's tip

In Unit A951 you may find questions about continuity. This is the idea in history that some things stay the same (continue) from one period to the next. Here is a question to help you practise thinking about continuity:

What continuity can you see between pilgrimages and the cult of Asclepius?

6.3 Medical schools and surgery

In this lesson you will:
- see that there was development in medicine in the Middle Ages
- write answers supported with facts and evidence.

The Middle Ages was a time of change in medicine, though this change was slow. The training of doctors was one of the first things to change.

The first medical school of the period was set up in around 900 at Salerno, in southern Italy. There is some evidence that it trained women as well as men, although these women doctors may just have treated women, especially during childbirth. The students worked with translations of the works of Galen and Hippocrates, which were later used in other medical schools. Many of these books had been saved only because they had been translated into Arabic. They were often then translated back from Arabic into Latin. The rediscovery of the works of the ancient Greeks and Romans, and the discovery of the works of the Arabs, were useful in many ways.

- The idea of clinical observation of the patient was stressed.
- The idea that cleanliness affected health gained a wider acceptance.
- The theory of the four humours and balance in the body was revived.

Less useful was the fact that, for many teachers in the medical schools, what was in the books became 'the truth'. They taught students to believe everything written in the books, sometimes despite clear physical evidence to the contrary.

The medical school at Salerno became so influential and well known that, in 1221, the Holy Roman Emperor Frederick made a law that only doctors who were approved at Salerno could practise medicine. This was an important step forward, although it applied only to the doctors who treated the rich and powerful, and it took many years for the practice of licensing doctors to be adopted in all countries. Gradually other medical schools were started, first in Montpelier (12th century), then in Bologna, Padua and Paris (13th century).

Slow acceptance of new ideas

With more schools, the number of trained doctors increased, as did the number of teachers and researchers. By the 14th century, there were many universities in Europe where students could train to become doctors. They were even

SOURCE **K**

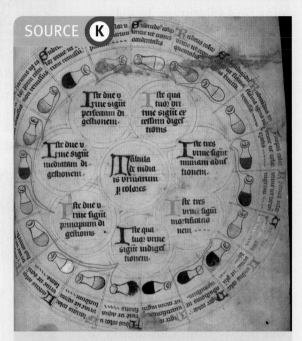

In the Middle Ages trained doctors used charts like these to diagnose disease by the colour, smell and taste of urine.

ACTIVITIES

1. How did the medical school at Salerno help to improve medicine?
2. Did it improve medicine for everybody?
3. How does Source K show both change and a return to old ideas?
4. What were the two types of surgeons?
5. Why were some doctors unwilling to practise surgery?
6. How did Galen's ideas come to dominate medicine?
7. 'Galen could not base his anatomy on human dissection. Medieval medical schools were allowed to use human dissection. Therefore medieval anatomy must have been better than Galen's.' Explain why you agree or disagree with this statement.
8.
   a. Why do you think de Mondeville (Source N) gave the advice he did?
   b. What effect might this have had on the development of medicine?

allowed to witness dissection and take part in debates challenging the ideas of Galen and Hippocrates. It was largely as a result of these debates that some of the ideas that had been accepted for years were revised. New ideas, such as using urine colour as an aid to diagnosis, were developed as a result of close observation of the progress of diseases.

Not everyone accepted the new ideas, and the ideas of Hippocrates and Galen still formed the basis of the textbooks from which student doctors were taught. Also, while ideas were debated, the debates were not always resolved in favour of the new ideas. They tended to be judged on the debating skills of the debaters, not on the medical evidence provided to support the claims of each side.

Surgery and anatomy

In the Middle Ages surgery was beginning to become a profession. Surgeons fell into two groups: a small number of university-trained, licensed, well-paid surgeons and a larger number of unqualified 'barber surgeons'. Patients operated on by either type of surgeon were more likely to die than not. Surgeons still had limited anatomical knowledge, so made mistakes. Also, fatal infections of wounds and deaths from the shock of the pain were common.

Anatomy

Medieval surgeons could have made some progress in understanding the human body, because medical schools were allowed to dissect a limited number of corpses. However, the lecturers did not dissect or learn from dissection. As Source M shows, they simply read from the works of Galen, while a 'demonstrator' dissected the body, pointing to the parts that the lecturer was describing. Books were scarce and copied out by hand. This meant that students could not consult the precious books. Also, each time a book was copied, there was a chance that mistakes would be made.

If anyone pointed out that what Galen described was not, in fact, what was inside the human body, they were told that either their perception was wrong or the demonstrator had made a mess of the dissection. Either way, Galen was not to be contradicted.

Surgeons had most success in surgery that didn't involve opening the body – treating cataracts or hernias. Some medieval surgeons tried using wine as an antiseptic to prevent infection. (Hugh of Lucca and his son Theodoric did this in the late 13th century.) Others, such as John of Arderne in the 1370s, used drugs to anaesthetise patients against the shock and pain. However, these were not widely used.

When they could, armies took surgeons with them when they went to war. When Edward I invaded Scotland in 1299, he took a surgeon with five assistants, just for himself. Practice made these surgeons more skilled at treating broken limbs. They learned to remove arrows and cauterise wounds to stop bleeding. Unfortunately, this caused infection, but the pus produced by the infection was seen as a good thing, a sign that healing was taking place.

A drawing of a skeleton from a 14th-century manuscript.

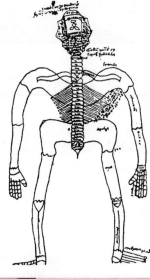

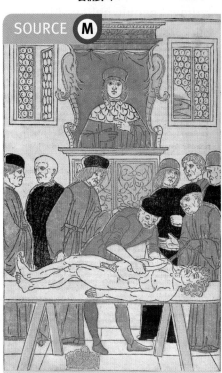

A lecturer reads from a book while his assistant dissects a body. This is the title page of a 1493 printing of Mondino de Luggi's *Anatomy*, written in 1316.

It is dangerous for a surgeon who is not famous to operate in any way different to that method in common use.

Henri de Mondeville (1260–1320), a master surgeon at the University of Bologna

ACTIVITIES

9 How did war improve surgery?

10 What might limit the spread of the ideas of surgeons like Hugh of Lucca and John of Arderne?

6.4 Disease and treatment

LEARNING OBJECTIVES

In this lesson you will:
- learn about the different types of treatment used in the Middle Ages
- look at how to 'use a source and your knowledge to explain your answer'.

Medieval people believed in a variety of causes of disease. We can group many of these together and call them magical or supernatural. Others were physical. There were also various types of people to go to for diagnosis and treatment. There were doctors (usually very expensive), monks from the local monastery, apothecaries (people who sold herbs and drugs) and local wise men and women. There was no simple link between the theory about disease and the type of person offering treatment. Doctors could prescribe charms, while many monks diagnosed and treated illness according to the theory of the four humours, as well as giving simple herbal remedies.

The Church taught that God could send disease and misfortune as a punishment or as a test of faith, and so prayer and pilgrimage were said to be helpful. This was especially true for people who had diseases that could not be cured in any other way. The planets were also held to be responsible for disease, and so medieval doctors were expected to have a good knowledge of astrology and astronomy. They needed to be able to chart the progress of the planets in the sky. This ability was seen as being just as important in diagnosing illness as examining the patient – maybe more so.

There were also physical or natural theories about the cause of disease. The theory of the four humours was accepted by most better-trained doctors. Urine analysis also played an important role in diagnosis. However, seemingly physical treatments, such as herbal cures, were often given for their supposed magical properties (herbs with a bitter taste, for example, were believed to drive away evil spirits), rather than for their actual scientific ones. Many doctors used a *vade mecum* to help them diagnose illness. This was a book containing tables of the planets, a urine chart, and a set of rules for bleeding patients.

SOURCE P

A doctor bleeding a patient. This picture is from the Luttrell Psalter, made in England about 1340.

GETTING STARTED

Study Source O. Is this an old idea or a new idea?

ACTIVITIES

1. a Make a list of the different beliefs about causes of disease in the Middle Ages.
   b For each belief on your list, explain why you think it was an old or a new idea.

SOURCE O

In this illustration from a 13th-century manuscript, Edward the Confessor touches a man to cure him from scrofula. Many kings and queens of England were believed to have the power to cure this disease, known as the 'King's Evil', by touch.

ACTIVITIES

2. What theory about the causes of disease lies behind the treatment in:
   a Source O?
   b Source P?
   Give reasons for your answers.

Trained doctors from medical schools were not available for everyone. While we know about the doctors who treated rich and powerful people, such as popes and kings, we do not know how much the treatment of ordinary people was affected by the changes in thinking in medieval times. The group of university-trained doctors at the top of the medical profession, who treated the upper classes, had little in common with most people who practised medicine.

The changes in ideas had least effect in the countryside, miles from the universities, where villagers continued to treat diseases in the same way as they had for centuries. For minor ailments, many people relied on cures passed down in their family or suggested by friends, and which were known to have worked in the past. They relied on local people, men and women, who had learned healing as a practical craft and had a reputation for successful magical or herbal cures. These people cared for the sick throughout the Middle Ages, but very few records of them or their activities have survived.

As towns grew, they attracted doctors. Doctors' fees were high. Many people could not afford a doctor when they were sick. Townspeople could ask the local apothecary to suggest a cure. But they would have to pay for the drugs he suggested, even if the advice was free. Medical care, even at this level, was becoming specialised and beginning to be carried out by men rather than women. There were surgeons, barber-surgeons and doctors of physic. Women tended to act specifically as midwives. Some of these people had their skills passed on to them informally; others became apprentices and had a more formal training, at the end of which they joined a guild.

SOURCE Q

An illustration from a 15th-century Italian medical manuscript. It shows the doctor (in red) seeing patients in a pharmacy. At the counter, the pharmacist mixes remedies made from the large collection of ingredients on the shelves.

ACTIVITIES

3 Did all people in the Middle Ages get the same level of treatment when they were ill?

4 Does Source Q show medicine for the poor or the rich? Give reasons for your answer.

5 What theory about the cause of disease was the doctor in Source Q likely to believe in? Give reasons for your answer.

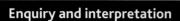

GradeStudio

Enquiry and interpretation

In the first question on Unit A951 you will be asked to show that you understand a source *in its context*. For example:

Study Source P. What theory of the causes of disease lies behind this treatment, and where did it come from? Use the source and your own knowledge to explain your answer.

Very often the best way to make sure that you score top marks is to break the question down into the steps that you will need in your answer. For the question about Source P, the steps are:

a What is the treatment? *Bloodletting*.

b What theory of the causes of disease is this treatment associated with? *Balance and the four humours*.

c Where did this idea start? *The Greeks, with Hippocrates and Aristotle*.

d How did the idea get to doctors in the Middle Ages? *Through Roman medicine, Galen's books, and either monasteries or Islam preserving the books, and the medical schools translating them and using them to train doctors*.

Notice how the answer will include what you can see in the source and information from your knowledge.

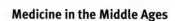

Medicine in the Middle Ages 59

6.5 Public health

LEARNING OBJECTIVES

In this lesson you will:

- learn about the different types of treatment used in the Middle Ages
- see how to 'use a source and your knowledge to explain your answer'.

GETTING STARTED

Study Source R. Why are the pipes shown in different colours?

The Romans provided piped water, public baths, toilets and sewage systems for their towns. This made it easier for people to follow the advice that most doctors gave about keeping clean. People did not want to live in dirty conditions. But in the Middle Ages, without government provision of any of these facilities, especially running water, cleanliness was a privilege of the rich.

Towns

Ordinary townspeople found it hard to obtain clean water for cooking, brewing and washing. Each town was run by a corporation of rich men from the town. They had to decide how much sanitation to provide, and how to raise the money to do it.

People put their household rubbish and sewage onto the street or into a nearby river. Sometimes houses shared a cesspit, or had privies built out over a stream, which should have washed the sewage away. This simply delayed the problem. Cesspits needed to be emptied, or they overflowed. Streams often got choked with sewage and became little better than open sewers.

Some corporations knew that it was not healthy to have rubbish and sewage in the streets. They also knew that the river water was not healthy. They passed by-laws to try to stop people throwing rubbish and sewage onto the street – but these were hard to enforce. Little was done unless there was a serious outbreak of disease in the town. Then the corporation would clear the streets and collect and burn the rubbish. Concern about public health was sporadic, and only came to a head with the horror at the huge numbers who died in the plague epidemic of 1348.

Monasteries

Monasteries were often rich, even if, individually, the monks were supposed to be poor. They had their own drainage and water supply systems installed in the monasteries. If their monastery was near a river, they could take the water from there. If not, they had to have more complicated systems. The water system at Canterbury Cathedral (a monastery, see Source R) was very complicated. The water was piped through five settling tanks, to purify it. It could then be used to wash, cook and brew beer. Dirty water was used to clear the toilets which were housed in a separate building. One of the monks was in charge of making sure that the *laver* (the place where the monks washed their hands and faces) was clean and always had clean towels. He was also in charge of supplying clean sheets.

Hospitals

Some hospitals for the sick were set up by the Church, including St Bartholomew's Hospital in London. Although never as rich as the larger monasteries, they were given money and usually had effective sanitation. There were only a few of them at this time, but those that existed were highly thought of by the public. They provided nursing, clean and quiet conditions, food, warmth, and sometimes surgery and medicine. Not all hospitals had doctors or surgeons – some were only for the care, not the treatment, of the sick.

ACTIVITIES

1. Describe how the problems of water supply and sanitation were dealt with in towns.
2. Why do you think the provisions for public health in the Middle Ages were so different from those in Roman times?
3. Describe how the problems of water supply and sanitation were dealt with in monasteries.
4. Why were monasteries better than towns in this respect?

ACTIVITIES

5 What are the similarities and differences between modern hospitals and hospitals in the Middle Ages?

6 Source S is like a cartoon with three frames on the top and two on the bottom. What is happening in each frame?

7 What theories about the causes of disease fit with what is shown in Source S?

Grade Studio

Examiner's tip

How reliable, or useful, is a source?

In Unit A952 you will probably be asked questions about the reliability or usefulness of a source. These two things can be a little complex. Take Source S. Is it reliable? It is certainly not literally true: hospitals didn't have angels and black-winged devils wandering round.

Start by not treating the source as one single thing. It shows us beds and bedclothes, for instance, as well as devils. If we want to know what hospital wards *looked like*, this source will be useful and reliable, even if not everything in it is true.

That shows another important thing: you can't just say whether a source is reliable or useful; you need to start by answering the question, 'What do I want to find out about?' Only when you know that can you decide whether a source is reliable or useful.

So, looking at Source S, it is a useful source for studying medieval hospitals, although not everything in it is true. If we were studying 13th-century painting though, it would be completely reliable. What we want to find out about can change whether the source is reliable or not.

SOURCE R

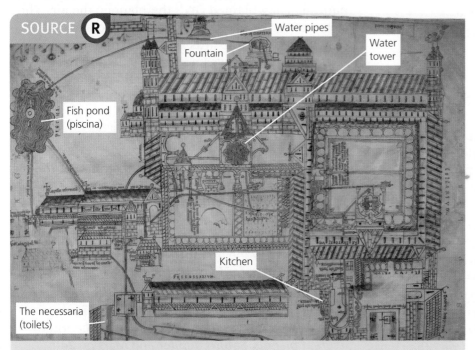

A plan of the water system of Canterbury Cathedral, drawn by the engineer who designed it in 1153.

SOURCE S

A 13th-century French manuscript showing a hospital.

Medicine in the Middle Ages   61

6.6 The Black Death

LEARNING OBJECTIVES

In this lesson you will:

- study sources about the Black Death
- see what makes a good answer to the last question in Unit A952.

GETTING STARTED

The population of Florence fell by 60 per cent because of the plague. How many people would be in your next history lesson if the class was down by 60 per cent? What would it feel like?

The Black Death is the name people gave to the plague. In 1347–9 the Black Death arrived in Eastern Europe and spread westwards in waves, first arriving in Britain in 1348. People became ill with a temperature, headache and vomiting. This was rapidly followed by the appearance of lumps (buboes), usually in the armpit or groin. The lumps then went black and lumps broke out on other parts of the body. After a few days the patient either began to recover or developed black bruises all over their body and died. Symptoms appeared in rapid succession. A patient could be dead within a day. The Black Death killed between a quarter and a third of the population of Europe.

We now know that there were two main types of plague. Pneumonic plague was spread by sneezing. Bubonic plague was spread by flea bites. The plague-carrying fleas came from black rats which infested towns and travelled from country to country on trading ships. The fleas could live for some time away from a living body, as long as they kept warm. They were carried from place to place on people and animals and in bales of wool, cloth and bedding.

People at the time did not know what caused the plague, how to cure it, or even how to slow down its progress. Despite their best efforts, its effect was devastating. Between one third and one half of the population of Britain died. Sometimes whole villages were wiped out, but the plague's effects were even worse in towns. The following sources show various ideas from the time about the causes and cures of the disease.

Causes

People did not know what caused the plague. They had a variety of explanations, supernatural and natural. They blamed God, the planets, the air. They saw that the disease was contagious, so avoided plague victims. This was a sensible precaution, even if the reason for it was not understood. Even so, none of the reasons they gave could fully explain the way in which the sickness spread.

SOURCE

Many people were unsure about the cause of the great death. In some places they believed that it was the Jews poisoning people. In other places it was the cripples or the nobles. If they found people carrying powders, or if ointments were found on anyone, that person was made to swallow them for fear they might be poisonous.

Whatever people say the truth is that there were two causes, one general, one particular. The general cause was the close position of the three great planets, Saturn, Jupiter and Mars on 24th March 1345, in the 14th degree of Aquarius. Such a coming together of planets is always a sign of wonderful, terrible or violent things to come.

The particular cause of the disease in each person was the state of the body – bad digestion, weakness and blockage, and for this reason the people died.

From *On Surgery*, a book written in 1363 by a French doctor, Guy de Chauliac

ACTIVITIES

1 What were the symptoms of the Black Death?
2 We now know that the Black Death was two different diseases.
   a What were they?
   b How were they spread?

Whoever touched the sick or dead was immediately infected and died. I, waiting for death 'till it come, have put these things in writing.

John of Clyn, an Irish friar who died from the Black Death in 1349

Flagellants whipping themselves. These people thought that the Black Death was sent by God because people were sinful. They paraded through towns punishing themselves and hoped this would persuade God to be merciful and end the plague. This group of Flagellants were Germans.

The pestilence comes from three things. Sometimes from the ground below, at others from the atmosphere above. Sometimes from both together, as we see a privy next to a chamber, or anything else which corrupts the air. Sometimes it comes from carcasses or the corruption of stagnant water in the ditches.

Written in 1485 by the Bishop of Aarhus in Denmark

Many wise people think that the Jews are not guilty of poisoning the water with plague, and that some Jews only confessed to doing so because they were tortured. Wise people think the plague was due to the great earthquake which took place in January of last year, 1348. This burst open the crust of the earth and allowed the bad, noxious poisons and vapours to enter the wells and the springs. A large proportion of the Jews are doctors, and they therefore know how to avoid the plague.

From *Chronicon Helveticum*, a history of Switzerland, written by Aegiolius in about 1560. He included many contemporary documents.

ACTIVITIES

Study Sources T to X.

3 What medieval ideas about the cause of the plague can be seen in each source? (There is more than one idea in some of the sources.)

4 Are these old or new ideas in the history of medicine? If they are old ideas, when was such an idea first held?

5 We now know that all of these theories about the way the plague was spread are wrong. Does this mean that these sources are not important in the history of medicine?

GradeStudio

Enquiry and interpretation

In the last question on Unit A952, you will find a statement that you have to test against all the sources in the paper and your own knowledge. For example:

Study all the sources.

  'In the Middle Ages people had very little understanding of the causes of the plague.'

How far do the sources on this paper support this view? Use the sources and your own knowledge to explain your answer.

Remember to identify the sources you use. **[10 marks]**

What is the best way to answer this?
• Make sure you understand what the statement means.

• Think about each of the sources in turn. Does the source support, prove, or offer evidence against the statement? Is the source reliable as evidence for the statement?
• Is there anything you know from studying the course which helps to prove or disprove the statement?
• The question asks 'How far?', so it is not asking for a yes or no answer. It wants you to explain the ways in which the sources do, and don't support the statement.

When you discuss a source in your answer, always name the source ('Source X shows the Flagellants', not 'The Flagellants ...'). Explain how the source supports or does not support the statement and why it is reliable or not reliable.

Now write a high-scoring answer to the question above.

What caused things to stay the same or change?		What ideas did people have about causes of disease?		New Features	
Factor	**Effect**	**Cause of Disease**	**Evidence**	**Feature**	**Evidence**
1 Chance		**1** Supernatural	a) b) c)	**1** Use of wine as a simple antiseptic	
		2	a) Bad air (Source W, X) b) c)	**2**	a) Salerno (11th century) b) Montpellier (12th century) c) Bologna, Padua, Paris (13th century)

What ideas did people have about treatments?		

2	Trade with the Arabs meant: a) Works by Galen and other Classicial authors returned to the West b)

Treatment	**Illness**	**Evidence**
1 Pilgrimage	Any	
2	Scrotula	
3 People punishing themselves so God would forgive sins.		

3 Books for doctors to carry round with them and use to help in diagnosis
4 Urine used as a guide to diagnosis

Did new ideas and treatments affect most people?

Special reasons for health or disease	
Reason	**Evidence**
	Between a quarter and a third of the population of Europe were killed

Who provided medical care?		
Group	**Patients**	**Evidence**
Trained doctors		page 58
Church hospitals		Source S
Local wise women and men		page 59

GradeStudio

Study Source Y.

'This source is about London, a city hundreds of miles away from Germany, so there is nothing it can tell us about the Flagellants in Germany.'

Use the sources and your knowledge to explain whether you agree with this statement. [8]

Source V

Flagellants whipping themselves. These people thought that the Black Death was sent by God because people were sinful. They paraded through towns punishing themselves and hoped this would persuade God to be merciful and end the plague. This group of Flagellants were Germans.

Source Y

About Michaelmas 1349, over six hundred men came to London from Flanders. Sometimes at St Paul's, and sometimes at other points in the city, they made two daily public appearances wearing clothes from the thighs to the ankle, but otherwise stripped bare. Each wore a cap with a red cross in front and behind. Each had in his right hand a whip with three tails. Each tail had a knot and through the middle of it there were sometimes sharp nails fixed. They marched naked in a file one behind the other and whipped themselves with these scourges on their naked and bleeding bodies. Four of them would chant in their native tongues, and four would chant in response. Three times they would all cast themselves on the ground in this sort of procession, stretching out their hands like the arms of the cross. The singing would go on and on and each of them in turn would step over the others and give one stroke with his scourge to the man lying under him. This went on from the first to the last until each of them had observed the ritual.

A description of the Flagellants in London, as witnessed by the chronicler Robert of Avesbury. Flanders is modern Belgium.

GradeStudio

The questions in Unit A952 are designed to make you really think about sources, for example the question on page 64 and what they can and can't help you understand. For example:

Look at the four examples of answers to this question. Rank them, from best to least good, and give a reason why each answer is better than the one you have ranked below it.

Answer 1
I agree. This source doesn't tell us anything about Germany, so it is no use.

Answer 2
It is quite useful because it tells me that people didn't know what was causing the plague so they did things like praying and this whipping.

Answer 3
It is useful because London and Germany are so far apart so it shows us how these ideas have spread.

Answer 4
It is useful because many people at the time thought that the plague was so terrible it must have been a punishment from God, so they were apologising to God for their sins, in the hope he would end the plague. This was quite normal in the Middle Ages and really the same as going on a pilgrimage to get cured, and that happened all over Europe too.

7 The Medical Renaissance

7.1 The Renaissance world

GETTING STARTED

Study Sources A and B. In what ways are they different? How might this difference affect medicine?

ACTIVITIES

1 What were the two key ideas of the Renaissance?
2 Why did artists want to attend human dissections?
3 How did this help the study of anatomy?

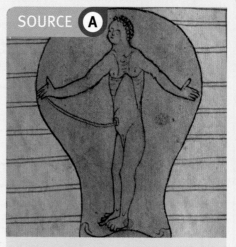

SOURCE A

A drawing of a fetus, from a medieval book for midwives, 1292.

The Middle Ages was a period of slow change. By contrast, between 1430 and 1750 Europe was in a ferment of change. Old ideas were being challenged. New ideas were proclaimed and challenged in their turn.

Renaissance means re-birth. It describes the new interest that was taken in the culture and science of the Greeks and Romans. Scholars of the Renaissance started by going back to the original Greek or Latin texts. The scholars not only read the texts but also began to adopt the enquiring attitudes of the classical authors. They accepted the importance of the close observation of nature and the need to make theories that explained the world. The movement which began by looking backwards finished by looking forwards.

There were important developments in art during the Renaissance. The great artists of the period insisted that art had to be based on the most accurate observation possible. Artists attended human dissections so that they would understand the structure of the body and be better able to paint it. This, in turn, helped medicine. The artists who worked with anatomists were able to bring a new realism to their work.

The Reformation was an equally dramatic change, this time in religion. Again it started by looking backwards. Thinking about how the Church should be organised, people concluded that the early Church, in the years immediately after the death of Christ, must be the best blueprint and that later changes should be swept away. The Pope, who was one of the later changes, did not agree.

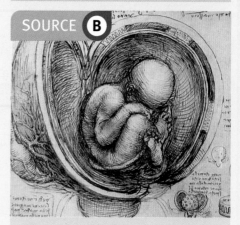

SOURCE B

A drawing of a fetus by Leonardo da Vinci, about 1510. Before making the drawing, he was able to dissect the body of a woman who had died during pregnancy.

TIMELINE

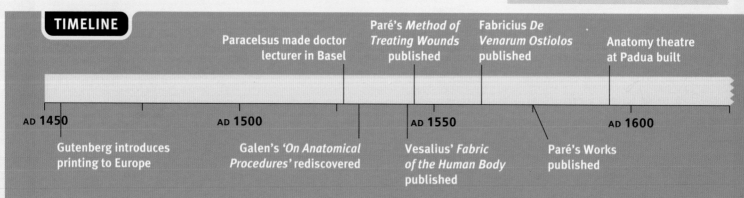

Paracelsus made doctor lecturer in Basel

Paré's *Method of Treating Wounds* published

Fabricius *De Venarum Ostiolos* published

Anatomy theatre at Padua built

AD 1450   AD 1500   AD 1550   AD 1600

Gutenberg introduces printing to Europe

Galen's 'On Anatomical Procedures' rediscovered

Vesalius' *Fabric of the Human Body* published

Paré's *Works* published

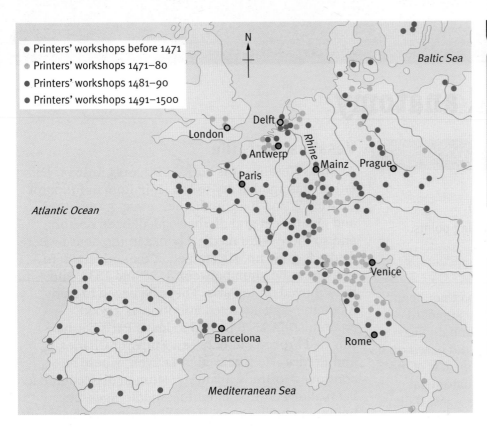

Printers' workshops before 1471
Printers' workshops 1471–80
Printers' workshops 1481–90
Printers' workshops 1491–1500

ACTIVITIES

4 How quickly did printing develop in Europe?

5 'Medicine has often been affected by changes in technology that are not changes in medical technology.' Can this be true? Explain your answer.

VOICE YOUR OPINION!

Within a year of his first lecture, Paracelsus was forced to flee from Basel, at dead of night, in fear of his life. Does this mean that his lecture cannot have been important in the development of medicine? Explain your answer.

Printing

There were important changes in technology as well. Johann Gutenberg introduced printing into Europe in 1454 and it spread very quickly. Its effects were enormous. Books were the best way to spread knowledge and ideas. Before Gutenberg, making a book, especially an illustrated one, had been a very labour-intensive process. Each picture had to be copied again, by hand. Illustrations were hugely important in books on anatomy. It is not surprising that, before printing, there were very few copies of most books and the illustrations in medical books were often poor. The skill of medieval artists and the time it took for their pictures to be copied meant that illustrations in medical books looked like Source A. Printing and the new skills of Renaissance artists resulted in medical drawings looking more like Source D on page 69.

Paracelsus

The ferment of ideas affected medicine. The changes in attitude happened gradually, over half a century, but they can be summed up by the events of one month, in 1527. Paracelsus was appointed town physician and lecturer to the university in Basel. He nailed an invitation to all people, including barber-surgeons, not just students, to the door of his lecture theatre. Three weeks later he started his first lecture by burning books by Galen and Avicenna. He then lectured in German, the language of the region, not Latin. He went on to say, 'Galen is a liar and a fake. Avicenna is a kitchen master. They are good for nothing. You will not need them. Reading never made a doctor. Patients are the only books. You will follow me.'

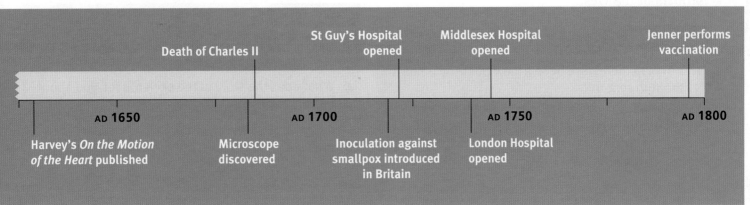

Death of Charles II

St Guy's Hospital opened

Middlesex Hospital opened

Jenner performs vaccination

AD 1650   AD 1700   AD 1750   AD 1800

Harvey's *On the Motion of the Heart* published

Microscope discovered

Inoculation against smallpox introduced in Britain

London Hospital opened

7.2 Vesalius and anatomy

LEARNING OBJECTIVES

In this lesson you will:
- look at the life of Vesalius (1514–64)
- use the concepts of trends and turning points.

A new book by Galen

Most of Galen's anatomical writings had not been available during the Middle Ages. The standard textbook on anatomy had been Mondino de Luzzi's *Anatomy*, which was written in 1316 and based on a translation from Arabic of half of *On the Use of the Parts*, one of Galen's less important anatomical books. Through the rest of the Middle Ages, Galen's anatomy was studied through Mondino's version. It was this book that professors read from while dissections were demonstrated.

After 1500 there was a new interest in anatomy. People wanted to get back to the 'pure' works of the classical masters. *On the Use of the Parts* was translated into Latin and published in full. In 1531, Johannes Guinter, Professor of Medicine at Paris, published a Latin translation of Galen's *On Anatomical Procedures*, his major work on anatomy – which had been lost in the West since the fall of the Roman Empire. This book now transformed the study of anatomy. It was vastly superior to Mondino's. Galen urged that the study of anatomy must start with the skeleton. He regretted not being able to use human dissection as the basis for his work, insisting it was necessary. His system for the study of anatomy was quite different from Mondino's. It was adopted without reservation throughout the West.

ACTIVITIES

1 How can there have been a 'new book' by Galen in the 16th century?
2 What was the effect of Galen's *On Anatomical Procedures* in the 16th century?

Vesalius' early life

Andreas Vesalius was born in Brussels in 1514. His father was apothecary to the Holy Roman Emperor Charles V, and his grandfather, great-grandfather and great-great-grandfather had all been doctors, and so there were medical books in the house where Andreas grew up. He studied at the university in Leuven in Belgium between 1528 and 1533, and then moved on to Paris. There he began to study medicine, and attracted attention as a good anatomist. In 1536 he had to leave Paris because war had broken out between Emperor Charles V and France. He returned to Leuven, where he continued to study anatomy. Human dissection had been allowed throughout the Middle Ages, but boiling up bodies to produce skeletons had been forbidden since 1300. While at Leuven, Vesalius went to great lengths to obtain a skeleton. He went to a gibbet outside the town where executed criminals were displayed. He wrote:

> I happened upon a dried cadaver. The bones were entirely bare, held together by the ligaments alone.... I climbed the stake and pulled off the femur from the hip bone. While tugging at the specimen, the shoulder blades together with the arms and hands also followed... After I had brought the legs and arms home in secret and successive trips (leaving the head behind with the entire trunk of the body), I allowed myself to be shut out of the city in the evening in order to obtain the trunk, which was firmly held by a chain. The next day I transported the bones home piecemeal through another gate of the city.

ACTIVITIES

3 Draw a timeline of Vesalius' life. Mark on it the events of his early life.
4 What does the story of the skeleton tell you about Vesalius?

Vesalius at Padua

Vesalius did not stay in Leuven long. He fell out with the professor of medicine over the correct way to bleed patients. He left in 1537 and went to Padua in Italy. Although still a young man, he was appointed professor of surgery. In Padua the professor of surgery was also responsible for teaching anatomy. The next five years in Padua were the most creative of Vesalius' life.

He taught anatomy, breaking with tradition by doing his own dissections, and then by publishing drawings. Many doctors at the time argued that drawings had no place in proper science. Vesalius disagreed. He felt that drawings of various parts of the body would help students watching a dissection, and help them learn about the body before and after dissections. In 1538 he published his *Tabulae Sex*, six large sheets of anatomical drawings. Source D shows part of one of these sheets. Imagine trying to describe what is shown in words, without the use of pictures or diagrams.

The *Tabulae Sex* showed that Vesalius was starting to see some problems in Galen's anatomy, but that he was not yet ready to reject Galen's theories openly. In Source D he shows a five-lobed liver, as described by Galen. In the first sheet, he shows two more views of the liver. The main one shows a five-lobed liver, but the smaller view shows a two-lobed liver of the type found in humans, not animals.

In 1539 Vesalius published his *Letter on Venesection*. Venesection was the practice of bleeding patients. Medical books of the Middle Ages, following the work of Arab doctors, said that the vein to be opened for bleeding should be on the opposite side of the body from the site of the illness, and that only a small amount of blood should be taken. This theory was criticised by doctors who wanted to get back to the 'pure' medicine of Hippocrates and Galen. Hippocrates and Galen had not said that bleeding should happen on the opposite side of the body, and had suggested taking more blood. This was the argument that had got Vesalius into trouble with the professor in Leuven. Vesalius was on the side of the purists. Other books on this controversial subject had based their arguments on what Galen and Hippocrates had actually written, or on the evidence that certain patients had got better when bled in one way or the other. Vesalius put the argument on a more scientific basis. He showed, again through illustrations, how the veins are connected. He provided an anatomical reason to accept the theories of Galen and Hippocrates.

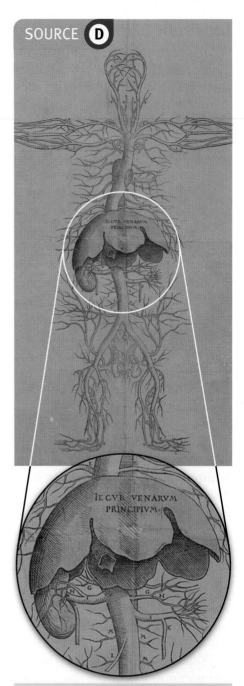

SOURCE **C**

As poles to tents, and walls to houses, so are bones to living creatures, for other features naturally take form from them and change with them.

From *On Anatomical Procedures*, written by Galen in about AD 200 but lost, after the fall of Rome, until 1531

ACTIVITIES

5 When Vesalius published the *Tabulae Sex*, did he agree or disagree with Galen? Explain your answer.

6 Add the events of this page to the timeline.

7 What was important about Vesalius' contribution to the arguments about venesection?

The Fabric of the Human Body

Vesalius spent his time in Padua working on his book, *The Fabric of the Human Body*. It was a comprehensive study of human anatomy, illustrated throughout by first-class artists from the studio of the Renaissance painter Titian. The publication of this book in 1543 was one of the great moments in the history of medicine.

- It offered a complete human anatomy, based on a comprehensive programme of human dissection. In each section, Vesalius starts with the most complete picture and works down from this. Thus the section on muscles begins with a flayed body displaying all the surface muscle groups, and ends, after each layer of muscles has been removed in turn, with a few individual muscles.
- It corrected some errors in Galen's anatomy.
- It offered a method by which the study of anatomy could progress – public dissection and the publication of work backed up with illustrations.
- It broke new ground in the relationship between illustrations and text. All Vesalius' illustrations have letters on them. These letters were not just used to key in a list of the names of the parts. Vesalius constantly referred to the letters in his text, so that the pictures and text in his book were integrated into one complete explanation.
- Vesalius painstakingly oversaw the preparation of the wood-block engravings that were used to print the illustrations and every stage in the publication of his work. In 1543 he left Padua to spend months with the printer in Basel so that everything was checked and correct.
- Because Vesalius' theories were in printed-book form, there was no shortage of copies. They were quickly distributed around the great centres of learning in Europe, and other anatomists could judge Vesalius' work for themselves, studying the text and illustrations in their own time.

The Fabric of the Human Body was not the only book that Vesalius published in 1543. At the same time he produced the *Epitome*, which was a small summary of *The Fabric*. The publication of *The Fabric* and the *Epitome* did not change the study of anatomy overnight. Many other anatomists of the day, whose work was challenged and contested by Vesalius, put up a strong fight. However, it was difficult to argue successfully with Vesalius' method – dissection and illustration.

Vesalius' later life

Vesalius dedicated *The Fabric* to the Holy Roman Emperor Charles V. He hoped for, and was given, a job at Charles' court. A second edition of *The Fabric*, published in 1555, included a number of new observations, but Vesalius worked on as a doctor, not an anatomist. He left the court in 1564, intending to return to Padua and teaching. However, he died before he could return.

The 16th plate from Vesalius' description of the muscles. Notice the letters and numbers so the parts can be named and referred to in Vesalius' text.

KEY WORDS

Trend – *a gradual change, happening over a long time, and made up of a series of events.*

Turning point – *a change that happens quickly and may be just one event. Afterwards, things are different in at least one important way.*

ACTIVITIES

8 Why is the publication of *The Fabric of the Human Body* so important in the history of medicine?

9 Complete the timeline of Vesalius' life.

10 Was there a turning point in Vesalius' life? If so, when was it? Give reasons for your answer.

SOURCE F

ANDREAE VESALII
BRVXELLENSIS, SCHOLAE
medicorum Patauinæ profefforis, de
Humani corporis fabrica
Libri feptem.

The title page of the 1543 edition of *The Fabric of the Human Body*. Vesalius is shown doing the dissection, which is taking place outdoors. This was common at the time, and temporary wooden stands were built to enable as many as possible to watch the dissection.

ACTIVITIES

11 Which of the following do you think was the most important book in helping to bring about developments in medicine?
   - *Tabulae Sex*
   - *Letter on Venesection*
   - *The Fabric of the Human Body*

   Explain your answer carefully.

12 Vesalius was a highly talented anatomist, whose books helped to correct long-standing mistaken ideas about how the human body worked. Why, then, did he face so much opposition to his work?

13 'The main reason why Vesalius was successful was because improved drawing techniques made it easier for people to understand anatomy.' Explain how far you agree with this statement.

GradeStudio

Understanding

Explain whether Vesalius' work should be seen as a **trend** or a **turning point** in the development of anatomy.

Explain

We have looked before at the 'explain' questions you will meet in the second question in Unit A951 (Lesson 4.4). The question above is a little more difficult because you have a concept to explain as well as some history. Remember to plan your answer in your mind before you write it.

7.3 Ambroise Paré

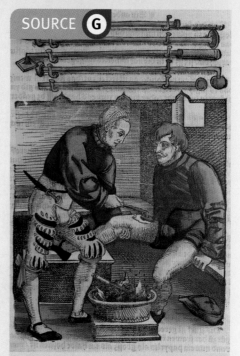

LEARNING OBJECTIVES

In this lesson you will:

* study the career of Ambroise Paré (1510–90) through his own writings
* practise answering 'explain' questions.

Ambroise Paré, the son of a barber-surgeon, was born in a small village in France in 1510. Barber-surgeons were the lowest of the low in 16th-century French medicine. However, by the time he died, aged 80, Paré had been surgeon to four successive kings of France, and was the most famous doctor of his age.

Paré went to Paris to train as a barber-surgeon in 1533. In 1534 he became the surgeon to the *Hôtel-Dieu*, which was the only public hospital in Paris. He left there in 1537 and joined the French army as a military surgeon. He was very successful, and, as France was usually at war, there was plenty of opportunity to practise. The musket was becoming the key weapon on the battlefield and Paré developed a new way of treating gunshot wounds. In 1545 he published his first book, *The Method of Treating Wounds*. It was written in French, not Latin, the usual language of medical books, as Paré did not speak Latin.

In 1552 Paré was appointed surgeon to Henri II of France. He continued to develop new treatments and to publish books about them. The first edition of his collected works was published in 1575. This led to an attack on him by the Faculty of Physicians, the people at the top of France's medical tree. Étienne Gourmelen, Dean of the Faculty, said that Paré was an ignorant fraudster and insisted that no medical books could be published without the Faculty's approval. This was the law, but Paré had the king's support. Nothing was done to stop the sale of his works, and three more editions of them were printed during his lifetime. The attack did spur Paré to write his own life story, *The Apology and Treatise of Ambroise Paré*, which was published in 1585. Because Paré was such a determined author, we can study some of his most important cases in his own words.

The treatment of gunshot wounds, before Paré. This print, from a manual for surgeons, shows the accepted treatment. Gunshot wounds were thought to be poisonous. They were either burnt with a red-hot iron (called a cautery) or filled with boiling oil. People believed that this would counteract the poison.

Dare you say you will teach me surgery, you who have never come out of your study? … Surgery is learned by the eye and the hands. I can perform surgical operations which you cannot do, because you have never left your study or the schools. Diseases are not to be cured by eloquence, but by treatment well and truly applied. You, my little master, know nothing else but how to chatter in a chair.

[Later Paré describes the scene after the battle of St Quentin, when the ground was covered with so many dead men and horses and] … so many blue and green flies rose from them they hid the sun; where they settled there they infested the air and brought the plague with them. My little master I wish you had been there.

From *The Apology and Treatise of Ambroise Paré*, 1585, in which he refers to Gourmelen ('my little master') who had criticised and tried to suppress his writings. 'My little master I wish you had been there' is a phrase that runs through the book.

Now at that time I was a fresh water soldier, I had not yet seen wounds made by gunpowder at the first dressing. I had read that wounds made with weapons of fire were poisoned, by reason of the powder, and they should be treated by cauterizing them with oil scalding hot, in which should be mingled a little treacle. Before I used this treatment, knowing it would cause the patient great pain, I wanted to know what the other surgeons did. They applied the oil, as hot as was possible, into the wounds. I took courage to do as they did.

Eventually I ran out of oil. I was forced instead to use an ointment made from yolks of eggs, oil of roses, and turpentine. That night I could not sleep, fearing what would happen because the wounds were not cauterized and that I should find those on whom I had not used the burning oil dead or poisoned. This made me rise up very early to visit them. To my surprise I found those to whom I gave my ointment feeling little pain, and their wounds without inflammation or swelling, having rested reasonably well during the night. Whereas the others, on whom I used the boiling oil, were feverish, with great pain and swelling about the edges of their wounds. And then I resolved with myself never so cruelly to burn poor men wounded with gunshot.

Paré's account of discovering his improved method for treating gunshot wounds, from *The Apology*, 1585. Paré had published an account of this method of treatment as early as 1545.

1 Briefly describe Paré's life.
2 How was Paré's treatment of gunshot wounds different from the treatments used before?
3 How was Paré's method for amputations different from the method used before?

Where the amputation is to be made
Let us suppose that the foot is mortified, even to the ankle. You must carefully mark in what place you must cut it off. You shall cut off as little that is sound as you possibly can.

How the amputation must be performed
The first care must be of the patient's strength. Let him be nourished with meats, yolks of eggs, and bread toasted and dipped in wine. Then let him be placed as is fit, and draw the muscles upwards toward the sound parts, and let them be tied with a ligature a little above the place which is to be cut. This ligature has three uses. First to hold the muscles and skin drawn up so that later they may cover the ends of the cut bones. Second to slow the flow of blood by pressing and shutting up the veins and arteries. Third it must dull the sense of the part. When you have made your ligature cut the flesh even to the bone with a sharp and well-cutting knife or with a crooked knife.

If you leave anything but bone to be cut by the saw you will put the patient to excessive pain. When you come to the bared bone cut it with a little saw, some foot and three inches long. Then you must smooth the front of the bone that the saw has made rough.

How to stop the bleeding
Let it bleed a little then let the veins and arteries be tied up as speedily as you can so that the course of the flowing blood may be stopped. This may be done by taking hold of the vessels with your Crow's Beak, which looks like this.

The ends of the vessels lying hidden in the flesh, must be drawn out with this instrument. When you have so drawn them forth bind them with double thread.

Formerly I used to stop the bleeding in another way, of which I am ashamed, but what should I do? I had observed my masters whose method I intended to follow, who used hot irons. This kind of treatment could not but bring great and tormenting pain to the patient. And truly of those that were burnt, the third part scarce recovered. I entreat all surgeons to leave this old and too cruel way of healing, and embrace this new.

From *Of Amputations*, which appeared in *Paré's Works*, 1575

Some years ago a certain gentleman who had a bezoar stone bragged before King Charles of the most certain effect of this stone against all manner of poisons. Then the king asked of me, whether there was any antidote which worked against all poisons. I answered that nature could not allow it, for neither do all poisons have the same effects, nor do they arise from one cause. Thus each must be withstood by its proper and contrary antidote, as to the hot, that which is cold. And that it was an easy matter to test this on someone condemned to be hanged.

The idea pleased the king. There was a cook brought in who was to have been hanged for stealing two silver dishes out of his master's house. The king desired first to know whether he would take the poison on this condition, that if the antidote, which was said to work against all poisons and which would be given to him straight after the poison, worked he should go free. The cook answered cheerfully that he was willing to undergo the hazard.

Therefore he had poison given to him by the apothecary, and presently after the poison some of the bezoar. After a while he began to vomit and move his bowels with grievous torments, and to cry out that his inward parts were burnt with fire. Because of this he was thirsty and asked for water which was given to him.

After an hour I went to him. I found him on the ground like a beast on his hands and feet, with his tongue thrust forth out of his mouth, his eyes fiery, vomiting, with cold sweats, and blood flowing from his ears, nose, mouth, anus and penis. I gave him eight ounces [227 grams] of oil to drink, but it did him no good for it was too late. At length he died in great torment seven hours after he took the poison. I opened his body and found the bottom of his stomach black and dry as if it had been burnt. From this I understood that he had been given sublimate, which the bezoar could not overcome. Wherefore the king commanded to burn it.

From *Of Bezoar*, which appeared in *Paré's Works*, 1575

The importance of Paré

Paré understood how to test a theory to see whether it was worth following or not. This is at the heart of modern scientific thinking, and it was a major development in the 16th century. Paré's story of the cook (Source K) seems brutal, but he proved false the idea that the bezoar stone was an antidote for all poisons. Many more lives could have been lost if it had just been accepted that the bezoar stone was a universal antidote. Doctors would have found explanations for why it didn't work, and carried on using it. In fact, they did carry on using it in all sorts of treatments.

Paré was also careful to make all his ideas public. He wanted other doctors to accept them and start using them (and, of course, to accept that he was a great doctor and surgeon). In order to progress, medicine needs this free flow of ideas.

ACTIVITIES

4 What was the role of chance in Paré's treatment of gunshot wounds?

5 Was chance the only factor involved in the success of this new treatment?

6 Paré said that he got the idea of using ligatures to stop bleeding after amputations from Galen's writing about the best way to stop wounds bleeding. Why might he have mentioned Galen?

7 What is important about Paré's test of the bezoar stone?

GradeStudio

Explain interpretations

In Lesson 6.2 we looked at one 'explain' question from Unit A951. Sometimes, as in the example below, the 'explain' question concentrates on a concept, such as chance, and you have to select information from any point in the course to support your answer. Think carefully about the examples you should use, and then answer this question.

Explain ways in which chance has had an impact on the development of medicine.

HISTORY DETECTIVE

Find out what medical discovery was made by Peter Chamberlen the Elder (1560–1631). Why is Paré more important in the development of medicine than Chamberlen?

7.4 William Harvey

LEARNING OBJECTIVES

In this lesson you will:

- see how understanding of the heart developed
- write clear explanations of what happened and why.

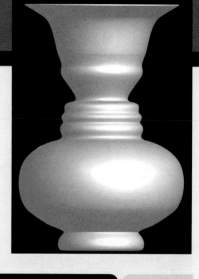

Believing and seeing

Sometimes knowing what you are looking at helps you to see it. The drawing on the right illustrates this point. Is it a vase, or is it the silhouettes of two people facing each other? You can see it either way. This is because seeing, for us, is not just the same as a camera taking a picture. Our brains interpret what we see, fitting it in with our understanding of the world. This is one reason why anatomists did not instantly solve all the problems of how the body worked. They understood the body through Galen's system, and so they tended to see things that Galen's system made them expect to see.

Also important in our ability to understand things is our ability to use ideas we already have. We think of something as being like something else. In the previous paragraph, seeing is described as 'not just the same as a camera'. Because we all know roughly what a camera does, this makes sense. An eye might be like a camera, but seeing isn't. Obviously, before cameras were invented, this example would not have been possible. All anatomists have used examples like this. Galen's included fire, and what happens in brewing and metal smelting. Just before William Harvey (1578–1657) was born, pumps were developed, for pumping water out of mines, or pumping water onto fires for firefighting. Because of this, Harvey had a possible comparison to help him to explain what the heart does, which had not been available to Galen.

Vesalius changes his mind

In *The Fabric of the Human Body*, published in 1543, Vesalius accepted Galen's theory that blood passed from one side of the heart to the other through the septum. He admitted that the holes in the septum were so small that they couldn't be seen, but still accepted that they were there. In the second edition of *The Fabric*, in 1555, he went one step further and said that, as there were no holes in the septum, blood could not pass from one side of the heart to the other. Vesalius' successor at Padua, Realdo Colombo, showed that the blood passed from one side of the heart to the other via the lungs. This was published in *De Re Anatomica*, in 1559. A later professor of anatomy at Padua, Geronimo Fabricius, identified the valves in the veins. Fabricius taught William Harvey, and also designed a new anatomy theatre at Padua.

GETTING STARTED

Look at the drawing above. What do you see? Does everyone see the same thing?

SOURCE L

The anatomy theatre at Padua, designed by Fabricius and built in 1594. Before this theatre was built, human dissection was usually carried out in the open air, with temporary stands erected for those watching (see Source F, page 71). Fabricius' theatre enabled everyone in the audience to have a close view of what was going on.

ACTIVITIES

1   What is the significance of the following in the study of the heart and blood:
    a   Vesalius' changed view of the septum
    b   Colombo's work
    c   Fabricius' work?

SOURCE M

The first illustration of a suction pump in a mine, from a book published in 1556.

Fact file

The development of the pump

As deeper mines were dug in the 16th century, flooding became a big problem. By 1556 early suction pumps had been developed. Water was sucked into a chamber by raising a piston; it came in through a one-way valve, which only allowed the water to pass in one direction. When the piston fell, it squeezed the water out of the chamber via a second valve, which only let water out. The water came out of the second valve at pressure, and in the mines it could be forced upwards. Portable versions of the pump were developed as fire engines, because the pressure was enough to send a jet of water out of the hose.

Harvey's early life

William Harvey was born in 1578 and studied medicine at Padua between 1598 and 1602. Fabricius taught him anatomy. After leaving Padua, Harvey worked in London, first as a doctor and later as lecturer in anatomy at the Royal College of Surgeons. From 1618 he was also physician to James I and then Charles I.

Harvey's theory

Most great scientists are great designers of experiments that will give them evidence to test or prove their theories. Harvey had many problems that needed careful testing. He wanted to study the body as a living system. Dead bodies do not have a heartbeat. He worked out when it was acceptable to base his conclusions on animals, and when it was essential to use humans. He did comparative studies of the hearts of humans and animals, and reached the conclusion that he could study the way the heart worked by experimenting on animals. The advantage of this was that he could do experiments on live animals, exposing their hearts in order to study them while they were still alive.

Unfortunately, the hearts of the first animals he worked on beat so fast that he couldn't see what was happening. He solved this problem by working on cold-blooded animals such as frogs. Their hearts beat more slowly, and so he could see each separate expansion and contraction.

Harvey's study of beating hearts showed him that the heart was pushing out large volumes of blood. He also realised that the blood flowed through the arteries with considerable force. Thinking of the heart as a pump helped him to understand, and explain, what was happening. The heart was pushing liquid (blood) round the body with a lot of force, just like a pump pushing water upwards out of a mine.

The blood was expelled, or pumped out, when the heart contracted, which happened at the same time as the pulse, which could be felt in the neck and at the wrist. Harvey next tried to calculate how much blood the heart was pumping out. He realised that so much blood was being pumped that it could not be being used up and replaced by new blood all the time, as Galen had thought. This suggested that there was a fixed volume of blood in the body. It was circulating.

ACTIVITIES

2 How did pumps work at the time when William Harvey was studying the heart?

Harvey still needed to explain how this worked, before his theory could be said to make sense. He turned his attention to the flaps or valves in the veins that his old teacher, Fabricius, had discovered. Harvey devised an experiment that showed that the valves allow blood to flow only one way. Now the theory fitted together. Blood flowed out from the heart through the arteries. It flowed back through the veins, and the valves in the veins ensured that blood could only flow back to the heart through them.

Harvey's theory replaced Galen's, which had itself been a refinement of earlier Greek theories. Harvey showed that blood was not continually being made and used. There was a fixed volume of blood in the body. By implication, his theory also meant that the practice of bleeding did not make sense. It was unlikely that there could be too much blood in a person's body, since it was circulating, not being made all the time. Harvey announced his theory in 1616, and first published it in 1628, in *On the Motion of the Heart*.

VOICE YOUR OPINION!

Harvey announced his theory of the circulation of blood in 1616, while he was still working as a doctor. Would you expect him to have gained or lost patients after this?

ACTIVITIES

3   Explain the importance of the following steps in Harvey's theory.
   a   the use of animals
   b   the use of frogs
   c   the force with which the blood moves in the body
   d   the volume of blood that the heart pumps
   e   the valves in the veins
4   How is a pump similar to the heart?
5   Comparing the heart to a pump is an analogy (see page 16). What analogies does Harvey use in Source O, and how does this help him?
6   Galen's idea that blood moves through the septum was wrong. Does this mean that his views about the heart are not important in the history of medicine? Explain your answer.

SOURCE N

These two movements happen one after the other, but so quickly that both [appear to] happen together and only one movement can be seen, especially in warmer animals in rapid movement. This is comparable with what happens in machines in which, with one wheel moving another, all seem to be moving at once. It also recalls that mechanical device fitted to firearms in which, on pressure to a trigger, a flint falls and strikes and advances the steel, a spark is evoked and falls upon the powder, the powder is fired and the flame leaps inside and spreads, and the ball flies out and enters the target; all these movements, because of their rapidity, seeming to happen at once as in the wink of an eye.

From *An Anatomical Treatise on the Motion of the Heart*, by William Harvey, 1628

SOURCE O

An illustration from Harvey's *An Anatomical Treatise on the Motion of the Heart*, 1628. It is entitled 'A simple experiment to show how valves in the veins allow blood to flow in one direction but not the other.'

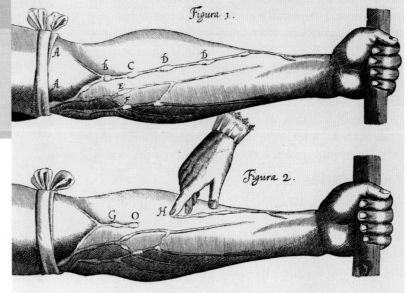

7.5 Treatment

Important advances in medicine were made during the Renaissance. The work of Vesalius and Harvey, in particular, meant that great progress was made in anatomy. Also a more scientific approach was adopted, with Paré and Harvey using experiments. However, these new ideas didn't help treatment, because doctors still did not know what caused disease. The treatments used were still a mixture of physical ideas, like the theory of the four humours, and spiritual cures.

Self-treatment

Letters and diaries from the time show that the sick often tried a variety of treatments. Many began by treating themselves – the cheapest, easiest route. Household recipe books that have survived often include medicines such as 'a syrup for the head ache' or 'a salve for wounds'. These were usually simple herbal remedies. If self-treatment failed, people needed outside help.

Trained doctors

From 1600 the Royal College of Physicians trained and licensed university-educated doctors, who practised mainly in towns and cities. There were about 50 of these doctors in London in the early 17th century (one for every 4000 people). They wanted to stop other people working as healers and claimed that untrained healers were dangerous. In fact, patients were usually better off with an experienced healer than with a doctor. A licence did not guarantee the best treatment, just the most expensive one.

Apothecaries

Apothecaries mixed medicines, were trained through an apprenticeship, and were mainly based in towns and cities. They used herbs, fruits, vegetables and spices, which they boiled, dried, pressed and distilled to make pills, syrups, ointments (mixed with fat) and poultices. They also mixed chemical, even toxic cures, which were often prescribed by doctors who believed that the body was a collection of chemicals, not humours, which needed to be kept in balance. The chemical cures included mercury, lead, gold, pearls (dissolved in vinegar) and even nitric acid. As well as mixing medicines to fit the prescriptions given out by doctors, many apothecaries gave medical advice and sold medicines to patients directly.

Other healers

After licensed doctors and apothecaries, the sick could turn to many different kinds of people who called themselves healers. There were far more 'amateur' healers than licensed doctors and apothecaries. In England in around 1600 there was about one healer for every 400 people in rural areas, and one for every 250 in the towns.

The local gentry often treated the poor in their area, usually with herbal medicines. Then there were the wise women and men, who may have learnt their skills from their parents. Their treatment was often a mixture of magic and some common-sense and herbal remedies. The supernatural cures, and healers, varied wildly. Some simply suggested that praying to God would be the most effective cure. Some healers claimed to be witches. They had a range of cures, from magical spells to ointments and potions that were made under 'magical' conditions – with herbs picked during a full moon while chanting spells. There were also faith healers, who believed that their faith gave them the power to heal the sick.

Women

Licensed doctors tried to stop women practising medicine. However, in rural areas, women probably still made up the largest number of healers. Even in the towns, women kept their traditional role as midwives. Some towns employed poor women to act as nurses. These women also looked after people who were isolated in 'lazar houses' because they had infectious diseases.

The range of treatments

The same treatments, such as bleeding and purging to get the humours in balance, were used by many licensed and unlicensed healers. At the beginning of the Renaissance period, trained doctors and apothecaries worked to keep the patient 'in balance', according to the four humours theory. Some, but not all of them, tied this balance to the movements of the stars and planets.

The end of the period saw more magical practices in use than at the beginning. For example, King Charles II (1630–85) re-introduced the practice of touching people to cure scrofula. This idea had been common in the Middle Ages, but lapsed in Tudor times. Similarly, while there had been a tendency for the most important people to use licensed doctors, Charles II sent for an Irish faith healer, Valentine Greatrakes, so that he could see him perform his miracles.

HISTORY DETECTIVE

Kings would get the best available treatment. See if you can find out how Charles II and William III were treated in their final illnesses.

SOURCE **Q**

This engraving, made in 1580, shows a woman giving birth. She is being helped by a midwife and comforted by her friends. The doctors in the background are working out the baby's horoscope.

SOURCE **P**

Unlicensed doctors are but charlatans. Women, especially, should not practise medicine because they do not have the natural authority of men. Also, they do not have enough understanding or a large enough capacity for reasoning. In this way, they might misdiagnose the disease and kill the patient.

Cotta practised as a doctor in Northamptonshire from about 1570. He followed his book about unlicensed healers with two more, about how to recognise and counteract witchcraft.

John Cotta, a licensed doctor, writing in a book about unlicensed healers in 1612

GradeStudio

Empathy

In history, to show empathy, you have to reconstruct the thoughts and feelings of the people at the time you are studying. For example, think about the two answers to the question below. Which is better, from the point of view of showing empathy?

The two trained doctors in Source Q are studying the stars, not helping with the birth. How do you think a woman at the time would feel about that?

Answer 1

It would make them angry. They would think the doctors should be looking after them not studying the stars.

Answer 2

They thought the stars affected medicine, and some doctors carried zodiacs, so this would have seemed all right.

People in the past acted in the way they did because of what they thought and believed. An ancient Egyptian who believed that evil spirits caused disease might reject modern drugs, because they don't deal with the spirit. Prayers and spells would make more sense.

7.6 Professionalisation and quacks

LEARNING OBJECTIVES

In this lesson you will:

- see how medicine developed in the 18th century
- learn how a Unit A952 question is marked.

Interest in science and experimentation continued into the 18th century. The microscope was invented in 1683, by the Dutchman Antony van Leeuwenhoek. This was followed by the thermometer, invented by the German Daniel Gabriel Fahrenheit in 1709.

Nevertheless, the 18th century was a time when old ideas about medicine were questioned. Physicians such as Hermann Boerhaave were stimulated into observing patients more closely and keeping accurate records. In physiology, Albrecht von Haller, a student of Boerhaave's, investigated breathing and digestion. In the USA, in 1822, William Beaumont had a patient whose stomach did not heal after a gunshot wound. He was able to observe the digestive system at work. Yet none of this resulted in doctors discovering the real cause of disease.

The medical profession did become more organised during the 18th century. Surgeons at last gained equal status with physicians. Organisations representing surgeons were set up in Britain and Europe. The Company of Surgeons was established in 1745 and, in 1800, it became the Royal College of Surgeons of London. This set the standards for surgical training.

People were beginning to feel that society should care for its members. Several new hospitals were founded in London at this time, including Guy's in 1721, The London Hospital in 1740, and the Middlesex Hospital in 1745. These hospitals were charities, set up with donations from the rich and offering free treatment to the poor.

'Quackery'

Despite the search for new knowledge, many old ideas continued in use during the 18th century. Many doctors clung to the theory of the four humours and their associated treatments. To explain the mystery of how disease spread, many adopted the idea of 'miasmas' – colourless, odourless gases in the air, which spread infection. 'Quack' doctors, in search of profit, peddled all sorts of nonsense. For example, 'piss-prophets' emphasised diagnosis by examining urine. Other 'quacks' recommended useless pills or claimed that evil worms caused illness. A German doctor, Franz Mesmer (1734–1815) claimed that he could cure patients by hypnotism.

GETTING STARTED

Study Sources R and S. Do they suggest that the medical profession was well thought of at the time?

ACTIVITIES

1. What were the main technical and scientific advances of the eighteenth century and why didn't they have much effect on medicine?
2. Briefly describe the work of Boerhaave.
3. What things happened in the 18th century that could be thought of as progress in medicine?

HISTORY DETECTIVE

Find out what 'Resurrectionists' were and what part they played in medicine. An interesting place to start is the Department of Anatomy at the University of Bristol's website.

You can access this by going to www.heineman.co.uk/hotlinks, entering the express code 8949P and finding the link for this lesson.

Physic for Man and Horse!!

Pills for Members of Parliament. | Digestive Boluses for Aldermen.
Scandal Drops for Old Maids. | Court Plaister for Short Winded Patriots.
Strengthening Plaister for Tender Consciences | Lawyers Elixir NB Very bracing in Term Time.
Electioneering Ointment NB Very much called for. | Young husband Pills for Widows.

Will Nobody Buy? — Will Nobody Buy!

Kill or Cure!!

A cartoon from 1802, making fun of quack doctors. The brown sign, above the door, says, 'Daniel Drug, dealer in patent medicines'.

An engraving from 1751, by William Hogarth, called 'The Reward of Cruelty'. It shows an anatomy demonstration. Doctors, in wigs and with canes, are in the background, ignoring what is happening. This picture was one of a series depicting the life of the person who is now the corpse. The series was intended to warn people against a life of crime, because you would end up hanged and having your body anatomised.

ACTIVITIES

4 In what ways is the doctor in Source R a quack doctor?

GradeStudio

Unit A952 questions are often concerned with what sources do or don't prove. Here is an example:

Study Sources R and S.

Do you agree that these sources prove that medicine was held in very low esteem in the 18th century? Use the sources and your knowledge to explain your answer.

Answers to questions are marked using a 'Levels of Response' mark scheme. The examiner has a list of five types of answer, with the number of marks that each type is worth. These descriptions of the types of answer are shown on the right, but they have been mixed up. What do you think is the proper order, from Level 1 (the least good type of answer) up to Level 5 (the best)?

A Answers which use common sense to interpret the sources. For example, 'The sources are cartoons so are not reliable about what all people think.'

B Yes, because they are both disrespectful to doctors.

C No. Answers supported by reference to the purpose of the sources and with reference to the candidate's knowledge of other developments in the 18th century.

D Generalised answers with no reference to the sources.

E Answers based on the purpose of the sources. For example, 'The sources were not produced to show what all people thought, but to make fun of doctors, and to warn people not to be criminals. They will exaggerate.'

7.7 Vaccination

LEARNING OBJECTIVES

In this lesson you will:
- study the work of Edward Jenner and the discovery of vaccine
- sharpen your skills at answering Unit A952 questions.

During the 18th century smallpox had taken over from the plague as the major killer-disease. Smallpox victims suffered from a high fever, and sores full of pus appeared all over their body. If the heart, brain and lungs became infected, death was certain. Some people who survived were left disfigured and, often, blind. Many had tried to make themselves immune from smallpox by inoculation.

Edward Jenner (1749–1823) was a country doctor from Berkeley in Gloucestershire. He studied under John Hunter, a famous surgeon, and learned from him the importance of scientific observation and experiment. Hunter once advised Jenner, 'Don't think, try the experiment'. Jenner was aware of a local belief that milkmaids who suffered from cowpox, a mild disease, never caught the dreaded smallpox. Years of observation confirmed this belief. So, in 1796, he decided to move on from observation to experiment. For the experiment to work, he needed to use a person who had never had cowpox or smallpox. He chose a young boy, James Phipps, and injected him with pus from the sores of Sarah Nelmes, a milkmaid with cowpox. Phipps developed cowpox. When he was fully recovered, Jenner gave him a dose of smallpox. If the idea he was testing was true, all would be well. If not, Phipps would develop smallpox and probably die.

It worked. Jenner had found a way to make people immune from a deadly, infectious disease. He called his method vaccination, after the Latin word *vacca*, which means 'cow'.

The reaction to Jenner's discovery

Despite the success of Jenner's experiments, some doctors were against vaccination. Some did not believe that a country doctor could discover something so important, and some could not accept new ideas. Others had a vested interest in supporting inoculation. Many had become rich and famous from this technique and feared that they would lose everything to the new methods of an unknown country doctor. However, Jenner had powerful supporters. Some members of the royal family were vaccinated. Vaccination was widely accepted abroad. A group of American Indians travelled to Britain to thank Jenner and the French Emperor Napoleon released a prisoner of war at Jenner's request. In 1802 Parliament gave Jenner £10,000 and in 1806 a further £20,000. In 1840 vaccination was made free for all infants and, in 1853, it was made compulsory. This was especially surprising at a time when the government usually refused to interfere in people's lives, even for the good of their health. Smallpox was on the way to being defeated, even though nobody had the faintest idea how vaccination worked.

Fact file

Inoculation

Lady Mary Wortley Montagu learned of inoculation against smallpox when she was in Turkey with her husband. In 1718 she introduced the idea into England. A cut was made in the patient's arm and a thread soaked in pus from the sores of someone with a mild form of smallpox was drawn through the cut. The patient became ill and was kept in a warm room until the symptoms had disappeared. Inoculation became popular, although some patients died.

ACTIVITIES

1. Explain which is better evidence of the danger of smallpox: the information in the text, or the information in the fact box about inoculation.
2. Describe the inoculation process.
3. What were the advantages and disadvantages of inoculation?
4. Describe vaccination.
5. What part did observation play in Jenner's discovery of vaccination?
6. What part did experiment play in Jenner's discovery of vaccination?
7. Give three reasons why some people opposed vaccination.
8. What evidence is there that vaccination was a success?

SOURCE T

The Cow Pock — or — the Wonderful Effects of the New Inoculation!

A cartoon by James Gillray, 1802. Opposition to vaccination continued throughout the nineteenth century.

SOURCE U

This day is published, price one shilling [5p], a letter from John Birch, Esquire. In this publication it is noticed that there was a Parliamentary grant of £30,000 to Dr Jenner for an unsuccessful experiment. There is also a letter proving the production of a new and fatal disease called the 'vaccine ulcer' described by Astley Cooper, Esquire, surgeon of Guy's Hospital. There is a letter from Mr Westcott of Ringwood proving the failures of the experiment there. A list of those who died of cow pox there. A list of those who were defectively [ineffectively] vaccinated and caught smallpox; and those who died of smallpox after having been vaccinated and told that they would be protected. There is also a list of other failures under the Treatment of the Jennerian Institution.

John Birch, the author of the anti-vaccination pamphlet described, was the surgeon at St Thomas' Hospital, London, and also the surgeon of the Prince of Wales.

A newspaper report of the publication of an anti-vaccination pamphlet in 1806

GradeStudio

Explain interpretation

On page 81, you looked at the way a Unit A952 question is marked. The question there was about what two sources proved. Below is a similar question. Using what you have learnt about the way to answer this type of question, write your own answer to this one.

Study Sources T and U.

Do you agree that these sources prove that vaccination was seen to be a stupid idea when Jenner first made his scheme public? Use the sources and your knowledge to explain your answer.

VOICE YOUR OPINION!

Jenner cannot have known that James Phipps would survive. Should he have made this experiment?

BRAIN BOOST THE MEDICAL RENAISSANCE

What caused things to stay the same or change?

Factor	Effect

1 Communications:
  a) development of printing
  b) accuracy of drawing	

2	Harvey could use the working of the pump as an analogy to help understand and explain the working of the human heart
3	Wounds treated led to new treatments being developed, such as Paré's use of ligatures
4 Chance	

Special reasons for health or disease

Reason	Evidence

What ideas did people have about causes of disease?

Cause of Disease	Evidence
Physical causes: The Four Humours	
Supernatural causes	

What ideas did people have about treatments?

Treatment	Illness	Evidence
1 Cautery		
2		Paré (Source I)
3	Amputations	Paré (Source J)
4 Magical cures	Any illness	
5	Any illness where the humours were out of balance	

Who provided medical care?

Group	Patients	Evidence
1 Trained doctors		
2 Apothecaries		page 78
3 All types of healers		
4 self treatment		

New Features

Feature	Evidence
1	*Publication of Tabulae Sex* (1538) and *Fabric of the Human Body* (1543)
2	Harvey, *Motion of the Heart*, 1628
3	Paré, *On Amputation*, 1576
4 A more scientific attitude to proof – especially the growing use of experiments	a) Vesalius' use of public dissection to prove his theories b) c)
5 Printed books make new ideas more widely available more quickly	Any medical book from the time

Did new ideas and treatments affect most people?

These new ideas don't really affect treatments

GradeStudio

In Unit A951 you have to answer one three-part question with sources, and then a choice of one from three questions, also three-part, but this time without sources. At this point in the course we have looked in detail at all the questions except the last part of the first question. So, what are the secrets of question 1, part c?

Question 1 will give you three sources, but since this question only uses two of them, only two are printed here.

Source V

A 14th-century illustration of a doctor bleeding a patient

Source W

The Death of Charles II

2 February 1685

At eight o'clock His Majesty King Charles, having just left his bed, was walking about quietly in his bedroom, when he felt some unusual disturbance in his brain, soon followed by loss of speech and convulsions.

Two of the king's doctors were present at the time. They, so as to prevent a serious danger to the king, opened a vein in his right arm and drew off about 16 ounces of blood. Meanwhile, the rest of the doctors had been summoned by express messengers, and flocked quickly to the King's assistance. After they had held a consultation together, they endeavoured to afford succour to His Majesty in his dangerous state.

Indeed they prescribed three cupping-glasses to his shoulders, and about eight ounces of blood were withdrawn.

From an account of the death of Charles II written by Sir Charles Scarburgh, one of the doctors who attended him in his final illness

GradeStudio

The first thing is to work out exactly what the question wants.

It asks 'Do these sources prove?', not 'How far?', and so there should be a 'yes' or 'no' answer.

'Prove' is a strong word. If the answer is 'yes', there can be no doubt this is true, and the evidence given is all you need.

The two sources give you your time period, between the 14th century and the 1680s – so through the end of the Middle Ages and most of the medical Renaissance.

c Study Sources V and W.

Do these sources prove that in the 1680s medicine had improved little since the 14th century? Use the sources and your knowledge to explain your answer. **[5 marks]**

The question isn't just a source question. The best marks will go to answers that use the sources here AND examples you have learnt from the course.

This is the statement you have to test.

Which of these sample answers is best, and why?

Answer 1

No because lots of things got better, Vesalius and anatomy and Pare and Harvey.

Answer 2

Yes, this does prove 'medicine has improved little' because in Source A the doctor is bleeding the patient, and what happens to Charles II? The first thing they do is bleed him, then they bleed him again.

Answer 3

No, there had been some improvements in medicine, like Harvey's work on the circulation of the blood, which showed that bleeding didn't really make sense, but this improvement didn't come with any ideas that helped treatments. Doctors carried on using the same old treatments, because there were no better ones, so Charles II's doctors still bled him.

8.1 The impact of the Industrial Revolution

The situation in 1820

Despite the advances of the 17th and 18th centuries, medical practice and knowledge were still limited.

- People still did not know what really caused disease. Doctors had an insufficient knowledge of chemistry and biochemistry. There was also a lack of technical aids for doctors. Although microscopes existed, they were not very powerful. Further developments in physics were needed if they were to be improved.

- Surgical operations were still carried out in filthy conditions as surgeons did not realise the need for cleanliness. Infection, therefore, was rife. Operations had to be carried out in haste because there were no effective anaesthetics. Patients often died from the trauma of the pain. Blood loss during an operation was another problem. Although surgeons knew there was a problem with losing too much blood, they were unable to carry out successful transfusions. They were not aware at this time that there were blood groups which had to be matched.

By the early 20th century, however, most of these problems had been overcome. How and why was this able to happen?

In the late 18th century a number of changes took place that turned Britain into an industrialised society. The population began to increase rapidly and there was an increase in demand for all types of goods. Factories full of machinery sprang up. These machines were powered at first by water, then by steam and latterly by electricity.

Large towns grew up very rapidly around the factories. Initially this brought slum housing, poor public health and epidemics of infectious diseases.

On the other hand, industrialisation stimulated the rapid development of the sciences and technology. New machines and new materials were brought into use. For example, a deeper knowledge of physics and improvements in glass-making led to the manufacture of more powerful microscopes. This, in turn, was a vital factor in scientists discovering that germs caused disease. Once this breakthrough was made, new cures and vaccines followed.

The growth of industry

The web of factors which enabled medicine to progress very quickly after about 1850.

Chemistry also made advances during this period. Chemists, working in teams, began research into drugs.

When electricity came into use in the late-19th century, it opened the way for new machines and technical aids to help medicine.

As well as industrialisation, other factors were also at work (see diagram). Combinations of these factors enabled medicine to progress very quickly from the mid-19th century, compared with the slow pace of change over the previous 3000 years. This rapid progress – sometimes called the 'medical revolution' – is dealt with in the next three chapters.

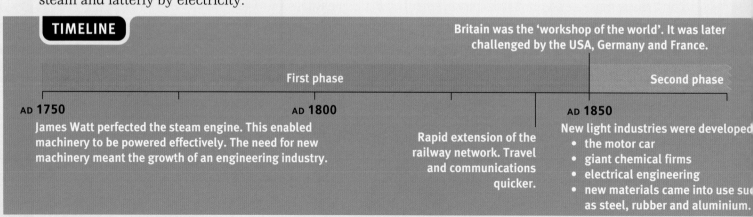

TIMELINE

Britain was the 'workshop of the world'. It was later challenged by the USA, Germany and France.

First phase | Second phase

AD 1750 — AD 1800 — AD 1850

James Watt perfected the steam engine. This enabled machinery to be powered effectively. The need for new machinery meant the growth of an engineering industry.

Rapid extension of the railway network. Travel and communications quicker.

New light industries were developed
- the motor car
- giant chemical firms
- electrical engineering
- new materials came into use such as steel, rubber and aluminium.

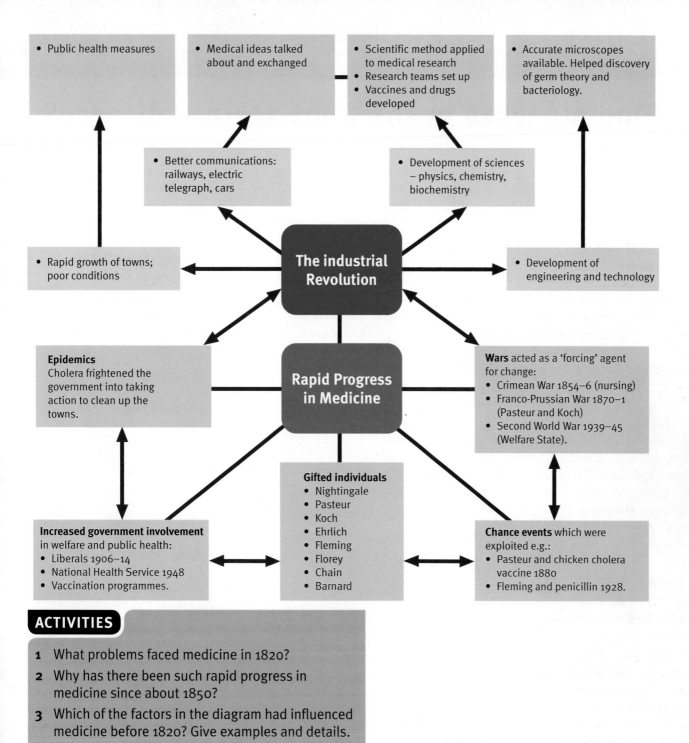

- Public health measures

- Medical ideas talked about and exchanged

- Scientific method applied to medical research
- Research teams set up
- Vaccines and drugs developed

- Accurate microscopes available. Helped discovery of germ theory and bacteriology.

- Better communications: railways, electric telegraph, cars

- Development of sciences – physics, chemistry, biochemistry

The industrial Revolution

- Rapid growth of towns; poor conditions

- Development of engineering and technology

Rapid Progress in Medicine

Epidemics
Cholera frightened the government into taking action to clean up the towns.

Wars acted as a 'forcing' agent for change:
- Crimean War 1854–6 (nursing)
- Franco-Prussian War 1870–1 (Pasteur and Koch)
- Second World War 1939–45 (Welfare State).

Gifted individuals
- Nightingale
- Pasteur
- Koch
- Ehrlich
- Fleming
- Florey
- Chain
- Barnard

Increased government involvement in welfare and public health:
- Liberals 1906–14
- National Health Service 1948
- Vaccination programmes.

Chance events which were exploited e.g.:
- Pasteur and chicken cholera vaccine 1880
- Fleming and penicillin 1928.

ACTIVITIES

1 What problems faced medicine in 1820?
2 Why has there been such rapid progress in medicine since about 1850?
3 Which of the factors in the diagram had influenced medicine before 1820? Give examples and details.

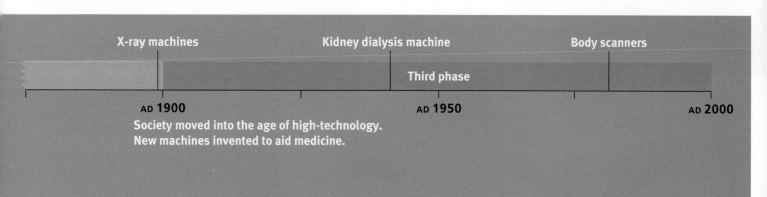

X-ray machines   Kidney dialysis machine   Body scanners

Third phase

AD **1900**   AD **1950**   AD **2000**

Society moved into the age of high-technology.
New machines invented to aid medicine.

9 Fighting disease

9.1 Who did what in the fight against disease?

Before

The medical profession has little idea about the cause of disease, and even less about how to prevent or cure it. They often believe that disease is caused by poisonous smells, evil spirits or even God. The work of Edward Jenner has shown a way forward through scientific methods and vaccination, although many doctors oppose his ideas.

Improved microscopes are starting to have an impact, and other improvements in technology are also likely, in time, to help doctors and scientists to gain a better understanding of disease.

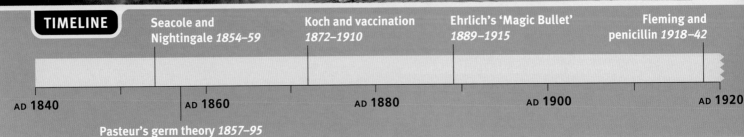

TIMELINE	Seacole and Nightingale *1854–59*	Koch and vaccination *1872–1910*	Ehrlich's 'Magic Bullet' *1889–1915*	Fleming and penicillin *1918–42*

AD **1840**   AD **1860**   AD **1880**   AD **1900**   AD **1920**

Pasteur's germ theory *1857–95*

HISTORY DETECTIVE

Find out what you can about each 'guardian angel'. Each represents a doctor or scientist who tackled infectious disease. Each 'demon' represents a killer disease.

Which 'demons' did each 'guardian angel' attack?

What weapons did each 'guardian angel' use?

Complete a brief profile of each 'guardian angel', including the diseases they battled against, how they carried out their work, whether they were successful and what factors helped them in their work. You can find out more about each of the diseases and doctors in the pages that follow. You might also like to find out more from other sources of information.

After

The medical profession understands that germs cause disease. The work of Louis Pasteur, Robert Koch and others has finally led to a scientific understanding of the causes of disease and helped in the development of treatments and cures. Sophisticated vaccines and chemical cures have reduced the death rate from infectious diseases. Some of the killer diseases of old have now almost disappeared. However, antibiotics are still to come and illness is still prevalent. Some of the 'demons' have returned.

AD **1920**   AD **1940**   AD **1960**   AD **1980**   AD 2

9.2 Opposition to vaccination in Britain in the 19th Century

GETTING STARTED

Look at the picture in Source A.

What can you learn from this source about how people reacted to Jenner's development of vaccination?

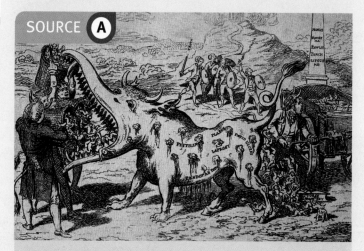

SOURCE **A**

'The Vaccination Monster' a cartoon published in 1807

You read about Jenner's development of vaccination on pages 82–83. Despite his successes, Jenner faced a good deal of opposition. On page 82 you read about two pieces of government legislation, in 1840 and 1853, which made vaccination for all infants free and compulsory. This caused an outcry in Britain from some powerful opponents of vaccination. A further Act of 1867 extended the compulsory vaccination requirement to age 14, with stiff penalties for those who did not obey the law. Resistance to these laws began immediately after passage of the 1853 law, with violent riots in Ipswich, Henley, Mitford, and several other towns. Opposition was particularly well organised in Leicester, where the first imprisonment under the 1853 Act is recorded; William Johnson served 14 days after refusing to allow his child to be vaccinated. In the village of Walsham le Willows, John Finch objected to vaccination. When he was asked to explain why, he said, 'I do not believe in it. I had two children one of which was vaccinated and died of diphtheria. The other child didn't have it and is still alive.'

The AntiVaccination League was founded in London in the same year. Then, in 1867 the AntiCompulsory Vaccination League was founded. Faith in vaccination was challenged by a smallpox outbreak in 1870 affecting some 44,000 people. In 1871 another Act was passed that attempted to strengthen previous legislation by making it mandatory for local Poor Law Boards of Guardians to appoint vaccination officers. Fines of up to £1/5s were introduced for parents who refused to have their offspring vaccinated. The anti-vaccination protesters based their objections partly on individual freedom,

partly on resistance to interference in the sanctity of the home and family, and partly on the medical opinion that there were alternative means to limit and control smallpox. The passion of the debate increased in the latter part of the 19th century.

A large number of antivaccination books and journals appeared in the 1870s and 1880s. The journals included the *AntiVaccinator* (founded 1869), the *National AntiCompulsory Vaccination Reporter* (1874), and the *Vaccination Inquirer* (1879). Pressure from the antivaccination movement was increasing. There was a massive antivaccination demonstration in Leicester in 1885 that attracted up to 100,000 people. On 23 March these demonstrators proceeded from the Temperance Hall to the Market Place where copies of the Vaccination Acts were burnt in full view of the Mayor and Chief Constable of Leicester. The cause, according to *The Times*, was '…a widespread belief that death and disease have resulted from the operation of vaccination…'. Compulsory vaccination had failed to prevent the smallpox epidemics of 1857–59, 1863–65 and 1870–72. Attacks on vaccination became increasingly personal and critical of events that occurred many decades previously. Doctors were accused of spreading smallpox in the 18th century by inoculation and Jenner was still being criticised nearly 90 years after he published his inquiry in 1798.

A cartoon about vaccination published in France in 1800

In Leicester, the decline in the take-up of vaccination was so steep that in 1890 only 3 per cent of babies were vaccinated in their first year. Nationally, the number of vaccinated infants declined, from 96 per cent in England and Wales in 1875 to 78 per cent in 1889. This can be partly explained by the increasing apathy of parents at a time when smallpox was steadily declining. In addition, many believed that government should advise, persuade and provide rather than coerce both parents and local government into compliance with the law.

In 1889, a royal commission was appointed to investigate the evidence for and against vaccination. The commission sat for seven years, studying the arguments from opponents and supporters of vaccination. Its report in 1896 concluded that vaccination protected against smallpox, but it recommended the abolition of penalties. A new Vaccination Act in 1898 removed penalties and introduced a conscience clause, allowing parents who did not believe vaccination was safe to obtain a certificate of exemption. Now that the compulsory element of vaccination had been removed, opposition to vaccination declined.

GradeStudio

Look at the cartoon in Source B. It represents vaccination as a strange group of sinister creatures chasing after innocent and terrified children with a large syringe, ready to vaccinate the helpless victims. It was published in France in 1800.

Study this question and read the examiner's tip before answering it.

This cartoon was published in France in 1800, so it has no value to the historian studying opposition to vaccination in Britain in the nineteenth century.

Explain fully whether you agree or disagree with this view.

Examiner's tip

It would be easy to dismiss this source and say it is irrelevant. However, answers to questions in Unit A952 are rarely that simple! This question is asking you to consider the usefulness (or utility) of the source. Although it is a French source, the historian studying opposition to vaccination in Britain in the 19th century would still find some value in it. A good answer would use details from the source to show that opposition to vaccination spread as far as Europe. In France, just as in England, opponents of vaccination published cartoons that tried to make vaccination appear ridiculous and perhaps even frightening. You could use your knowledge of the topic to explain how this cartoon matches the details of anti-vaccination protests in England and is very similar to other cartoons published in England, like the Gilray cartoon on page 83, or the cartoon of the 'Vaccination Monster' in this chapter.

Now have a go at answering the question for yourself.

9.3 Pasteur and the germ theory of disease

LEARNING OBJECTIVES

In this lesson you will:

- find out how Louis Pasteur developed his **germ** theory and which factors helped him to succeed
- use sources to form opinions about Pasteur.

Pasteur and the germ theory

Louis Pasteur was the scientist who first linked germs with disease, but he did not set out to do this. His research was driven by the needs of the brewing industry, which asked him in 1857 to investigate a problem. Sugar beet, used to make alcohol, often went sour during fermentation and could not be used. Pasteur thought that the souring was caused by germs in the air and he proved this by experimenting with liquid in a swan-neck flask. Source C is Pasteur's description of the results of his experiment.

When this discovery was announced, many scientists and doctors refused to believe it – even though Pasteur had successfully carried out the experiment in public. Others saw that Pasteur had made a definite link between germs and decay.

In 1865 Pasteur began to study a silkworm disease called *pébrine*. His studies were disrupted by the deaths of his father and two of his daughters but, by 1867, he was able to demonstrate that germs were the cause of *pébrine*. The link between germs and disease had been made.

Fact file

Spontaneous Generation

By 1800 most scientists and doctors knew that micro-organisms called germs or microbes existed, but many of them thought germs were the *result* of disease, not the *cause* of it. This idea was called Spontaneous Generation. Some believed that disease was caused by gases called miasmas, others believed different theories, but none of them thought germs were the cause.

SOURCE C

I place some liquid in a flask with a long neck. I boil it and let it cool. In a few days little animals will grow in it. But by boiling it I had killed the germs. If I repeat the experiment but draw the neck into a curve, but still open, the liquid will remain pure for three or four years. What difference is there between them? They both contain the same liquid and they both contain air. It is that in one the dust in the air and its germs can fall in, in the other they cannot. I have kept germs out of it and, therefore, have kept Life from it – for Life is a germ and a germ is Life.

Pasteur's description of an experiment he carried out in public at the University of Paris on 7 April 1864

KEY PEOPLE

Louis Pasteur 1822–95
Nationality: French.
Occupation: Chemist. He made many investigations for businesses which needed solutions to problems that were losing them money.
1849 Made Professor of Chemistry at Strasbourg University.
1854 Moved to Lille University. Here he proved the connection between germs and decay (1864) and then the connection between germs and disease (1867).

1865–67 Studied silkworm disease. His research was interrupted by deaths in his family.
1868 A brain haemorrhage left him paralysed on one side. He stopped working, but by 1877 he was back at work, investigating anthrax.
He discovered vaccines for chicken cholera (1880), anthrax (1881) and rabies (1885).
1888 The French government set up the *Institut Pasteur* in Paris, for Pasteur and others to carry on medical research.

VOICE YOUR OPINION!

When Pasteur announced his discovery in 1864, many scientists and doctors refused to believe it. Why do you think this happened?

KEY WORDS

Germ – *a very small organism that causes disease. Some other terms for 'germ' include 'microbe', 'bacterium' and 'bacillus'.*

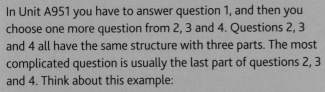

GradeStudio

In Unit A951 you have to answer question 1, and then you choose one more question from 2, 3 and 4. Questions 2, 3 and 4 all have the same structure with three parts. The most complicated question is usually the last part of questions 2, 3 and 4. Think about this example:

Between the time of the Ancient Greeks and the end of the nineteenth century there has been more continuity than change in ideas about the causes of disease? Explain how far you agree with this statement. [8 marks]

You will need good knowledge and ideas about the causes of disease across a large period of time. You don't need to know everything in detail, but you will usually be expected to know about at least two examples of changing ideas about the cause of disease, and two examples of continuity in ideas about the cause of disease. You could choose any from the following list:

1 Building Asclepions.
2 Theory of the Four Humours.
3 Roman belief in bad air as a cause of disease.
4 Roman belief in bad water as a cause of disease.

5 Belief in the Middle Ages that plague was sent by God.
6 The theory of miasma.
7 Spontaneous generation.
8 Jenner and vaccination.
9 Pasteur and germ theory.

Start by working in pairs.

- Can you give a brief description of each example?
- List the examples in two columns, those that show continuity over this period and those that show change.
- Can you explain your reasons for your choices to each other?
- Now share your ideas with another pair of students and discuss any similarities and differences in your answers.
- Now try to put together a written answer to this question.
- When you have finished, swap your answer with that of another pair of students.
- Mark their answer using the mark scheme.
- Try to write some constructive comments about the answer, and explain how you think it can be improved.

Mark Scheme AO1 and AO2

Level 1: General assertions
Valid, but general answers. No specific contextual knowledge. E.g. *'I think there has been much more change. This is because people in the nineteenth century did not believe the same as people in Greek times about disease.'* [1 mark]

Level 2: Identifies or describes examples of continuity and/or change
Specific contextual knowledge demonstrated but no explanation. 2/3 marks for 1/2 examples of continuity or change. 4 marks for examples of both continuity and change. Examples might include: continuity – Four Humours, dirt, bad air; change – spontaneous generation, miasma, and germ theory. [2–4 marks]

Level 3: Explains example(s) of continuity or of change
E.g. *'Continuity is more important because for most of that period ideas did not change much at all. The Greeks came up with the idea of the Four Humours. This said that you became ill because the humours in your body were out of balance. This was still believed even in the nineteenth century when many doctors still used bloodletting as a treatment.'* [5–6 marks]

Level 4: Explains the importance/lack of importance of both Jenner and Pasteur
Award 7 marks for explanation of long-term impact of one of them. [7 marks]

Level 5: As for Level 4 and comes to a supported conclusion
To get into this level reasons must be given to support the conclusion. E.g. *'I think there has been much more change than continuity. This is because although some beliefs have stayed the same for all this time for example the Romans believed that bad air spread disease. They always made sure they built towns away from swamps because they thought that the bad air and smells from swamps caused disease. At the beginning of the nineteenth century people still believed bad air caused disease. Even when John Snow showed that cholera was spread by water and not air a lot of people did not believe him. However, when Pasteur came along and proved that disease was spread by germs most people had to accept it. This was a revolution and opened up new kinds of treatments that are still used today like drugs and vaccinations. This is why I think change is more important because when there was this change it was so basic as to change the whole way that medicine worked.'* [8 marks]

9.4 Koch and bacteriology

LEARNING OBJECTIVES

In this lesson you will:
- find out how Robert Koch linked particular germs to particular diseases
- use sources to form opinions about Koch.

Robert Koch

By 1870, the chemist Louis Pasteur had shown the connection between germs and decay and disease. The next step – linking a particular germ or microbe to a particular disease – was made by a German doctor, Robert Koch, who had more detailed medical knowledge than Pasteur. In 1872 Koch began to study anthrax, a fatal disease which affects cattle and sheep and can also spread to humans. By 1875, by studying the blood of affected and unaffected animals, he had identified the microbe that causes anthrax.

Koch moved on to study the germ that causes blood poisoning, or septicaemia, in wounds. It was impossible for him to see this microbe at first, even with a microscope, but then new technology came to his aid. He used new industrial dyes to stain the microbe, so that it became visible. Koch devised a way to grow the germs and then used his daughter's pet mice to experiment with them. Soon he had a fluid that contained only one kind of germ. Mice injected with the fluid developed septicaemia. Koch knew that he had to *prove* that he had identified the right germ. Again, new technology helped. He connected a new type of lens to his microscope and photographed the whole process.

Koch developed superb experimental methods. As well as the use of dyes and photography, he developed a solid **culture** for breeding colonies of germs. This was more reliable than Pasteur's liquid culture. Koch went on to isolate other germs. In 1882 he discovered the germ that causes tuberculosis (TB) and in 1883 he identified the germ that causes cholera.

KEY WORDS

Bacteriology – *the scientific study of bacteria and other microscopic living things, especially those that cause disease.*

Culture – *a growth of micro-organisms in the laboratory. They may be grown in either a solid or a liquid.*

GETTING STARTED

Louis Pasteur was French. Robert Koch was German. Both scientists worked in the second half of the 19th century. In 1870, a war broke out between France and Germany.

How do you think a war might affect scientists in the countries involved and their work together? Think about the impact war would have on scientists in the 19th century and in the 21st century.

KEY PEOPLE

Robert Koch 1843–1910

Nationality: German.

Education: Graduated in medicine from Gottingen University.

1870 Joined the Prussian army in the war against France. The French were beaten within 6 months.

1871 Became the medical officer in Wollstein, a town near the border with Poland.

1872 (29th birthday) His wife bought him a microscope, which would affect his life greatly.

He identified the microbes that cause TB (1882) and cholera (1883).

1891 German government set up the Institute for Infectious Diseases in Berlin. Koch was selected to work there.

1905 Awarded a Nobel Prize for his work.

Look back at the picture on pages 88–89. It shows some 'guardian angels' trying to protect a patient from 'demons'.

1   List the 'weapons' the angels are using.

2   Do you think Pasteur and Koch used any of these 'weapons'? If so, which did they use in their work? Which of these 'weapons' was the most important in helping them to make their discoveries?

Grade Studio

Explanation

Here is an example of an examination question from Unit A951 that requires you to compare the relative importance of three men in the development of vaccination. You will need to apply your knowledge of key individuals across different periods and judge their long-term impact. Here is the question:

Who contributed more to the development of vaccination, Jenner, Koch or Pasteur?
Explain your answer.   **[8 marks]**

Examiner's tip

When answering a question like this, you must do more than just show your knowledge of the topic. You must explain the importance of each individual by saying how each made their own unique contribution to the development of vaccination. Examples might include:

• Jenner made the first discovery, tested it, published his work and his vaccine became widely used.
• Pasteur used Jenner's work, but he improved it by explaining how it worked, which led to further work on vaccines for other diseases.
• Koch was able to identify the germs that caused specific diseases like TB and cholera which enabled scientists to produce specific vaccines.

To get a top-level answer you need to explain either why one is more important than the others, or why they are equally important. Look at this answer, which is worth full marks:

Candidate answer

Pasteur was more important than Jenner because although Jenner discovered vaccination in the first place he did not understand how it worked. This meant that he could only develop a vaccine against smallpox and not other diseases. There could not be other vaccines unless someone worked out how vaccination worked. This is what Pasteur did. He knew that weak forms of the germ protected people against the disease. Even so, he was not able to identify the germs that caused specific diseases like TB and cholera. Koch used new industrial dyes to stain microbes so that they became visible. With these discoveries, other vaccines were developed against killer diseases like TB, rabies and anthrax.

9.5 Searching for vaccines and curing disease

LEARNING OBJECTIVES

In this lesson you will:

- find out how Pasteur and Koch developed vaccines and cures for human diseases
- use information from lessons 9.1 to 9.4 to analyse why Pasteur and Koch were successful.

GETTING STARTED

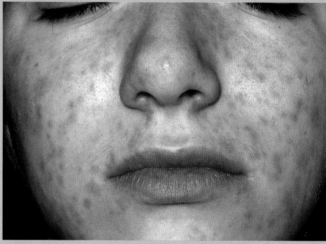

This person has measles.

Did you know that measles can kill? In the 19th century, there were several measles epidemics which killed tens of thousands of people. Have you had measles? Do you remember what it was like? You might have younger relatives who have had measles more recently. What treatment is given in this country today to a person suffering from measles? How do you think treatment might have been different in the 19th century?

Chicken cholera

Pasteur read of Koch's achievements. He was determined to make more discoveries, to win prestige for France, which had lost land to Germany at the end of the Franco-Prussian war of 1870–71. Pasteur built a research team and, in 1877, began work on the anthrax germ. In 1880 he was asked to stop work on anthrax and investigate chicken cholera, a fatal disease that was sweeping through the chicken population and losing French poultry farmers a lot of money. The germ had already been isolated by the professor of a veterinary school in Toulouse, but Pasteur and his team needed to find a liquid culture for the germs to grow in. The usual liquids – water, urine and yeast – did not work. A sterile broth of chicken gristle and potash did.

One of Pasteur's team, Charles Chamberland, was made responsible for injecting some chickens with this liquid culture, to see if it infected them with cholera. However, he forgot to inject the chickens before he went on holiday and the liquid stood uncovered on the bench for many days. On his return, Chamberland injected the chickens, but they did not die. He told Pasteur what had happened and Pasteur instructed him to inject the chickens with a fresh, strong culture. The chickens still did not die. Pasteur left a new culture exposed to air for several days. New chickens were injected with this culture and did not die. Pasteur then injected these chickens and another new batch with a fresh culture. The new chickens died. Those that had been injected with the exposed culture did not. The germs had been weakened by exposure to air. They were not strong enough to kill, but they were strong enough to give **immunity** to a strong dose. This is the principle of **attenuation**. Pasteur called the weaker culture a '**vaccine**', as a tribute to Jenner.

KEY WORDS

Attenuation – *thinning something out or weakening. In medicine, attenuation refers to the idea of weakening a germ, so it loses its effectiveness.*

Immunity – *protection against disease through the body's own defences.*

Vaccine – *killed or weakened forms of bacteria which are injected into the body to give it resistance against disease.*

Pasteur in his laboratory in 1884.

Will you have some microbe? There is some everywhere. Microbiolatry [the worship of microbes] is the fashion, it reigns undisputed; it is a doctrine which must not even be discussed, especially when its Pontiff [Pope], the learned Monsieur Pasteur, has pronounced the holy words, 'I have spoken.' The microbe alone is and shall be the characteristic of a disease; that is understood and settled; the microbe alone is true, and Pasteur is its prophet.

Rossignol ridiculed the germ theory and this led to his challenge to Pasteur to demonstrate his experiment at Pouilly-le-Fort.

Rossignol's article in the *Veterinary Press*, 31 January 1881

ACTIVITIES

'The information on this page explains how Pasteur made a breakthrough in the fight to find a vaccine against chicken cholera. Since this picture shows Pasteur inspecting rabbits in 1884, it has no relevance to his work on the chicken cholera vaccine.' Explain whether you agree or disagree with this statement. Explain your answer fully.

Anthrax – the experiment at Pouilly-le-Fort

After the discovery of the chicken cholera vaccine, Pasteur returned to his work on anthrax, seeking a vaccine for that. His team, led by Dr Emile Roux, managed to produce a weakened strain of anthrax by keeping the germs at a temperature of 42–43°C over a period of eight days.

In 1881 a French journalist named Rossignol challenged Pasteur to test this vaccine in public. (See Source E.) Pasteur accepted and the tests were set for 5 May, on Rossignol's farm at Pouilly-le-Fort, near Paris. The event attracted huge interest throughout Europe and was attended by politicians, farmers and journalists. Pasteur

Pasteur vaccinating sheep against anthrax at Rossignol's farm.

was provided with 60 sheep, 25 of which would be vaccinated and then given deadly anthrax germs. Another 25 would just be given a fatal dose of anthrax germs. The remaining 10 sheep were left alone so that they could be compared with any survivors. The experiment was carried out. By 2 June the unvaccinated sheep were dead and those that had been vaccinated were fit and well. It was a triumph. Reports of the event were sent out by electric telegraph and the world soon knew of Pasteur's success. Robert Koch also tried to find a vaccine for anthrax, but failed. He resorted to attacking Pasteur in the medical press.

Pasteur's vaccine greatly reduced the death rate from anthrax in animals and saved the French farming industry large amounts of money. The experiments on animals had an important influence on human medicine too. Once people were confident that vaccination worked on animals, they were more likely to accept the use of vaccination for humans. Also, the techniques and equipment developed would be the same, whether the patient was a chicken, a sheep or a person.

STRETCH YOURSELF

Read the text about Pasteur's experiments at Pouilly-le-Fort and study Sources E and F. Write a front-page report for a newspaper, broadcasting this famous discovery to the public.

A vaccine for rabies

In 1882 Pasteur's team got ready to produce a vaccine for rabies, a terrible disease that is always fatal once symptoms develop. Emile Roux made the most progress at first, devising a way of drying the spines of rabies-infected rabbits in a glass flask to see how long the rabies virus remained dangerous. Pasteur saw this and copied Roux's idea. It caused a furious row, but Pasteur began to make vaccines from the infected spines and to test them on animals. First he used germs from a spine that had been drying for 14 days, which would not pass the disease on. Next he used a 13-day-old spine, and so on, until the last vaccine he injected was made from a fresh spine, which would definitely cause the disease. Gradually increasing the strength of the germs injected resulted in immunity from rabies. The team, and Pasteur himself, had doubts about this method but, in 1885, their hand was forced by a chance happening. On 6 July a woman from Alsace turned up at Pasteur's laboratory with her son, who had been bitten by a rabid dog. Joseph Meister was doomed unless Pasteur tried the untested vaccine on him. Two doctors advised Pasteur to try. The boy was given a series of injections, which proved successful as he survived. In his later life, Joseph Meister served as a caretaker at the *Pasteur Institut* in Paris!

SOURCE G

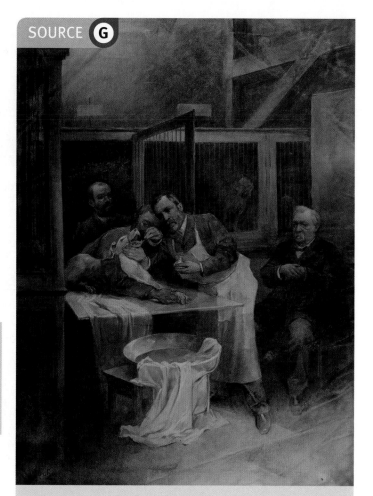

In this engraving, saliva is being removed from a rabid dog.

SOURCE H

Joseph Meister, aged nine years, was bitten on 4 July, at eight o'clock in the morning. This child had been knocked over by the dog and showed numerous bites, on the hands, legs and thighs, some so deep as to make walking difficult. The dog was certainly rabid. Joseph Meister had been pulled out from him covered in foam and blood. The death of this child being certain, I decided to try the method which had been successful with dogs. Young Meister was inoculated under a fold of skin with half a syringeful of the spinal cord of a rabbit which had died of rabies and had been preserved for 15 days in a flask of dry air. Joseph Meister has survived not only the rabies from the bites but also the rabies with which I inoculated him.

Pasteur's description of the rabies injection, from 'A Lecture on the Prevention of Rabies', 1885

Conquering diphtheria

Diphtheria was conquered not by one person but by several, each building on the discoveries of the others. The diphtheria bacillus was discovered by a German doctor, Edwin Klebs. Freidrich Loeffler then bred the germs but could not work out how they killed. He guessed that they produced some kind of toxin or poison. The search was taken up by Roux, who was able to prove that it was the toxin, not the germs, that was fatal. Emil von Behring, a former member of Koch's team, used the blood of animals that survived the disease to develop a **serum**, which he called 'anti-toxin'. When this was injected, it prevented the germs from producing toxin in the body.

Tuberculosis

Koch tested a vaccine for **tuberculosis** (TB), called 'tuberculin', which seemed to work on animals. The German government pushed him to announce the success at the 10th International Medical Congress in 1890. It caused great excitement and thousands of sufferers flocked to Berlin for treatment. However, tuberculin did not work for them and Koch was blamed. His own career waned, but his team continued to succeed.

Government help

The governments of France and Germany realised that the work of Pasteur and Koch brought prestige to their countries. Each government set up a research institute with the latest technology – the *Institut Pasteur* in Paris and the Institute for Infectious Diseases, in Berlin – to enable the scientists to continue their pioneering work.

BACK TO THE START

Study the diagram below and also look back to the opening of this chapter where you saw a desperate patient who was being protected by 'guardian angels'. Each was using weapons to try to fight off 'demon' diseases. Look also at your own answer to activity 2 on page 95. Having reviewed the work you have done so far in Chapter 9, try to answer the GradeStudio question. It is typical of an examination question in Unit A951 and focuses on 'Knowledge and Explanation' skills.

GradeStudio

Exam style question

Which was the most important factor which enabled Pasteur and Koch to succeed: war, or their personal qualities? **[8 marks]**

Industry, science and technology
- The much improved microscope allowed bacteria to be studied.
- Koch used industrial chemical dyes to stain bacteria.

Communications
- The results of experiments and research were spread quickly via telegraph, newspapers and journals. Railways enabled scientists to meet regularly.

Research techniques
- Both Pasteur and Koch devised experiments to prove theories.
- Both had research teams.

Factors that enabled Pasteur and Koch to succeed

Personal qualities
- Both men were intelligent, persistent and determined.
- Both spoke in public at the risk of abuse from doubters.

Chance events
- Chamberland's 'mistake' when Pasteur was researching a vaccine for chicken cholera.
- The surprise arrival of Joseph Meister allowed Pasteur to test his rabies vaccine on humans.

War
- The Franco-Prussian War (1870–71) ended in a disastrous defeat for the French. Tension between the two countries followed.
- Pasteur and Koch were spurred on by this tension. They became rivals; a new discovery brought prestige for their country.

A diagram to show the factors that had an impact on the work of Pasteur and Koch.

9.6 The development of drugs – Paul Ehrlich

LEARNING OBJECTIVES

In this lesson you will:

- find out why Paul Ehrlich is an important figure in the development of drugs
- understand and classify the reasons why some people opposed Salvarsan 606.

Progress in the fight against infectious diseases

By 1900 the germs that caused the most common diseases had been discovered. Koch, Pasteur and others had developed vaccines that could prevent people from catching these diseases. Governments were also introducing preventative measures against disease, by ruling that councils must provide clean water and efficient sewage disposal. Doctors and scientists now needed to find effective cures for people with infectious disease.

There was some knowledge to build on. Drugs made from natural substances had been used for centuries in the treatment of illness. For example, opium (made from poppies) was used as a painkiller. However, these drugs did not combat the bacteria that caused the diseases. By about 1890, most doctors accepted the work of Joseph Lister, who showed that germs outside the body could be killed with carbolic acid – but this chemical was too toxic to use internally. A chemical was needed that could be used safely to kill bacteria inside a person.

KEY PEOPLE

Paul Ehrlich 1854–1915

Nationality: German.

Education: University of Leipzig, researching in chemistry and bacteriology.

Worked as a doctor.

1886 Caught TB, and took three years to recover.

1889 Joined Robert Koch's research team at the Institute for Infectious Diseases in Berlin.

1899–1915 Director of the Royal Institute of Experimental Therapy in Frankfurt. Here he carried out research into chemotherapy (the treatment of disease by chemical drugs).

1908 Shared the Nobel Prize for medicine with the Russian bacteriologist Elie Metchnikov.

1909 Developed a cure for syphilis, which was produced and went on sale in 1910.

GETTING STARTED

This picture shows an actor in the role of Paul Ehrlich in the 1940 Warner film *Dr Ehrlich's Magic Bullet*. Some historians argue that Hollywood movies should not be used as evidence for the lives and deeds of famous people from history. In that case, is this picture of no use to the historian studying the life and work of Paul Ehrlich?

KEY WORDS

Antibodies – *proteins produced in the blood which fight diseases by attacking and killing harmful bacteria.*

Arsenic – *a chemical element which, though poisonous, is sometimes used in small quantities in medicines.*

The search for a magic bullet

By the late 19th century the German chemical industry was progressing rapidly, particularly in the manufacture of synthetic dyes. Koch was experienced in using synthetic textile dyes to stain microbes, to make them easier to study under the microscope.

Paul Ehrlich joined Koch's research team in 1889 and began working with Emil Behring on a diphtheria vaccine. He became fascinated by the fact that the body naturally produces **antibodies** to ward off specific germs, without damaging the rest of the body. He referred to such antibodies as 'magic bullets' because, like bullets from a gun, they seek and hit only their specific target. However, antibodies did not always kill off bacteria that invaded the body. Ehrlich began to think that there must be a chemical dye that could be used to kill specific bacteria inside the body, without harming the rest of the body. This would be a synthetic 'magic bullet'.

In 1899 Ehrlich and his team of researchers started to test different dyes to see if they would kill microbes. They had limited success at first, as dyes were found that attacked malaria and sleeping sickness germs.

The syphilis microbe

In 1906 the microbe that caused syphilis was identified. Syphilis was a sexually transmitted disease which killed thousands of people each year. In 1907 Ehrlich decided to search for a magic bullet to kill the syphilis germ. His team made and tested over 600 **arsenic** compounds. All were said to be useless.

In 1909 Sahachiro Hata, a Japanese bacteriologist, joined Ehrlich's team. Hata was asked to re-test the compounds that had been discarded. He found that compound 606 did in fact kill the syphilis germ. Ehrlich called the new drug Salvarsan 606. He was concerned that doctors might give the wrong dose, or that the drug might be harmful in other ways. He insisted on repeated testing on many hundreds of animals which were deliberately infected with syphilis. He found that the compound always targeted the syphilis germ without harming the rest of the body. Salvarsan 606 was first used on a human patient in 1911.

Opposition

Not everyone welcomed the discovery of Salvarsan 606. Some doctors were not keen to use the new drug; it was not very soluble and was difficult and painful to inject into veins. The use of the new drug led to a number of deaths due to it being administered incorrectly. Some doctors believed that people would become promiscuous now that they knew that syphilis could be cured. Some French doctors were opposed to the drug, developed by Ehrlich, because of their antagonism towards German ideas. Despite Ehrlich's rigorous testing, many doctors did not like the idea of giving their patients arsenic, in any form.

ACTIVITIES

1 What progress had been made in the fight against infectious diseases by 1900?

2 **a** What factors enabled the discovery of Salvarsan 606 to be made?

   b Was any one of these factors more important than the others? Explain your answer.

3 Explain the reasons why people were opposed to Salvarsan 606.

SOURCE

Salvarsan's success represented the promise of modern medicine – that effective synthetic drugs could be devised to treat disease. But it fell short of being a perfect magic bullet. Patients with later stages of syphilis didn't respond as well to the drug. And physicians found the drug difficult to handle and administer properly. Salvarsan was distributed in powdered form; doctors had to dissolve it in several hundred milliliters of pure, sterilized water and then inject it intravenously, taking care to minimize air exposure.

From an article by Amanda Yarnell in the journal *Chemical and Engineering News*, 20 June 2005

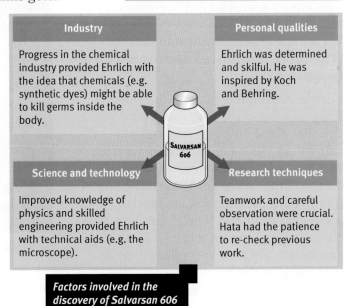

Industry	Personal qualities
Progress in the chemical industry provided Ehrlich with the idea that chemicals (e.g. synthetic dyes) might be able to kill germs inside the body.	Ehrlich was determined and skilful. He was inspired by Koch and Behring.
Science and technology	**Research techniques**
Improved knowledge of physics and skilled engineering provided Ehrlich with technical aids (e.g. the microscope).	Teamwork and careful observation were crucial. Hata had the patience to re-check previous work.

Factors involved in the discovery of Salvarsan 606

9.7 The development of drugs – Gerhard Domagk

LEARNING OBJECTIVES

In this lesson you will:

- find out how Gerhard Domagk developed sulphonamide drugs
- analyse the reliability of sources assessing the impact of Domagk's work.

GETTING STARTED

About 30 million pills per hour are taken around the world today. We now have a multitude of drugs to relieve pain, cure illness, prevent sickness, make us feel good or look better, or help us to live longer. Chemical firms spend millions of pounds on the development of new drugs, which are helping doctors to reduce deaths from disease.

Prepare a brief statement summing up your views in response to the following: 'Drugs – necessary medicine or wasteful luxury?'

Domagk and sulphonamide drugs

Gerhard Domagk worked for a large chemical firm in Elberfeld, Germany. Inspired by Ehrlich's work, he carried out a programme of systematic research, looking for dyes that might destroy microbes which infect the body. Domagk, like Ehrlich, was conscientious and determined.

His first success was the discovery of germanin, a drug effective against sleeping sickness. Then, in 1932, he discovered that a red dye, called prontosil, stopped the streptococcus microbe (which causes blood-poisoning) from multiplying in mice, without causing any harm to the rest of the body. He had no idea whether this drug would work on humans. One day, in 1935, Domagk's daughter, Hildegarde, pricked herself with an infected needle and blood-poisoning set in. The girl was seriously ill and Domagk, with nothing to lose, gave her a huge dose of prontosil. Although her skin turned slightly red, she made a rapid recovery.

Further research by a team of French scientists found that the compound in the dye that acted on the germs was sulphonamide, a chemical derived from coal tar. Soon other sulphonamide-derived drugs were developed, capable of fighting diseases such as tonsillitis, puerperal fever and scarlet fever. In 1938, chemists working for a British firm, May and Baker, discovered a sulphonamide-derived drug that worked against the microbe that causes pneumonia. They tried the drug on a Norfolk farm labourer, who had severe pneumonia, and it worked. They called the drug M&B 693, as it was the 693rd compound they had tested before meeting with success.

Sulphonamide drugs had disadvantages, however. They sometimes caused damage to the kidneys and liver and they were ineffective against more virulent microbes. An even more powerful magic bullet was needed if infectious disease was to be conquered.

SOURCE J

A painting from the 1860s, called 'An Anxious Hour'. It shows a child in a critical condition, suffering from flu.

Why do you think Source J has been included here?

Source K

Paul Ehrlich had a most weird and wrong-headed and unscientific imagination. Ignorant, he lacked Koch's clear intelligence. Then too, Paul Ehrlich was a disgusting doctor because his brain was in the grip of dreams. There was no dignity about Paul Ehrlich. He would draw pictures of his theories anywhere – on his cuffs, on the bottom of his shoes and on the shirt fronts of his colleagues if they did not dodge quickly enough! Just the same he was the most exact of men in his experiments.

From Microbe Hunters by Paul de Kruif (1926).

Source L

The views of Ehrlich's colleagues were united. Behind the eccentric façade there was an exceptionally able mind capable of working brilliant pieces of practical creative chemistry. His methods were highly refined and he carried out his experiments with enormous care.

From Microbes and Men by Robert Reid (1974).

Source M

There can be no doubt that Domagk's influence on the battle against infectious disease was huge. Before his development of sulphonamides, many diseases like meningitis, pneumonia and tonsilitis were killers. From 1935 onwards, the proportions of patients dying from these diseases dropped dramatically. It has been claimed that Domagk saved millions of lives.

From a worksheet written by a history teacher in 2009.

Study these sources and use the knowledge you have acquired in the last four lessons to answer the questions in the activities box.

ACTIVITIES

1   Study Source K. Would Koch have approved of the methods described in Source K? Use the source and your knowledge to explain the answer.

2   Compare Source L with source K. How are the interpretations of Ehrlich both similar and different?

3   Read page 102, headed 'Domagk and sulphonamide drugs'. Now look again at Sources K and L. How different were the scientific methods of Ehrlich and Domagk?

4   Study Source M. Does the teacher give a fair assessment of Domagk's work?

5   Study all of the sources and review your work from the last four lessons. Who was more important in the battle against infectious disease: Pasteur, Koch, Ehrlich or Domagk? Write an essay to explain your answer. It might help to look back to the Examiner's tip in the Grade Studio on page 95.

9.8 The development of penicillin (1)

LEARNING OBJECTIVES

In this lesson you will:

- investigate how penicillin was discovered
- conduct an enquiry into how much of Fleming's work was 'new' and how much was based on the work of others.

Penicillin was the world's first antibiotic – a drug that is derived from living organisms, such as fungi, and which will kill bacteria or prevent bacteria from growing. Penicillin is effective against a variety of germs, and its development involved three brilliant individuals: Alexander Fleming, Howard Florey and Ernst Chain.

'Alexander Fleming: the man who didn't invent penicillin'

Alexander Fleming is one of the most famous names in the history of medicine. If you ask people what he did, they are quite likely to say that he 'invented penicillin' – but this isn't true. Penicillin is not something that can be invented. It is a natural substance. For example, when cheese or fruit goes bad, mould grows on it. This mould has a Latin name, 'penicillium', and has become more commonly known as penicillin.

People might say that Alexander Fleming 'discovered penicillin' – but this isn't really true either. In 1871 Joseph Lister, who discovered antiseptic surgery (see Chapter 10.5), began experimenting with penicillium after he noticed that it seemed to weaken the microbes he was studying at the time. For reasons that we do not know, Lister did

KEY PEOPLE

Alexander Fleming 1881–1955

Born: Lochfield, Ayrshire.

Career: Joined military services but resigned in 1901 when he was left some money in a relative's will. Studied at St Mary's Hospital, London, and qualified as doctor in 1906.

Offered a job as a research assistant by Sir Almroth Wright, head of the Inoculation Department at St Mary's Hospital.

Worked in a military hospital in Boulogne, France, during the First World War.

Returned to St Mary's Hospital after the war and continued work as a medical researcher.

1944 Knighted (became Sir Alexander Fleming).

1945 Nobel Prize for Medicine (together with Florey and Chain).

GETTING STARTED

Think back to the work you did on Gerhard Domagk. Make a list of reasons why he was successful in his work. Keep this list so that, at the end of this lesson, you can compare the reasons for Domagk's success with the reasons for Fleming's success.

SOURCE N

In 1881 a young nurse, working at King's College Hospital, was injured in a street accident. Her wound became infected. Several antiseptics were used, but unsuccessfully. Then a different treatment was used. It was so effective that she wrote down its name. It was 'penicillium'.

Adapted from a book about Fleming published in 1985

SOURCE O

This stained-glass window, showing Alexander Fleming in his laboratory, was installed in St James' Church, Paddington, London, close to St Mary's Hospital, where Fleming had worked for 49 years.

not continue his studies into penicillium and did not leave detailed notes about his work. Several other scientists did work on using penicillium as a treatment, but were unable to find a way of making sufficient quantities to treat patients successfully. Although all this work on penicillin was done by others, before Fleming, it was he who became famous in connection with it. Why was this?

Fleming's discovery

During the First World War, Fleming worked in a military hospital in France, and was appalled to see that antiseptics such as carbolic acid did not prevent infection in deep wounds. Later he wrote in his memoirs: 'Surrounded by all those men suffering and dying, I was consumed by a desire to discover something which would kill the microbes'. After the war, Fleming returned to work at St Mary's Hospital in London, determined to find a substance that could kill germs more effectively. In 1922 he discovered that a natural substance in tears, lysozyme, would kill some germs, but not those that caused disease and infection.

In 1928 Fleming was carrying out research into staphylococci, the germs that turn wounds septic. This involved growing the germs on **agar,** in culture dishes. When Fleming came to clean a pile of discarded culture dishes, he noticed that a mould spore had lodged itself on one of them. It had grown to a size of about one centimetre across the dish. This was not unusual, but Fleming was quick to notice that, around the mould, the germs had stopped growing. Another, less astute, person might have thrown away the dish and thought nothing more about it, but Fleming was curious. The mould was a member of the *penicillium notatum* family. It produced a bacteria-killing juice which Fleming called penicillin.

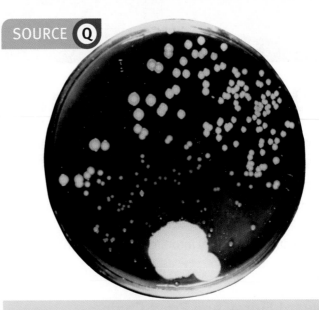

SOURCE Q

The dish with the 'abnormal' culture that caught Fleming's attention

VOICE YOUR OPINION!

Was it a lucky chance that Fleming discovered penicillin in the culture dish, or was it down to his individual brilliance?

Fleming grew further quantities of the mould and found that it stopped other deadly germs from growing, including anthrax and diphtheria bacilli. He injected it into animals and it did not harm them. However, if penicillin was to be of use in treating humans, a way had to be found of turning the mould juice into a pure drug. Fleming and his colleagues were unable to do this. No one would give them the specialist help or money needed for carrying out further experiments. Fleming wrote up his findings and published articles in the *British Journal of Experimental Pathology* in 1929 and 1931. He did nothing more about his discovery.

SOURCE P

Nothing is more certain than that when, in September 1928, I saw bacteria fading away from around the mould, I had no suspicion that I had got the clue to the most powerful substance yet used to defeat bacterial infection.

From a speech made by Fleming in 1943

KEY WORDS

Agar – *a jelly prepared from seaweed for bacteria to grow on for use in experiments.*

ACTIVITIES

Look at these statements:

The work of Fleming marked a complete change in the fight against disease. This was a new and significant breakthrough.

Fleming was simply continuing the work of those who had come before him. Even he did not realise how important his discovery was.

Which of these two opinions do you agree with more? Use evidence from the text and the sources to support your answer.

9.9 The development of penicillin (2)

LEARNING OBJECTIVES

In this lesson you will:

- understand and explain the contributions made by Fleming, Florey and Chain to the development of penicillin
- conduct an enquiry into the 'Fleming myth'.

Howard Florey and Ernst Chain

In 1935 Howard Florey, an Australian doctor, became head of the William Dunn School of Pathology at Oxford. He built a team of brilliant biochemists to carry out medical research, including Ernst Chain, a scientist who came to Britain to escape from Nazi persecution. In 1938 Florey's team decided to study germ-killing substances. Chain came across Fleming's articles on penicillin and the team then set out to produce pure penicillin from the mould juice. They managed to make small quantities of pure penicillin in powder form, and decided to test this on animals. On 25 May 1940 eight mice were injected with streptococci. Four were then given regular doses of penicillin and they survived. The other four mice all died within 16 hours. Florey claimed that they had witnessed a miracle.

Problems in the production of pure penicillin

Florey's team did not have the resources to manufacture large amounts of pure penicillin. They grew the mould in milk bottles, bedpans and milk churns, and turned it into pure penicillin by a process of freeze-drying devised by Chain. In October 1940 they tried using penicillin for the first time to treat a human – a policeman, Albert Alexander, who was suffering from blood-poisoning and close to death. He began to recover after receiving penicillin, only to die when supplies ran out.

War and the US chemical industry

The curative qualities of penicillin were now beyond question, but mass-producing the drug for commercial use remained a problem. Only large chemical companies had the resources to do so. By this time, Britain was deeply engaged in the Second World War and its chemical industry was too busy producing explosives to become involved in the manufacture of penicillin.

Florey realised that penicillin would cure the deep infections caused by war wounds. He visited the USA to try to persuade American chemical firms to invest in the mass-production of penicillin. At first he was unsuccessful. Then, in December 1941, the USA entered the war, and the US government made grants available to firms wishing to buy equipment for making penicillin. British firms began to mass-produce the drug in 1943. In 1945 the Americans estimated that

Stage 1 – 1928

Alexander Fleming discovered the penicillin mould. He was unable to produce pure penicillin from the mould. He published a report of his work but did no more.

Stage 2 – 1938–41

A team of researchers at Oxford University, led by Howard Florey and Ernst Chain, developed a method of making pure penicillin. They could not make large amounts, however.

Stage 3 – 1941–44

In 1941 the USA entered the Second World War. The US government funded research into methods of making large quantities of penicillin. By 1944 enough penicillin was available for Allied soldiers.

Stages in the penicillin story

almost one-sixth of all wounded men were saved from death from infected wounds, because they were given penicillin. After the war, more efficient processes for mass-producing penicillin were invented. The cost of the drug was reduced and it became used across the world to treat a whole range of diseases.

The 'Fleming myth'

In August 1942 a friend of Alexander Fleming lay dying in St Mary's Hospital, London. Fleming contacted Florey in Oxford and asked for some penicillin to treat his friend. Florey immediately obliged and the patient made a rapid recovery. The story appeared in *The Times* and, on 30 August 1942, Almroth Wright wrote a letter to the newspaper saying that Fleming was the person responsible for the drug. Source R is an extract from the letter. People began to believe that the development of penicillin was due entirely to Fleming. Even though Florey and Chain were awarded the Nobel Prize, along with Fleming, in 1945, their part in this medical breakthrough was played down.

ACTIVITIES

1 Make your own copy of the diagram of 'stages in the penicillin story'. Include details about other significant people who were involved, and fit their contributions into the appropriate stage in the diagram.
2 **a** What is the 'Fleming myth'? How did it come into existence?
   b Who do you think deserves the credit for penicillin? Give reasons for your answer.
3 Study Source R. Find out what you can about Sir Almroth Wright. Use this information to explain why you think he wrote this letter to *The Times* in 1942.
4 Would penicillin have been discovered even if Fleming, Florey and Chain had not lived? Explain your answer.
5 For many years before 1900, people in numerous parts of the world used mould from fungus to treat wounds. Knowing this, would you say that the work of Fleming, Florey and Chain was not really a breakthrough in the history of medicine? Explain your answer.

SOURCE R

Sir, In your article on penicillin yesterday you refrained from putting the laurel wreath for this discovery around anyone's brow. I would supplement your article by pointing out that it should be decreed to Professor Alexander Fleming of this laboratory. For he is the discoverer of penicillin and also the author of the original suggestion that this substance might ... have important applications in medicine.

From a letter to *The Times* by Sir Almroth Wright, published on 30 August 1942

SOURCE S

There has been a lot of most undesirable publicity in the newspapers and press about penicillin. The whole subject is presented as having been foreseen and worked out by Fleming. This steady propaganda seems to have its effect even on scientific people, in that several have now said to us, 'But I thought you had done something on penicillin too'.

From a letter from Howard Florey to Sir Henry Dale, President of the Royal Society (a body concerned with the advancement of science), December 1942

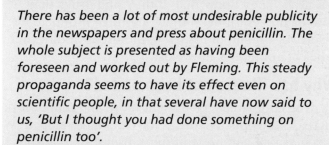

GradeStudio

Analysis of sources

Study Sources R and S. Are you surprised by what Florey says in Source S? Use the sources and your knowledge to explain your answer.
[9 marks]

Examiner's tip

This is an example of a question from Unit A952 which requires you to analyse and evaluate the two sources, using your knowledge of the topic to put what both sources say about the discovery of penicillin into historical context. This is not an easy skill and it is tempting to fall into the trap of either writing down everything you know about the discovery of penicillin and ignoring the sources or the question completely, or of analysing the content of the sources without thinking about the historical context at all. To achieve top marks, you will need to explain why Florey would have been unhappy that Fleming was getting all the credit for the discovery, since Florey and Chain had both played leading parts in its development.

9.10 The battle against infectious and non-infectious disease

LEARNING OBJECTIVES

In this lesson you will:

- understand why, despite all the medical advances of the 20th century, illness has not disappeared
- carry out independent research into hospital 'superbugs'.

GETTING STARTED

Drugs companies have made huge investments in drug research since 1945. Is this a good thing or a bad thing? Try to come up with points for and against.

KEY WORDS

Antibiotic – *a medicine that can destroy harmful bacteria in the body, or limit their growth.*

AIDS – *Acquired Immune Deficiency Syndrome. It is caused by HIV, a virus that attacks the immune system, leaving the sufferer exposed to infection.*

MRSA – *a 'superbug' which is resistant to many antibiotics. It stands for Methicillin-Resistant Staphylococcus Aureus.*

Antibiotics

When the Second World War ended in 1945, the companies producing penicillin for the military were able to mass-produce it for the general public. The first **antibiotics** had been born. Since 1945 drug companies have invested millions of pounds in research. They know that, if they find drugs that cure or prevent illness, there are huge profits to be made. As a result of research, hundreds of different types of antibiotics now exist.

Why has illness not been ended?

As drug companies have spent more and more on research, so increasingly effective drugs have been developed. We now have vaccines that can prevent most diseases, and drugs that can control irregular heartbeat or even help the heart to pump blood through damaged arteries. However, the story is not one of complete success. Sometimes new 'wonder drugs' turn out to be less effective than we would like.

Thalidomide

In the early 1960s a new drug, thalidomide, was introduced to help pregnant women who were suffering from morning sickness. The drug proved effective, but it had not been tested thoroughly enough. The makers did not realise that the drug caused harm to the fetus. A number of children were born with severely deformed limbs, as a result of their mothers taking thalidomide during pregnancy. Later it was discovered that the effects of thalidomide could be passed from generation to generation. The drug companies were made to pay millions of pounds in compensation. Following this, in 1964, the British government set up the Committee on Safety of Drugs, to screen all drugs that were developed.

SOURCE T

'GOOD NEWS DARLING! MY OPERATION HAS BEEN CANCELLED...'

This cartoon was published at a time when there was public concern about the presence of superbugs in hospitals.

Superbugs

Following the introduction of antibiotics, a worrying development was that busy people began to demand antibiotics as an instant cure for their illnesses. This has led to an overuse of antibiotics, with the result that some bacteria are developing a resistance to the drugs. Stronger antibiotics have meant that bacteria are developing even greater resistance. Scientists call bacteria that are resistant to antibiotics 'superbugs'. Hospitals have become fertile breeding grounds for these superbugs.

AIDS

AIDS (Acquired Immune Deficiency Syndrome) came to the attention of US doctors in 1981, when they realised that large numbers of young gay men were dying from unrecognised conditions involving the breakdown of the body's immune system. By 1983 the HIV virus had been discovered as the cause of AIDS. No one really knows where the disease has come from and various theories have been put forward. One suggestion is that it was previously restricted to small areas of African rainforest, but increased communication led to its spread across the world. Whatever the origin of the disease, it has killed tens of millions of people.

Tuberculosis

It isn't just new diseases that are causing problems. It was thought that we had conquered tuberculosis (TB), but now it is beginning to show signs of resistance to antibiotics. Between 1985 and 1991 tuberculosis increased by 12 per cent in the USA, 30 per cent in Europe and 300 per cent in parts of Africa. The disease kills more than three million people each year, 95 per cent of them in the less economically-developed world.

Genetic engineering – hope for the future?

With technological advances, in particular more powerful microscopes, scientists have been able to study human cells and the genes and chromosomes within them. This has allowed them to develop means of 'genetic engineering' where the genetic material in a person is altered by destroying specific damaged or diseased cells.

Such a practice is still in its early years, but has already proved valuable in the treatment of cancers, and blood, liver and lung disorders. Some medical experts believe that a time will come when spare body parts could be cloned to replace damaged or diseased organs. Perhaps in the future it will be possible to transplant parts grown in test tubes into our bodies.

ACTIVITIES

1. What is **MRSA**?
2. According to Source U, there is a 'cover-up' going on in connection with MRSA. Can you explain why the writer of the article believes this?
3. What is the main message of the cartoon, Source T?
4. Carry out your own research to find out about MRSA and other hospital 'superbugs'.

9.11 Hospitals and caring for the ill

LEARNING OBJECTIVES

In this lesson you will:

- find out about the development of nursing as a profession
- investigate why Florence Nightingale and Mary Seacole have been represented in different ways.

GETTING STARTED

Study Source V. Describe the similarities and differences between a 19th-century nurse and a modern nurse. What impression does this source give you of 19th-century nurses?

In 1850, nursing was looked on as a lowly occupation. Nurses were generally portrayed as uneducated and slovenly and they had a reputation for heavy drinking, although this image was not totally fair. The conditions under which they worked were often appalling and there was no proper training. However, in 1853, at Kaiserwerth in Germany, the local pastor, Theodor Fliedner, set up a small hospital and training school for nurses. He insisted that his nurses be of 'good character'. Elizabeth Fry, famous for her attempts to reform prison conditions in London's Newgate gaol, visited Kaiserwerth in 1840. She was so impressed that, on her return to England, she founded Britain's first nursing school, the Institute of Nursing Sisters. During the second half of the 19th century nursing underwent a revolution and developed into a respected profession. How did this change come about?

The Crimean War (1854–56): a tale of two women

Florence Nightingale (1820–1910) came from a wealthy middle-class family. In 1844 she told her parents that she wanted to become a nurse, but they had a low opinion of nurses and it took Florence seven years to persuade them to agree. She then visited Kaiserwerth, and from there travelled to Paris to study nursing. In 1853 she became the Superintendent at the Institution for the Care of Sick Gentlewomen in Harley Street, London, which she ran very efficiently. By now she was fully committed to a career training nurses.

In March 1854 Britain, along with France and Turkey, went to war against Russia. The war was fought in the Crimea, a peninsula on the Black Sea, 3000 miles from Britain. A scandal broke when the

SOURCE V

Nurses were often portrayed in this way in the 19th century.

public read news reports by William Russell, the war correspondent of *The Times*. He told of chaotic conditions in the Barrack Hospital in Scutari, near Constantinople, in Turkey. Wounded British troops were being kept there in overcrowded and filthy conditions. There were no nursing staff and no bandages, and men were dying in agony.

Nightingale's work at Scutari

The Secretary of War, Sidney Herbert, was a friend of the Nightingale family. He wrote to ask Florence if she would 'go and superintend the whole thing'. She agreed and, in the autumn of 1854, departed for Scutari with a team of 38 nurses whom she had personally selected. When they arrived, they were not warmly welcomed by the army doctors, who felt that female nurses were 'unfavourable to military discipline and to the recovery of the patients'. Despite this undercurrent of hostility, Florence made sure that the wards were clean, the patients well-fed, the sanitation and water supply improved and that supplies were plentiful. By early 1856 the death rate in the hospital had fallen from 42 per cent to 2 per cent.

The work of Mary Seacole

Mary Jane Seacole (1805–81) was born in Kingston, Jamaica. Her mother ran a boarding house for invalid soldiers, where Mary helped to care for the patients. In 1854 she went to England and told the War Office that she was willing to go to the Crimea as a nurse. She was rejected and felt that it was because her 'blood flowed beneath a somewhat duskier skin than theirs'. In other words, she was a victim of Victorian racism.

Not to be outdone, she made her own way to the Crimea, at her own expense. She set up a medical store and hostel near Balaclava, where soldiers could obtain medicines. She also tended the wounded on the battlefield and became known to the troops as 'Mother Seacole'. She met Florence Nightingale on several occasions but was not invited to join her team of nurses.

Seacole's fortunes after the Crimean War

In 1856 Mary Seacole returned to England, but not to a heroine's welcome. She went bankrupt and received a deal of sympathy from the English press, notably *The Times* and *Punch* magazine. A four-day festival of music was organised for her benefit in 1857, but it raised only £233. In the same year, Mary published her life story (see Source X) in an effort to raise money. She was quite well off when she died, but no one in the medical world had made use of her nursing skills since the end of the Crimean War.

SOURCE W

A legend grew up around Florence Nightingale. She became known as 'the lady with the lamp' and 'an angel of mercy'. She was said to tour the wards of the Scutari hospital at night, making sure that the patients were comfortable. This picture was painted in 1855.

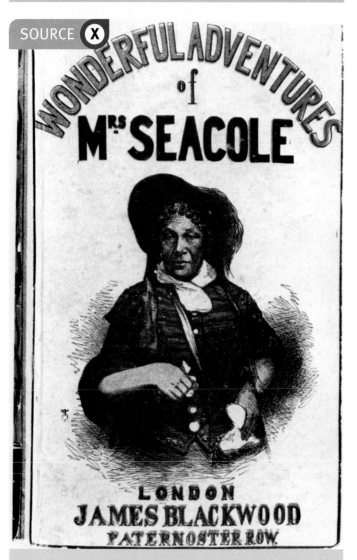

SOURCE X

This rare portrait of Mary Seacole appears on the title page of her autobiography, *The Wonderful Adventures of Mrs Seacole*, published in 1857.

Nursing becomes a profession

On her return to England, Florence Nightingale won huge public acclaim. However, *The Times* commented: 'While the benevolent deeds of Florence Nightingale are being handed down to posterity ... are the human actions of Mrs Seacole to be entirely forgotten?' (24 November 1856).

Florence had high hopes that her success in the Crimea would enable her to establish nursing as a respected profession. In 1859 she published a book called *Notes on Nursing*, which described her methods. It stressed the importance of professionalism and ward hygiene and became the standard text for trainee nurses. A public fund was opened to enable her to develop the training of nurses. It raised £44,000 and the money was used to start the Nightingale School of Nursing at St Thomas's Hospital in London. It was here that the standards were laid down for the training of nurses. Trainees had to be disciplined and willing to work hard. They served a one-year probationary period and then trained for a further two years in order to qualify. Other training schools followed this example and, by 1900, there were 64,000 trained nurses in Britain.

In 1919 the Registration of Nurses Act was passed. It laid down the qualifications needed to enter nursing. Today men also choose nursing as a career and it remains a highly respected profession.

Analysing sources

Study the source below and then look at the Examiner's tip before you try to answer the question that follows.

Source Y

Seacole kept – I will not call it a 'bad house' – but something not very unlike it – in the Crimean War… She was very kind to the men, and what is more, to the officers – and did some good – and made many drunk… [She was] a woman of bad character…

Extracts from letters written by Florence Nightingale to her brother-in-law Sir Harry Verney in 1870. A 'bad house' was a popular name at that time for a brothel, or a house of prostitution.

Question

Are you surprised by what Nightingale says in this source? Use the source and your own knowledge to explain your answer. **[9 marks]**

Examiner's tip

When answering questions like this on Unit A952, you must always remember to use your knowledge of this topic to help your explain why Florence Nightingale might have made these comments. Remember that she had refused to allow Mary Seacole to work with her at Scutari during the Crimean War, Look at the date of the source. These lines were written some time after the war had ended. Nightingale had had time to reflect on how popular Seacole had become immediately after the war. It was seen as something of a scandal that Seacole had not gained more recognition for her work. Remember also that Florence's comments are written in private letters to her brother-in-law. All of these points might help you to understand her motives for her comments. Look at this answer:

Candidate answer

Yes, I am surprised. She says Mary did some good. She says she was kind to the men and to the officers, but she seems to want to criticise her by saying that she gave them drink and generally ran a bad house. How could this be the case if she wanted to do the men some good? She seems to contradict herself.

This is not a bad start, and would probably score 4 marks, The problem here is the lack of knowledge to explain Nightingale's comments. By 1870 perhaps Florence was facing some awkward questions about why she refused to let Mary work with her during the war. That might help to explain why she is writing these things to a member of her family. Now have a go at answering the question yourself.

GradeStudio

Knowledge and Understanding

Explanation

Below is an example of a question that requires you to consider the importance of different factors in an historical development. This is a common type of question in Unit A951. You need to use your knowledge of the topic to give evidence about the relative importance of the different factors.

> The following factors were all of equal importance in the development of penicillin:
>
> **a** Chance
> **b** War and governments
> **c** Individuals and teams.
>
> Explain whether you agree or disagree with this view, giving reasons for your answer. **[8 marks]**

Examiner's tip

Think about everything you have learnt about the development of penicillin and decide which parts are relevant to this question. It's always a good idea to plan what specific evidence you are going to use to support each side of the argument. Look at this mark scheme before thinking about what you would need to do to answer this question.

Mark scheme

Level 1: General and vague assertions
Level 2: Identifies or describes factors supporting the development of penicillin
Level 3: Explains evidence for one factor in the development of penicillin
Level 4: Explains evidence supporting at least two factors in the development of penicillin. Higher marks will be awarded to candidates explaining all three factors.
Level 5: As level four, but also reaches and supports a final judgment in answer to the question.

Look at the example answer 1 below and think about how the candidate moves up these levels.

Examiner's comment

Answer 1

Chance (or luck) certainly played a part in the discovery of penicillin. This is the factor that is usually associated with Fleming's discovery. Certainly you can say that chance played a part because Fleming had not been looking for penicillin and had only found the mould by chance. But was it really chance? If Fleming had not been carrying out medical research, or if he had been a less observant person, then he might not have noticed the mould. So you could say it was the result of individual ability, not chance.

This is a good start. The candidate is using the principle of a three-part paragraph. They have made a clear point, supported it with specific evidence and then linked the evidence to the question in order to explain their ideas.

By giving an example of how chance was involved in the discovery of penicillin the candidate has achieved level two: identification.

The candidate explains their evidence and so the answer moves up to a level three. This will earn approximately half marks.

To go up to level four the candidate will need to explain more than one factor in the development of penicillin. Now look at answer 2.

Examiner's comment

Answer 2

Chance (or luck) certainly played a part in the discovery of penicillin. This is the factor that is usually associated with Fleming's discovery. Certainly you can say that chance played a part because Fleming had not been looking for penicillin and had only found the mould by chance. But was it really chance? If Fleming had not been carrying out medical research, or if he had been a less observant person, then he might not have noticed the mould. So you could say it was the result of individual ability, not chance.

War also had a big part to play in the development of penicillin because the British and US governments put large sums of money into mass-producing penicillin. Without this the drug would not have reached most of the people it saved. But Fleming didn't do his research because of war (although he was motivated by what he saw in the First World War) and Florey and Chain said they did their work because they enjoyed the science. So once again it's not so straightforward.

By explaining evidence for two factors the candidate moves up to level four. To strengthen this still further the candidate could explain more than one piece of evidence for each argument and put in more detail. To attain level five, the candidate needs to reach an overall judgment about the original question: were all three factors equally important? It is important to include something new in the conclusion, rather than just summarising what has already been said.

Now write a conclusion to this question. Highlight in your answer where you have made a clear judgement.

BRAIN BOOST   FIGHTING DISEASE

Now it is time to revise your work on the fight against disease. There is a lot to remember, so it is important to find methods that help you revise the work. You don't need to remember every single fact and date.

For Unit A951, it is important to be able to argue for or against a particular view, or to be able to explain the main factors that caused events to happen. If you are a visual learner, 'mind mapping' is a useful way of revising. Copy and complete the following mind map to show the factors involved in the fight against disease.

If you are an auditory or kinaesthetic learner, you might want to do something more active. Remembering the facts in a story can be easier if you make it more fun to do. You could make the story of the fight against disease into a rap.

Remember, it does not matter how unusual the method of revision is. If it works for you, then it is the right method!

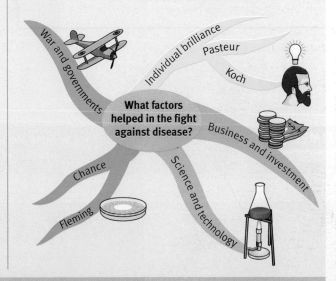

10 The revolution in surgery

10.1 How have operations changed?

Before

Surgery in the early 19th century is dangerous and painful. There is no way to relieve the pain felt by patients during operations. Surgeons do not yet know how to control blood loss or infection, and operating theatres are dirty and dangerous places to be.

Some surgeons superstitiously prefer to wear their 'lucky' coat in the operating theatre – a coat worn during a successful operation in the past. They do not wash their 'lucky' coat between operations in case this breaks their run of luck.

The operating table is often blood-stained. The floor around it is sprinkled with sawdust to stop the surgeon from slipping on blood and other waste as he speeds around the table, carrying out his operation at breakneck speed!

Surgery is usually a last resort, and the most common operations are **amputations**, which can be completed quickly. Robert Liston amputated a leg in two and a half minutes. Unfortunately, such was his haste that he cut off the patient's testicles as well. Patients are lucky to survive operations without any harmful side effects.

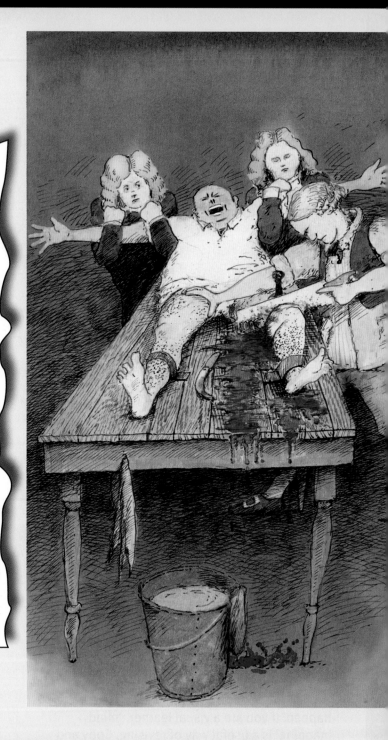

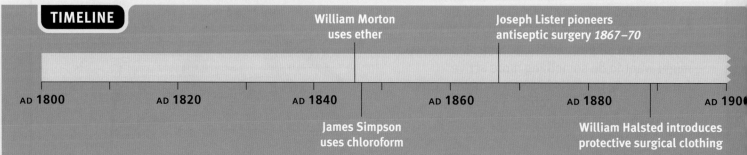

TIMELINE

William Morton uses ether

Joseph Lister pioneers antiseptic surgery *1867–70*

AD 1800   AD 1820   AD 1840   AD 1860   AD 1880   AD 1900

James Simpson uses chloroform

William Halsted introduces protective surgical clothing

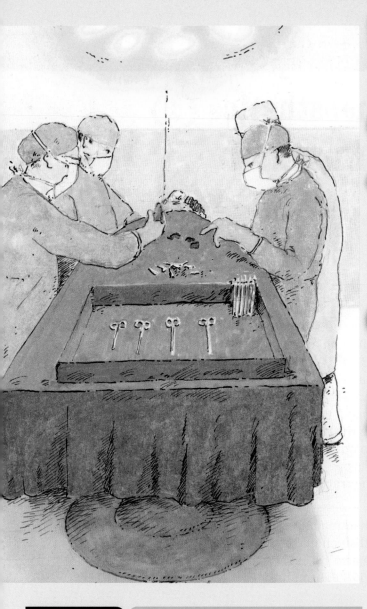

After

Modern operating theatres are clean and safe. State-of-the-art equipment helps surgeons to perform delicate and intricate operations using techniques like **keyhole surgery**. Some surgeons are experimenting with robotic parts to help them carry out operations. High-technology scanners enable surgeons to probe deep inside parts of the body.

Surgeons today can carry out operations that could only have been dreamt of 40 to 50 years ago. Although the first human heart transplant operation only took place in 1967, heart transplants are carried out quite frequently now. Transplants of other body organs are common. Many people agree to donate their organs when they die so that they can be used for transplants, helping other people to recover from illness and to stay alive. Some medical scientists hope that it will become possible to **clone** human organs for transplants.

ACTIVITIES

1 Look at the pictures. One shows an operation in about 1790. The other shows an operation in the early 21st century. What are the main similarities and differences between the two operations? Make a detailed list. This chapter will help you to understand the changes that brought about modern surgical techniques.

2 Some scientists want the government to change the laws on organ donation to make it easier for doctors to obtain organs from patients who have died in hospital. This is a controversial subject. What do you think are the arguments for and against these proposed changes? You might organise a class debate.

KEY WORDS

Amputation – *cutting off (all or part of a limb or digit of the body) through surgery.*

Clone – *to make an exact copy (a genetically identical copy) of cells or an organism. In recent years, scientists have been able to clone animals such as sheep.*

Keyhole surgery – *operating through a very small incision, perhaps only a few centimetres in size.*

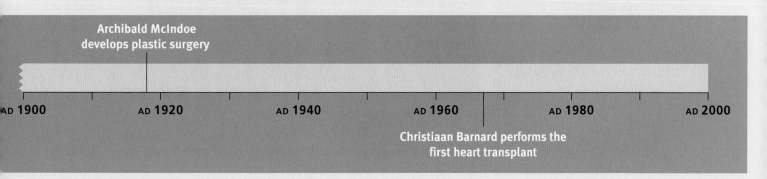

Archibald McIndoe develops plastic surgery

AD 1900   AD 1920   AD 1940   AD 1960   AD 1980   AD 2000

Christiaan Barnard performs the first heart transplant

10.2 Developments in anaesthetics (1)

LEARNING OBJECTIVES

In this lesson you will:

- find out how the problem of pain in operations had started to be tackled by 1846
- check the reliability of sources as evidence for a particular enquiry.

GETTING STARTED

What do you think surgery was like in the early 19th century? From your knowledge of medicine at that time, which four things do you think would have improved operations for patients and doctors?

The problem of pain

Surgeons had long had to face the problems of pain, infection and bleeding. This was still true in the early 19th century. There were no effective **anaesthetics**. To help numb the pain during an operation, surgeons gave their patients drugs like opium and mandrake, or tried to get them drunk. A few surgeons used 'mesmerism' (hypnosis), hoping this would lead the patient to ignore the pain. Surgery had to be quick. Deep internal operations were out of the question. Most surgery was limited to removing growths or amputating limbs. Even so, many patients died from the trauma of the excruciating pain.

During the late 18th century the science of chemistry had made some progress. In 1772 Joseph Priestley (1733–1804), an English chemist, discovered that oxygen was a gas. Other chemists were also investigating the properties of different substances. In 1799 Humphrey Davy (1778–1829) discovered that pain could be relieved by inhaling nitrous oxide ('laughing gas'). He wrote a pamphlet saying that nitrous oxide might be successfully used by surgeons as an anaesthetic. The medical profession ignored his suggestion.

KEY WORDS

Anaesthetics – *drugs given to patients to prevent them feeling pain. There are two types.* **General anaesthetics** *are usually inhaled and make the patient unconscious.* **Local anaesthetics** *are usually injected and have the effect of numbing the feeling in one particular part of the body, such as a tooth. They do not make the patient unconscious.*

ACTIVITIES

1 What problems of surgery are shown in Source A?
2 How reliable is Source A?
3 Imagine you are a relative of the person having the operation. Write an entry in your diary describing what you see, hear and smell during the operation.

SOURCE **A**

A cartoon drawn by Thomas Rowlandson, showing an operation in 1793.

Early successes

During the early 1840s a number of experiments were made to find an effective anaesthetic. In 1842 an American doctor, Crawford Long, found that ether was a useful anaesthetic, but he did not publicly announce his discovery.

On 10 December 1845 an American dentist, Horace Wells (1815–48), watched people inhaling nitrous oxide as an amusement at a fair. He noticed that, under the influence of the gas, they could injure themselves and feel no pain. The next day, Wells had a tooth painlessly taken out after inhaling the gas. He tried to demonstrate painless tooth extraction to some medical students at a hospital in Boston, USA. What he did not know was that some people are not affected by nitrous oxide. Wells' volunteer yelled as the tooth was taken out and the students left the demonstration shouting 'Humbug! Humbug!'

On 16 October 1846 William Thomas Green Morton (1819–68) persuaded John Warren, the head surgeon at Boston Hospital, to carry out an operation in public, using ether as an anaesthetic. Morton gave the ether through an inhaler to the patient, Gilbert Abbott. Then Warren removed a tumour painlessly from Abbott's neck. Warren turned to his audience and announced, 'Gentlemen, this is no humbug!'

News of Warren's success spread quickly to Europe. By 18 October, Dr Bigelow, who had seen the operation, had published an article about it. On 3 December a steamship carried a letter from Bigelow to Dr Boot in London. By 19 December Dr Boot had extracted a tooth using ether – and had written an article about this. On 21 December the surgeon Robert Liston successfully amputated the leg of Frederick Churchill (a butler), using ether as an anaesthetic. Liston removed the leg in 26 seconds! With the leg already on the floor, Churchill raised his head and asked Liston when he was going to begin the operation.

VOICE YOUR OPINION!

What impression does Source A give of operations in the late 18th century?

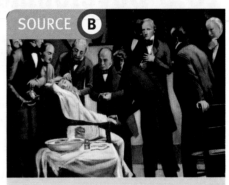

SOURCE **B**

Warren's operation on Gilbert Abbott, 16 October 1846, painted by Robert Hinckely in 1882.

ACTIVITIES

4 Before the introduction of anaesthetics, operations tended to be simple and quick. The most common operations performed were amputations. After anaesthetics were introduced, the death rate during operations increased at first. Why do you think that was?

5 Copy a chart like the one below to record the details you have learnt about the experiments people made with anaesthetics.

Date	Event	Person(s) involved	Was this work successful in tackling pain?

GradeStudio

Enquiry

Study Source B. This is a painting completed after the event. Is it a reliable source of evidence for an historian? Explain your answer.

Examiner's tip

Questions like this will appear on Unit A951 and A952 of the examination. Such questions require you to check how far you can trust the source to be accurate or truthful about the events it represents. To do this well, you need to do these things:

i   Check the content. Does it seem truthful? Is it exaggerated? Does it hide any facts? Does the content match other information that you can find about this operation from other sources, or from your own knowledge?

ii Look at the type of source it is and when it was produced. Source B is a painting produced 36 years after the event. Does this make it more or less reliable?

iii Work out who produced the source. Can you find out anything about the artist and why he painted the picture? Do your answers to these questions have a bearing on the reliability of the source?

10.3 Developments in anaesthetics (2)

LEARNING OBJECTIVES

In this lesson you will:

- investigate how opposition to anaesthetics was overcome
- compare sources of evidence that describe the same event.

GETTING STARTED

By 1846, the problems of overcoming pain during operations had been solved.

Do you agree with this statement? Take a class vote.

James Simpson and chloroform

James Young Simpson (1811–70), Professor of Midwifery at Edinburgh University, wanted to find something to relieve women's pain during childbirth. He disliked ether because it was flammable, had a pungent smell and irritated the lungs when it was inhaled, making the patient cough. He began to test the effects of different chemicals. On 4 November 1847 Simpson and two other doctors discovered the effects of chloroform (see Source C).

Simpson found chloroform easier to administer than ether. Less of it was needed and it appeared to take effect more quickly. By the end of November 1847 he had given chloroform to more than 50 patients and he declared himself pleased with the outcome.

Opposition to anaesthetics

The first anaesthetics meant painless operations, but they were not welcomed by everyone.

- Some people worried that surgeons were inexperienced in using the anaesthetics, and therefore unsure about the correct amount to give and about any side effects the drugs could have. There were even instances of explosions in operating theatres caused by the use of ether. Such fears appeared to be realised when, in 1848, 15-year-old Hannah Green died from an overdose of chloroform. Deaths also occurred from the overuse of ether.
- Members of the Calvinist Church in Scotland were outraged at the use of chloroform in childbirth. They pointed to the book of Genesis in the Bible, where God says to Eve: 'In sorrow shalt thou bring forth children.' To them, this meant that God intended women to bear pain when giving birth.
- Some people worried that anaesthetics placed patients under the total control of the surgeons. What if a surgeon did something against the patient's will?
- In the army, some officers regarded the use of anaesthetics as 'soft'. In 1854 John Hall, Chief of Medical Staff in the Crimea, told his team of doctors: 'A good hand on the knife is stimulating. It is much better to hear a fellow shouting with all his might than to see him sink quietly into his grave.'

SOURCE C

Late one evening Dr Simpson with his two friends and assistants, sat down to their somewhat hazardous work in Dr Simpson's dining room. Having sniffed several substances, but without much effect, it occurred to Dr Simpson to try a material which he had regarded as likely to be of no use whatever; that happened to be a small bottle of chloroform. It was searched for and recovered from beneath a heap of waste paper. [They inhaled the chloroform and passed out.] On awakening Dr Simpson's first thought was, 'This is far stronger and better than ether.'

From H.L. Gordon, *Sir James Young Simpson and Chloroform*, 1897

SOURCE D

This 19th-century drawing shows the effect of inhaling chloroform on Simpson and his assistants.

GradeStudio

Enquiry

Study Sources C and D. Working with a partner, read the exam question and the mark scheme and write an answer that you think would gain a high mark. When you have finished, swap your answer with another pair of students and mark each other's work. Try to give some constructive feedback on the answer you have marked.

'Source D was drawn to show the events described in Source C'. Explain whether you agree or disagree with this statement.

Mark scheme

Level One: Simple answer that makes little or no use of the sources.

Level Two: Agrees or disagrees with the statement, using information from the sources.

Level Three: Agrees and disagrees with the statement, using information from the sources.

Level Four: Level two or level three, plus uses details from the text about the sources to show that it is impossible to say which source came first and therefore that it is difficult to answer the question.

SOURCE **E**

A chloroform inhaler from 1879. It consists of a cotton face mask onto which the chloroform was poured.

SOURCE **F**

Modern anaesthetists at work.

The royal seal of approval

Some of the opposition to anaesthetics disappeared after Queen Victoria was given chloroform during the birth of her eighth child, Prince Leopold, on 7 April 1853. The anaesthetist was Dr John Snow (1813–58), who later did vital research into cholera. The Queen wrote in her journal that chloroform was 'soothing, quietening and delightful beyond measure.' As a result of her experience, chloroform became socially more acceptable. It became the most popular anaesthetic until about 1900, when it was realised that it could damage the liver. Surgeons then returned to using ether.

Anaesthetics from the late 19th century to the present day

Anaesthetics became accepted but problems remained in using them. Massive amounts were often needed, not to prevent pain, but to relax the muscles. Patients became saturated and slept for hours, even days. Recovery was slow and there were frequent complications.

From the end of the 19th century, anaesthetists became specialists. New substances were discovered and put into use. In 1884 cocaine was first used as a local anaesthetic, numbing one part of the body while the patient remained conscious. In Germany, in 1905, novocaine was proved to be more effective than cocaine. In 1942 curare, a South American poison, was first used as a muscle relaxant during operations; it remains in use today. A skilled anaesthetist is now a crucial member of every surgical team, responsible for monitoring the patient's well-being during operations.

ACTIVITIES

1 Why did Simpson dislike ether?

2 Does Source C show that chance played a part in the discovery of chloroform?

3 What other factors enabled Simpson to make his discovery?

4 Why was there fierce opposition to anaesthetics?

5 How was the opposition to anaesthetics overcome?

6 How is the work of a modern anaesthetist different from the work of pioneers in anaesthetics such as Horace Wells, William Morton and James Simpson?

10.4 The development of blood transfusions

LEARNING OBJECTIVES

In this lesson you will:

- discover how the obstacles to successful blood transfusions were removed
- perform research into aspects of the history of blood transfusion.

GETTING STARTED

Think of as many reasons as you can why a person might need a blood transfusion. Share your ideas with a partner.

The first transfusions

The practice of blood transfusion – transferring blood from the circulation of one person to that of another – is relatively recent. It only became a practical possibility during and shortly after the Second World War, and yet the concept of transfusion has origins much further back in history. The first successful attempts came in the 1670s. In 1628 William Harvey had proved that blood circulates (see page 75). This encouraged scientists to experiment with the idea of blood transfusion. Dr Richard Lower, a doctor in Oxford, performed one of the first transfusions from an animal to an animal. Then the first transfusion from an animal to a man was carried out by Jean Denys, a French doctor, in 1667. Denys continued to perform animal-to-human blood transfusions, some more successful than others.

Doctors in the 17th century did not understand why some blood transfusions went well, while others did not. Despite Harvey's discoveries, many doctors still believed Galen's ideas about how blood was produced (see page 44) and they continued to practise bloodletting. The most popular reason for carrying out a transfusion was to try to alter the mental state of the patient. Many believed that it could restore youth to the aged, and it was even suggested that marital discord might be settled by transfusing the blood of husband and wife! In

KEY WORDS

Anticoagulant – *a substance that prevents clotting.*

Freeze-dried plasma – *the yellow liquid part of the blood which has been separated and freeze-dried so that it can be stored and used later.*

SOURCE **G**

Physicians and a patient during a blood transfusion in 1667.

1679, the Pope issued a ban on blood transfusions, and interest in this area of research declined.

The work of James Blundell

James Blundell (1790–1877) was a noted doctor and obstetrician. He was the first to transfuse human blood and has been described as 'the father of modern blood transfusion'. The first documented transfusion of human blood took place on 22 December 1818. The patient was a 35-year-old man who was near to death. Blundell gave him approximately 14 ounces of blood from several donors. The blood was administered by syringe, in small amounts, at intervals of 5–6 minutes. Although his condition improved at first, the patient died 56 hours later. His disease was incurable and nothing could really have been expected from the transfusion. Between 1818 and 1829, Blundell established many techniques in blood transfusion which would continue to be used.

Further developments

Despite Blundell's work, the success of blood transfusions still seemed a matter of chance. One difficulty was that blood coagulates, or clots, making it impossible to transfuse. In 1860, J. Neudorfer recommended adding sodium bicarbonate to the blood to stop it clotting. Another problem was the danger of infection from unsafe transfusion methods, but this began to be resolved when Louis Pasteur proved that germs cause disease (see page 92) and Joseph Lister pioneered antiseptics (see page 124). As a result, doctors began to sterilise instruments and use antiseptic methods.

In 1900 Dr Karl Landsteiner (1868–1943) discovered different blood groups. It was then recognised that only compatible blood types could be successfully transfused. Scientific and technological advances became more and more involved in the development of transfusion during the 20th century. The voluntary blood donor scheme was pioneered in London, after the Red Cross, which had set up a blood transfusion service in 1926, had requested two blood donors at short notice. Shortly after the introduction of electrical refrigeration, the first 'blood bank' was set up in Barcelona in 1936. Many other major developments in transfusion medicine during the 20th century were given impetus by wars and major conflicts. **Freeze-dried plasma** was developed in 1940. ACD (acid citrate dextrose) **anticoagulant** solution for the storage of blood was developed in 1943, and the development of a method of freezing blood followed in 1944.

VOICE YOUR OPINION!

Why do you think 17th-century blood transfusions had limited success?

HISTORY DETECTIVE

Increase your knowledge of the history of blood transfusion by investigating one or more of the following topics.

1   Blood transfusions during the Franco-Prussian War (1866–70)
2   The work of Norman Bethune during the Spanish Civil War (1936)
3   The development of blood transfusions after the Second World War.

You should then prepare a presentation about your chosen topic for the rest of the class.

SOURCE **H**

Donated blood is loaded onto a truck to be refrigerated, in the Second World War.

10.5 Developments in antiseptic surgery

LEARNING OBJECTIVES

In this lesson you will:

• understand why there was opposition to antiseptic surgery and how that opposition was overcome

• make cross-references between two sources to explain why they appear to contradict each other.

GETTING STARTED

Look at this picture. It shows a typical operating theatre in about 1840. Explain as fully as you can why this operation might not be successful.

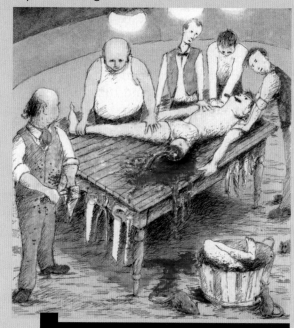

An artist's impression of an operating theatre in about 1840.

The problem of infection

The period between the first use of ether as an anaesthetic in 1846 and about 1870 has been called the 'black period' of surgery. Being able to remove pain made surgeons over-confident and they performed many operations that they would not have attempted before. However, operations were still carried out in unhygienic conditions, by surgeons wearing their everyday clothes. Instruments were not sterilised between operations. Before Pasteur proved the germ theory (see page 92), people did not understand the need for cleanliness. As a result, many patients died from infections that developed after an operation.

Ignaz Semmelweiss

Ignaz Semmelweiss was a young Hungarian doctor working in Vienna in the 1840s. He was worried about the high death rate of women from puerperal fever, an infection which set in after childbirth. Some doctors believed it was spread by miasmas (unhealthy smells or vapours) in the air of hospital wards. In 1847 Semmelweiss suggested that the doctors themselves might be spreading the infection by examining patients immediately after dissecting the bodies of women who had died from the fever. He ordered the doctors to wash their hands in a solution of chloride of lime before examining patients. This was unpleasant and many doctors resented it. But the death rate from puerperal fever in their wards fell dramatically. Other doctors did not accept Semmelweiss' method. The high death rates continued in most places.

Joseph Lister

The breakthrough in preventing infection was made by Joseph Lister (1786–1869). He had read of Pasteur's research and realised that the infections killing his patients were caused by germs. He knew that the operating theatre smelled similar to rotting sewage. To kill any germs that were present, he decided to use carbolic acid, a disinfectant that was used to combat the smell at sewage works. First Lister used bandages soaked in carbolic acid. Then he developed his technique to

SOURCE **1**

An antiseptic operation in Aberdeen in the 1880s. Lister's steam carbolic spray is being used.

ACTIVITIES

Why did Lister's carbolic spray meet with fierce opposition?

SOURCE J

Despite the [support] of statistical evidence, Lister's method met with interference and even violent opposition ... Fully twenty years of patient trial, improvement, demonstration and education were needed before British surgeons were won over to the idea, and not before many senior members of the profession had been replaced by a younger generation.

Leo M. Zimmermann and Ilza Veith, *Great Ideas in the History of Surgery*, 1961

include a spray of the acid that drenched the air, the surgeon's hands, the instruments and the patients. This was unpleasant for surgeons but the results were remarkable. Mortality plummeted. Between 1864 and 1866, of the amputations performed without antiseptics, 46 per cent of patients died. Between 1867 and 1870, when antiseptics were being used during amputations, only 15 per cent of patients died. By 1912, when Lister died, ten times as many operations were being performed as in 1867. For the first time, surgeons were able to operate without fear of infection killing the patient. The combination of anaesthetics and antiseptics meant that surgery was now much safer.

From antiseptic to aseptic surgery

Antiseptic surgery had its drawbacks, not least being the discomfort felt by surgeons and nurses as the carbolic acid burnt their skin and the spray irritated their lungs.

Rather than trying to fight germs, surgeons in Germany developed techniques for keeping them away. This is known as **asepsis**, and aseptic surgery quickly became the normal procedure in operating theatres. The idea of scrupulous cleanliness originated with Professor Gustav Neuber and was developed by Ernst von Bergmann (1836–1907). Surgeons' hands, clothes and instruments were all sterilised. A chamber was used to pass superheated steam over the instruments, thus killing the germs without the need for disinfecting chemicals.

The 'father' of American surgery, William S. Halsted (1852–1922), introduced a further innovation. In 1889 his nurse, Caroline Hampton, complained that antiseptic chemicals were harming her hands. Halsted asked the Goodyear Rubber Company to make some gloves. He had a particular interest as he was to marry Nurse Hampton in 1890. Halsted realised that the gloves were protecting the patient

GradeStudio

Enquiry

Study Sources I and J. Given what you can see in Source I, are you surprised by what you read in Source J?

Examiner's tip

Questions like this often appear on Unit A952. They test your ability to compare sources and to suggest reasons why they might appear to contradict each other. The trick is to get beyond the surface detail. Although Source I shows Lister's spray being used, and Source J suggests there was opposition to it, you need to notice that Source J does not say that the spray was never used. In addition, you need to notice the date of Source I. It shows an operation taking place several years after Lister first developed his spray. Perhaps the opposition had died down by then. To score really high marks in this question, you need to ask how typical Source I is. It only shows one operation in one hospital in the 1880s. Maybe it didn't catch on in other hospitals in other parts of the country.

as well as the nurse. He followed this by introducing caps, masks and gowns for surgery. Halsted also investigated cocaine as an anaesthetic but became a drug addict, taking both cocaine and morphine.

Today instruments are pre-packed in sterile containers. The air is sterilised before it enters the operating theatre. Some operations, especially on babies or for joint replacement, take place in sterile 'tents' to ensure that there is no risk of infection.

KEY WORDS

Asepsis – *sterilising the air, the clothing and tools of doctors in the operating room to remove the risk of germs.*

SOURCE K

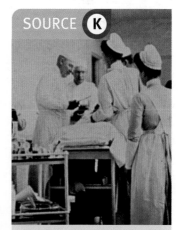

Halsted in the operating theatre at the Johns Hopkins Medical School, Baltimore, USA. He operated and taught his students at the same time.

10.6 Modern surgeries (1) – plastic surgery

LEARNING OBJECTIVES

In this lesson you will:

- investigate the development of plastic surgery techniques
- compare the usefulness of written and visual sources.

GETTING STARTED

Plastic surgery is not as important a development in the history of surgery as anaesthetics and antiseptics, since 'plastic surgery is only used to improve people's personal appearance, and not to save lives.'

Explain whether you agree or disagree with this view.

Plastic surgery

Grafting skin to repair damaged features was practised in ancient India and during the Renaissance, but infection was a major problem. In the 20th century, the development of new weapons led to an increase in the number and types of facial and skin wounds. In Britain, Harold Gillies set up a unit to treat horrific wounds inflicted during the First World War. He was the first plastic surgeon to consider the patient's appearance. Gillies' assistant was a New Zealander, Archibald McIndoe. In the Second World War, McIndoe set up a unit at East Grinstead in Sussex, where he treated over 4000 patients, mostly airmen, whose faces and hands had been disfigured by blazing petrol. His patients, known as 'guinea pigs', were helped by developments in drugs like sulphonamides and penicillin which helped to prevent infection. Since then plastic surgery has become a vital branch of surgery, giving a better quality of life to people whose lives would otherwise be shattered by injury or birth defects.

KEY WORDS

Grafting – *transplanting or implanting (living tissue, for example) surgically into a bodily part, to replace a damaged part or to compensate for a defect.*

ACTIVITIES

1 Why did 20th-century warfare speed up the development of plastic surgery?

KEY PEOPLE

Archibald McIndoe 1900–60

Born: Dunedin, New Zealand.

Career: Studied medicine at Otago in New Zealand, the Mayo Clinic in the USA and St Bartholomew's Hospital in London. After the First World War he worked with the British surgeon Harold Gillies, treating patients who had suffered disfigurement as a result of wounds received in the war.

He continued his work throughout the Second World War at East Grinstead, Sussex. (An example of his work was described in 2002, in the obituary of a former RAF pilot: 'the pilot's fuel tank caught fire, spilling fuel over the cockpit and the pilot himself. He was taken to East Grinstead, where the pioneering surgeon Sir Archibald McIndoe, rebuilt his hands and carried out skin grafts.')

Knighted in 1947 (became Sir Archibald McIndoe).

After his death, as a symbol of gratitude, his ashes were buried in the RAF church in London.

When a man is lying in bed bandaged from head to toe, with eyelids gone, without a nose, it is hard to think of a useful life to come, harder still to believe there might be love and joy in his future. His life has crashed and burned and he is perhaps nineteen, perhaps twenty-one. Does he want to die? Quite possibly. He is in agony. If he is from a farm he remembers the merciful way a gravely injured animal is put down. Does he want to live? Hard to imagine when everything he once saw in his future, a few days ago, has disappeared in a blinding flash.

Rita Donovan, *As for the Canadians: the Remarkable Story of the RCAF's "Guinea Pigs" of World War II*, 2000, pp. 18–19

Rebuilding a badly burned nose required a pedicle, or temporary bridge of tissue, between the chest and the nose. This shows Flight Lieutenant Charles Goldhamer with a pedicle.

Plastic surgery is much more common today. It can be used to repair skin damage from burns, disease or injury. High-technology tools are used to join up nerves and repair the skin. Plastic surgery can also be used to repair hands and fingers that have been torn off in accidents.

Face transplants

In 2006 French woman Isabelle Dinoire became the first person in the world to undergo a partial face transplant, after she had been savaged by a dog three years before. The procedure caused great controversy. Some people argued that it was wrong for surgeons to develop techniques that could enable people to switch their identity or 'trade their face'. There is still fierce debate today about whether it is ethical to transfer a key part of someone's identity from a dead body to a living person.

The doctors who treated Isabelle were convinced that they were justified in carrying out the operation. Professor Bernard Devauchelle, who led the operation, said: 'The transplant was very rapidly integrated into her life – it became a part of who she was.' French doctors have carried out more such operations. But although there are clear benefits for people who no longer have to live with a horrific disfiguration, there is strong opposition to face transplants.

The French doctors have been accused of 'ethical crimes'. In particular, people question whether it is right to use surgery that was developed during wartime to save people's lives purely for cosmetic purposes, to satisfy people who don't like their appearance.

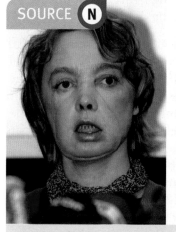

Photographs of Isabelle Dinare the first person in the world to undergo face transplant surgery.

VOICE YOUR OPINION!

Examine Sources L and M. Which is more useful to the historian studying McIndoe's methods? Explain your answer fully.

ACTIVITIES

2 'Without Pasteur, Fleming and Domagk, there might have been no McIndoe.' Explain fully whether you agree or disagree with this view.

3 Carry out further research into Archibald McIndoe's work at East Grinstead. In what ways were his methods unconventional?

10.7 Modern surgeries (2) – transplanting organs

LEARNING OBJECTIVES

In this lesson you will:

- find out about the development of transplant surgery
- analyse the significance of Christiaan Barnard in the development of heart transplant surgery.

GETTING STARTED

Discuss with a partner what you know about the ethical debates surrounding transplants between human beings and animal-to-human transplants. Can you decide what your view is? Is it different from your partner's?

Heart surgery

Before the Second World War, surgery on the heart was dangerous and rarely carried out. When surgeons opened the chest, the patient's lungs collapsed and when the heart was touched, it stopped. It was thought that nothing could be done about this.

The Second World War provided the stimulus for further research, as some soldiers had bullets and fragments of shrapnel lodged in their hearts. A US army surgeon, Dwight Harken, had the courage to try to save them. He cut into the beating heart and used his finger to remove the fragments. The problem in surgery to correct defects in the heart was that the patient's blood supply needed to be cut off when the heart was opened. Cutting off the blood supply for more than four minutes causes brain damage. A Canadian surgeon, Bill Biggelow, came up with the idea of lowering the patient's body temperature to increase the length of time for which it is safe to cut the blood supply. Nevertheless the problem remained.

At the University of Minnesota, Norman Shumway led a team specialising in pioneering heart surgery but there was sometimes a 50 per cent death rate. In 1960 the Methodist Hospital in Houston, Texas, became the centre for heart surgery, under Michael de Blakey. He worked at immense speed and used knitted Dacron, an artificial fibre, to replace diseased arteries. The problem of how to transplant a replacement heart remained to be solved. **Tissue rejection** made it seem impossible. However, research continued, despite a shortage of human hearts. In 1967 Norman Shumway announced that he was ready to try a human heart transplant. In New York, Dr Adrian Kantrowitz prepared to operate on a baby on 3 December. That same morning he heard that Christiaan Barnard had performed the world's first human heart transplant in South Africa.

KEY WORDS

Tissue rejection – *when a transplant recipient's immune system attacks a transplanted organ or tissue.*

KEY PEOPLE

Christiaan Barnard
1923–2001

Born: Beaufort West, South Africa.

Career: Walked five miles each day to study at Cape Town University and qualified as a family doctor.

1950s Went to the USA to study heart treatment at the University of Minnesota.

1967 Transplanted the heart of a female road accident victim into 59-year-old Louis Washkansky. Although Washkansky died 18 days later, Barnard had shown that the operation was possible. He became world-famous and was invited to meet the Pope in Rome and US President Johnson in Washington. He was surprised by the publicity. As he said, 'I didn't even inform the hospital superintendent what we were doing.'

Christiaan Barnard

Surgeons in the USA were disappointed, as they felt that they had done all the experimental work and Barnard had used their ideas. Barnard denied this. Shumway and Kantrowitz carried out their operations but their patients soon died. Barnard did another transplant and his patient lived for more than a year and a half. In Texas, Michael de Blakey and Denton Cooley also tried human transplants. Cooley was able to complete a transplant operation in 20 minutes. No one, however, could overcome the problems caused by the patient's immune system. The drugs the patients needed to take, to make their body accept the donor heart, left them open to infection. All the transplant patients died within a relatively short time.

Enormous public expectation had been shattered. The failure rate was too high. Barnard tried, without success, to keep transplants going. Some saw him as the villain. Heart transplant operations ceased. Some doctors turned to experimenting with artificial hearts and, in 1982, a plastic heart was given to Barney Clarke in Salt Lake City, USA. He died three weeks later.

The solution arrived by chance. In 1974, when looking for new drug substances in soil samples, a researcher in Norway came across the drug cyclosporin. It was found that cyclosporin controlled tissue rejection, but did not eliminate the body's resistance to disease. Cyclosporin then had a more dramatic effect on heart transplant surgery than the skills of Barnard and Cooley combined, because it meant that transplants were possible again. By 1987, 90 per cent of heart transplant patients lived more than two years. Heart transplants are now routine. Surgery, drugs, patient care and the control of rejection all interlink to give success.

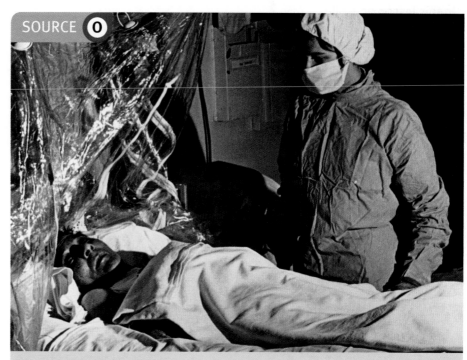

SOURCE O

A nurse cares for the first heart transplant patient, Louis Washkansky, after the pioneering operation by Dr Christiaan Barnard in December 1967.

GradeStudio

Explanation

Christiaan Barnard made the most important breakthrough in the history of heart surgery.

Do you agree or disagree with this view? Explain your answer.

Examiner's tip

This type of question requires you to write a two-sided argument. Write an answer to the question, using this mark scheme to help you aim for the highest possible mark.

Mark scheme

Level 1: General and vague assertions.

Level 2: Identifies or describes factors from at least one side of the argument.

Level 3: Explains evidence supporting one side of the argument.

Level 4: Explains evidence supporting both sides of the argument.

Level 5: As Level 4, but also reaches and supports a final judgement in answer to the question.

10.8 Modern surgeries (3) – high-technology surgery

LEARNING OBJECTIVES

In this lesson you will:
- find out about developments in high-technology surgery
- recall and communicate your knowledge about modern surgery.

GETTING STARTED

Look at Source P. Discuss with a partner how this source demonstrates the role of technology in the development of modern surgical techniques. How does it compare to the operating theatre in 1840? (10.5 page 124)

High technology surgery

Surgeons could often benefit from the rapid development of science and technology in the late 19th and 20th centuries. The increasing use of electricity meant that many machines could be developed to assist surgery. Plastics and steel enabled artificial joints to be made for replacement surgery.

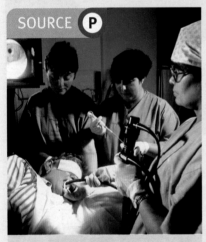

SOURCE **P**

A surgeon using an endoscope to look inside the patient. The endoscope is inserted through a small incision near the patient's navel.

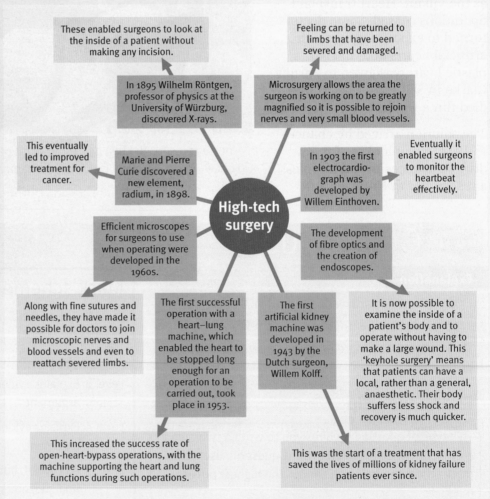

These enabled surgeons to look at the inside of a patient without making any incision.

Feeling can be returned to limbs that have been severed and damaged.

In 1895 Wilhelm Röntgen, professor of physics at the University of Würzburg, discovered X-rays.

Microsurgery allows the area the surgeon is working on to be greatly magnified so it is possible to rejoin nerves and very small blood vessels.

This eventually led to improved treatment for cancer.

Marie and Pierre Curie discovered a new element, radium, in 1898.

In 1903 the first electrocardio-graph was developed by Willem Einthoven.

Eventually it enabled surgeons to monitor the heartbeat effectively.

High-tech surgery

Efficient microscopes for surgeons to use when operating were developed in the 1960s.

The development of fibre optics and the creation of endoscopes.

Along with fine sutures and needles, they have made it possible for doctors to join microscopic nerves and blood vessels and even to reattach severed limbs.

The first successful operation with a heart–lung machine, which enabled the heart to be stopped long enough for an operation to be carried out, took place in 1953.

The first artificial kidney machine was developed in 1943 by the Dutch surgeon, Willem Kolff.

It is now possible to examine the inside of a patient's body and to operate without having to make a large wound. This 'keyhole surgery' means that patients can have a local, rather than a general, anaesthetic. Their body suffers less shock and recovery is much quicker.

This increased the success rate of open-heart-bypass operations, with the machine supporting the heart and lung functions during such operations.

This was the start of a treatment that has saved the lives of millions of kidney failure patients ever since.

Case study: the development of brain surgery in the early 20th century

American Harvey Williams Cushing (1869–1939) became a pioneer of brain surgery. He was probably the greatest neurosurgeon of the 20th century, and has been described as the 'father of modern neurosurgery'.

He was an ambitious man who seemed driven to develop pioneering surgical techniques. His colleagues noticed his limitless energy and fanatical work ethic. He was said to be egotistical and mean, and ruthless in promoting the importance of his own work. He threw himself into all aspects of his life, becoming an expert surgeon, teacher and author of many medical books.

In 1907 Cushing began to study the **pituitary gland**, at the base of the brain. He was able to diagnose many of the conditions that affect the operation of this gland. He was unique in providing evidence that it was possible to deal with these conditions by operating on the gland. He developed new techniques that enabled surgeons to open the skull, expose the brain and attack and remove tumours. His success rate was much higher than previously known. He and his team achieved a record of treating more than 2000 tumours. Many of the brains on which Cushing operated were stored in an archive, for him to use in future research and development, and they are still housed at Yale University today. Neurosurgeons continued to rely heavily on the methods developed by Cushing until the 1990s, when even more advanced methods using keyhole surgery were developed. You can read about some more recent developments in brain surgery on pages 132–3.

You can read about some more recent developments in brain surgery on pages 132–3.

HISTORY DETECTIVE

Find out more about the work of Harvey Cushing, or any of the other pioneers whose work is briefly mentioned in parts 10.7 and 10.8 of this chapter. In writing a report of your findings, try to cover the 'Five Ws':

- *Who* is the pioneer you have investigated?
- *What* was their area of work?
- *Where* did they carry out their main work?
- *When* was their main work carried out, and in what circumstances?
- *Why* were they successful?

Cushing was way ahead of his time in performing brain surgery with his patients given local anaesthetics only. In 1911 he introduced special **sutures** to control the severe bleeding that often made brain surgery impossible. Cushing turned neurosurgery into a separate and specialist field. His use of X-rays to locate the position and size of pituitary tumours paved the way for the use of more sophisticated scanners in more recent times.

KEY WORDS

Pituitary gland – *a small organ at the base of the brain which controls the growth and activity of the body by producing hormones.*
Sutures – *surgeons' stitches.*

SOURCE **Q**

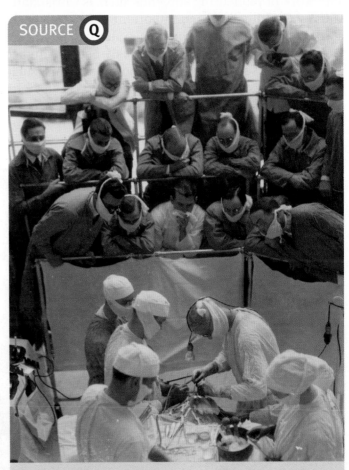

Harvey Cushing operates on 6 May 1932, before the 16 interested founding members of the Harvey Cushing Society – now the American Association of Neurological Surgeons.

10.9 The impact of high-technology surgery

In this lesson you will:

- consider the advantages and disadvantages of high-technology surgery
- analyse the factors that have played a part in the development of surgery since 1870.

Some obese patients have had fat sucked out of their bodies in a treatment called liposuction. Others have had their stomachs stapled, to make them smaller, so that they will only be able to eat small amounts of food. Should surgeons be spending time and money on procedures like these when people all over the world are dying from fatal diseases?

The work of pioneering surgeons such as Christiaan Barnard and Harvey Cushing has been important in expanding the boundaries of surgery. Improved technology has also had an enormous impact. For example, the use of lasers has quickly become an accepted part of treatment. Lasers are used in minor operations, such as to correct eye faults, and in treatment to control cancers, thus helping to save lives. Medical skills and technology have even increased to the point where it is possible to detect problems in an unborn baby and carry out corrective surgery before the child is born.

SOURCE **R**

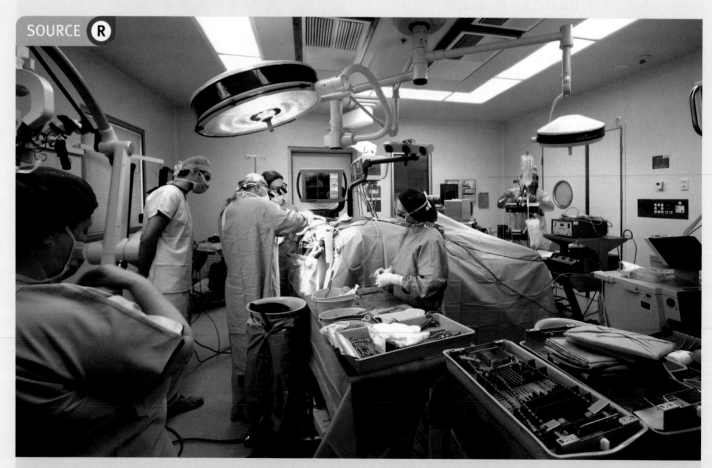

Dr Khurana performs a pioneering brain operation in 2008.

Lasers in cosmetic surgery

Since lasers were discovered in 1958, they have been used increasingly in medicine. Lasers can cut through tissue without causing excessive bleeding. Surgeons can reach areas within the body more easily with lasers than with a scalpel. But the ability of lasers to 'resurface' facial skin was discovered almost by accident. Surgeons treating acne scars with a laser noticed that, after they had resurfaced the skin around the scar to make the scar less visible, small wrinkles in the skin were also greatly reduced.

Since then, laser resurfacing to reduce wrinkles has become very popular among people who can afford it. It is a way of refreshing the skin's surface and can make patients look 10 to 20 years younger. The results can last for 8 to 10 years, provided that, after surgery, patients avoid sunbathing and so destroying their skin again. Patients can have a repeat treatment after one year, but usually the first procedure is so successful that a follow-up is not needed.

Lasers cannot rejuvenate skin on other parts of the body. Nor can laser treatment smooth out sagging neck skin. These conditions can still only be treated by traditional surgical methods.

Not everyone is suited to laser resurfacing. Certain people with very sensitive skin and those not mentally prepared for resurfacing are not good candidates. Patients can be left with bruising and swelling. It takes at least 10 days to heal before make-up can be used.

Brain surgery

In 2008 a pioneering surgical team in Canberra, Australia, led by Indian-born Australian neurosurgeon Dr Vini Gautam Khurana, performed a six-hour brain operation on a patient whilst he was still awake. His condition had been caused by the formation of a blister on a major vein in his brain, behind his right eye. Dr Khurana needed the patient to stay awake, because he needed to test his vision while the operation was progressing.

The surgical team was composed of three neurosurgeons, one plastic surgeon, two anaesthetists, and four nurses. Using keyhole surgery, they entered the patient's brain through a tiny opening in the frontal bone above the eyes.

The high-technology equipment used for the operation included an ultrasound probe to measure blood flow, eyepieces linked to scanners to display the head, and virtual reality software to create a three-dimensional image of the brain. The surgery was successful, and the patient was able to leave the hospital soon afterwards and make a good recovery.

The implications of modern surgery

The wide range of surgery now available has had a major effect on the finances of hospitals, and the National Health Service is facing great difficulties funding all the operations that could be carried out. A heart transplant is a wonderful thing, but is so expensive that it might take funds away from other, seemingly less important areas, such as hip replacements for the elderly. Many hospitals are forced to juggle their budgets to keep their operating theatres working. A tragic consequence of this is that surgeons sometimes have to 'prioritise' operations. There have been cases where treatment for 'self-imposed illness' (perhaps a condition that is a result of smoking) has been put lower down the list of priorities than other treatment. Surgeons and patients find this a very difficult situation to cope with.

SOURCE S

Administrators decided we were spending too much. They had the enormous stupidity to suggest that, if we kept patients out, we could work within budget. I said, 'No problem. We've got a shot gun. I'll load it. You fire it, because that's what you're planning. Now, out.'

Denis Melrose, a leading British heart surgeon, describing a difficulty he faced in the 1960s

ACTIVITIES

1 Study Source R. Compare it with Source Q and the information about Harvey Cushing on page 131. What similarities and differences can you see between Cushing's and Khurana's work?

2 'Modern surgery is getting out of control. There have been too many advances in surgical techniques and the government should make new laws to control what surgeons can and cannot do.' Write a short essay saying whether you agree or disagree with this view.

GradeStudio

The source-based examination paper, Unit A952, involves studying a range of sources about an issue or personality in British medicine in the period 1200–1945. Some of the questions in the paper may involve considering more than one source; some may involve using cross-references to other sources on the paper or your own knowledge. All the questions will expect you to use your knowledge of the period to interpret the sources.

Enquiry

Below is an example of a question based around a consideration of the importance of anaesthetics in the development of surgery. Study the source carefully and then answer the question that follows.

Source A

When the dreadful steel was plunged into the breast – cutting through veins – arteries – flesh – nerves – I needed no injunctions not to restrain my cries. I began a scream that lasted unintermittingly during the whole time of the incision – I almost marvel that it does not ring in my ears still so excruciating was the agony! When the wound was made and the instrument withdrawn, the pain seemed undiminished, for the air that suddenly rushed into those delicate parts felt like a mass of minute but sharp and forked daggers, that were tearing at the edges of the wound, but when I felt again the instrument… I thought I must have expired, I attempted to open no more my eyes – they felt so firmly closed, that the eyelids seemed indented to the cheeks.

From an account of a mastectomy (breast removal) operation in 1811 by the novelist Fanny Burney

Study Source A. How useful is this source to an historian studying the role of anaesthetics in the development of surgery? Explain your answer. **[8]**

Examiner's tip

This is a standard and relatively common question on utility. You have been asked about the usefulness of this source. Remember that you have been told in what context it is to be considered (in studying the role of anaesthetics in the development of surgery), so anything else (for example, what 19th-century novels are like) is irrelevant. You have also been asked 'how' useful, so you need to consider limitations on usefulness, not just ways in which the source is useful.

Answering the question

STEP 1: This is the same for any source work question you consider. Ask yourself 'What is the source? When and why do you think it was produced?' Here we have a really graphic account of an operation to remove a breast, written by a novelist in 1811.

STEP 2: Now you are ready to answer the question. Your answer about how useful the source is should be based on what it tells you, what you can work out from it and what you already know that the source doesn't tell you.

STEP 3: Now for the clever bit. In addition to Step 2, you need to know whether the source is reliable. If it is not reliable, that may make it less useful – or even useful in some other way!

Below are two students' answers to the question. How do you think you could improve Answer 1?

Examiner's comment

Answer 1

I think this source is very useful. It tells me how it must have felt to have an operation in 1811. It describes the pain felt when the incision was made – the agony was 'excruciating'. It describes how her body felt after the instrument was withdrawn – 'the air that suddenly rushed into those delicate parts felt like a mass of minute but sharp and forked daggers'. However, the source does not tell me whether any anaesthetics were used or not, and it also does not say how the rest of the operation went and whether it was a success or not. I don't know if I believe her account.

Answer 2 shows how the student might re-work the response in the light of these comments. Answer 2 is worth full marks.

Answer 2

I think this source is very useful. It tells me how it must have felt to have an operation in 1811. It describes the pain felt when the incision was made – the agony was 'excruciating'. It describes how her body felt after the instrument was withdrawn – 'the air that suddenly rushed into those delicate parts felt like a mass of minute but sharp and forked daggers'. However, the source does not tell me whether any anaesthetics were used or not. Since it was written in 1811, I know that this was before the use of ether and chloroform had become commonplace. This could give us a useful insight into the pain suffered by patients before anaesthetics were developed in the nineteenth century. It also does not say how the rest of the operation went and whether it was a success or not. This makes the source less useful than it might have been, since we cannot work out whether the lack of anaesthetics affected the outcome of the operation. I don't know if I believe her account. She uses very dramatic language. She describes the surgeon's instrument as 'the dreadful steel', and she goes on to add that when the air rushed in, it felt like daggers were 'tearing at the edges of the wound'. Being a novelist, she seems to be writing to entertain her audience, and I think her account is exaggerated.

BRAIN BOOST

Now it is time to revise your work on the development of surgery. It is important to be able to select the key dates, facts, personalities and events from the mass of detail that has been provided in this chapter. It is equally important to be able to analyse and explain the significance of the dates, facts, personalities and events. One way to do this is to summarise the information in a way that is effective for you. To get you started, make your own completed copy of this table.

Developments in surgery			
Aspect	Date	Details	Significance in the development of surgery
Anaesthetics	1845	Horace Wells uses nitrous oxide to extract a patient's tooth.	The nitrous oxide does not mask the pain and his work is discredited.
	1846	William Morton supervises an operation using ether.	The operation is a success and other surgeons in Europe carry out operations using ether.
	1847	James Simpson discovers the effects of chloroform.	The use of chloroform leads to painless surgery, meaning surgeons can perform more complex and longer operations. There was strong opposition to the use of anaesthetics.
	1853	Queen Victoria is given chloroform during the birth of her eighth child.	Opposition to the use of anaesthetics is overcome and chloroform becomes socially acceptable.
Antiseptics			
Blood transfusion			
Modern surgery			

GradeStudio

Summary checklist

- The combination of anaesthetics and antiseptics meant that surgery became much safer after 1870.
- Aseptic surgery, when no germs are allowed to be present, soon replaced antiseptic surgery.
- The discovery of the different blood groups allowed safe transfusions, thus reducing the risks from blood loss in surgery.
- Surgeons began to specialise as surgery became safer. Plastic, brain and heart surgery were developed by pioneering individuals.
- Developments in science and technology contributed to new techniques in medicine.
- The wars fought in the 20th century speeded up developments in surgery.

Think about these key questions and how you would answer them in an exam.

1 How important have individuals been in the development of surgery since 1870?

2 How have science and technology helped surgery to develop since 1870?

3 What other factors have played a part in the development of surgery since 1870?

4 Which of the following was the biggest turning point in the development of modern surgery?
   a Paré's work on ligatures
   b Lister's carbolic spray
   c Pasteur's discovery of the germ theory of disease
   d McIndoe's work on plastic surgery.

In your answer, explain how each of these developments was a turning point, transforming what had come before and what was to happen after in the development of modern surgery.

11.1 How has public health changed?

Before

Living conditions in 19th-century Britain are appalling. Many people live in new industrial towns, which have grown fast as they attract people looking for work in the factories. New houses have been built quickly to accommodate the extra people. These houses are overcrowded, with poor sanitation. People need to live near their place of work, because there is no cheap public transport. Terraces of back-to-back houses are built near the railway and many landlords make a quick profit. The back-to-back houses often house as many as 20 people in one room upstairs and one room downstairs. Reports on living conditions in the towns have found houses with five families crammed under one roof. The worst houses are in courts – enclosed passageways with houses built all round them. An open drain running through the middle of the court is often blocked with rubbish and sewage. Toilets are outside the houses and shared. There may be only one or two toilets for all the families in the court.

Public health in British towns is desperately poor. In Manchester, in the 1840s, 57 per cent of children die before the age of five. Typhus and typhoid flourish, and diarrhoea can also be a killer disease, especially where there is no regular supply of clean water. These diseases spread as a result of the dirt and rubbish. Tuberculosis, scarlet fever, whooping cough and measles are also common diseases, but no one really understands what causes them.

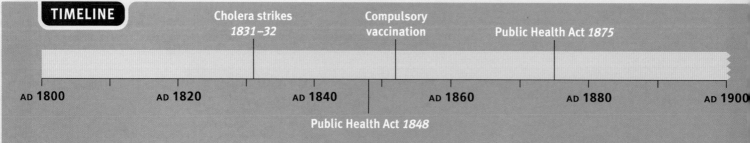

TIMELINE

Cholera strikes *1831–32*

Compulsory vaccination

Public Health Act *1875*

AD **1800** AD **1820** AD **1840** AD **1860** AD **1880** AD **1900**

Public Health Act *1848*

After

After the 1875 Public Health Act, town councils had to appoint inspectors and a medical officer of health. Councils began to lay sewers and drains, build reservoirs, parks, swimming baths and public conveniences. The Artisans' Dwellings Act of 1875 laid down laws about the standard of housing.

Today, Environmental Health Departments deal with refuse disposal, pollution of air and water, noise pollution, food inspection, pest control, slum clearance and the provision of a range of health services. This does not mean that all the problems of the past have been solved. For example, one community in Glasgow needs more than £187 million to bring slum homes up to standard. In July 2008 a detailed study of 131 typical tenement properties in Govanhill, Glasgow, found that even carrying out essential repairs would cost an average of £80,000 per home – and there are hundreds more just like them. However, unlike in the 19th century, council officials are aware of the problems. A council spokesperson said:

> Slum housing is just not tolerable in the 21st century and is the root cause of many of the problems we've got here. What has made it worse is the overcrowding in many privately rented flats. People new to the area have been squeezed into flats; many have Victorian conditions including cockroaches, rats, bed bugs, leaking roofs, no proper heating.

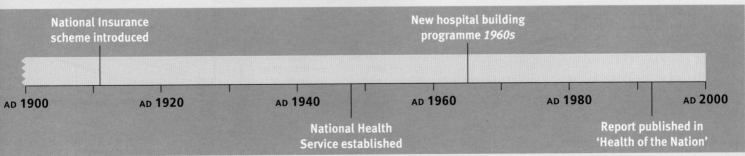

National Insurance scheme introduced

New hospital building programme *1960s*

AD 1900   AD 1920   AD 1940   AD 1960   AD 1980   AD 2000

National Health Service established

Report published in 'Health of the Nation'

11.2 The impact of industrialisation on living conditions and health and hygiene

LEARNING OBJECTIVES

In this lesson you will:

- understand why the Industrial Revolution had a negative effect on public health
- compare written and visual sources of evidence to assess their usefulness.

GETTING STARTED

Look at Source A. Why did the people who lived on Market Street allow their living conditions to become so bad? Think of as many reasons as you can.

From 1700 onwards, Britain was caught up in the Industrial Revolution. People no longer worked making things at home or in small workshops. They worked in bigger groups and in factories. As more and more machines were invented to help the manufacturing industries, especially the cloth industry, large factories were set up. These factories needed many workers, and so factory towns and villages grew rapidly. The workers, mostly badly paid, could not afford good housing. They were either crammed into old buildings, often more than one family to a room, or new houses were built for them as cheaply as possible. Little provision was made for fresh water or sewage disposal. The government had a policy of **laissez-faire**. This means that it was not prepared to interfere in people's lives, or in their working and living conditions.

KEY WORDS

Back-to-back houses – *a form of terrace, in which the houses are joined by their side and rear walls. The houses were built for working-class people and were usually of low quality.*

Laissez-faire – *an economic theory from the 18th century, which was strongly opposed to any government intervention in business affairs. 'Laissez faire' is French for 'leave alone'.*

SOURCE A

In one part of Market Street is a dunghill. Yet it is too large to be called a dunghill. I do not overestimate its size when I say that it contains 100 cubic yards [76 cubic metres] of impure filth which has been collected from all parts of the town. It is never removed. The moisture oozes through the wall and over the pavement. This place is horrible, with swarms of flies which give a strong taste of the dunghill to any food left uncovered.

A description of conditions in Greenock, Scotland, by Dr Laurie. It was included in Chadwick's 1842 Report to Parliament.

Town houses were often built on a **back-to-back** system. Sometimes they were built round a courtyard. Like the roads, these courtyards were unpaved and became muddy and contaminated with sewage. Houses were verminous, badly ventilated and overcrowded. Waste was piled in the courtyard or thrown into streams. Wells and watercourses quickly became polluted.

Industry made problems worse. Factory chimneys belched smoke and fumes into the air and other waste products from factories polluted the rivers.

SOURCE B

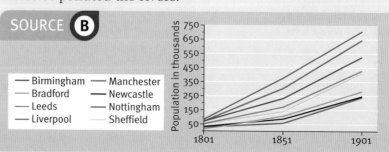

Population Growth in British Cities 1801–1901.

GradeStudio

Enquiry

Compare sources B and C. Which is more useful to the historian studying the growth of towns in the 19th century?

Examiner's tip

In questions like this, you need to do more than talk about what type the sources are. You need to show that both sources have their uses, because they provide different kinds of information. In the end, it depends on what the historian wants to know. What different things can you say about the growth of 19th-century towns from these two sources? Try to write an answer of your own.

Disease

Bad living conditions meant that infectious diseases spread easily. The scourge of smallpox in the 18th century was accompanied by tuberculosis, influenza and 'fever'. The fevers were typhoid, which was spread through dirty water, and typhus, which was spread by the bites of body lice – and most people had these lice, because of poor personal hygiene.

These **endemic** diseases, which were always present in the population, were joined in 1831–32 by a new **epidemic** – a disease that suddenly infected large numbers of people. This was cholera, which had been spreading from China and India across Europe since the beginning of the century and now finally reached Britain.

Cholera is caused by a germ that attacks the intestines and leads to diarrhoea, vomiting, cramps, fever and death. The disease is spread through water that is infected by sewage from the victims. Cholera was first known to have entered Britain when William Sproat, a sailor, died in the port of Sunderland.

Doctors at the time had no idea what caused cholera or how to cure it. In some places, barrels of tar were burnt in the streets to try to ward off 'poisonous miasmas', invisible gases that were thought to be the cause of disease. The disease spread rapidly, and so many people died that the government was forced to act.

Instructions were given that the dead should be buried immediately, and that graves must be a certain depth.

By the end of 1832, most places in Britain had been affected by cholera and over 21,000 people had died. Then the disease seemed to die out and the boards of health that had been set up to combat it were abolished. Cholera was to return, however, in 1848, 1854 and 1866.

ACTIVITY

Which of Sources D and E would be most useful to the historian studying the spread of cholera in Exeter in 1832? Why? Look back at the examiner's tip on page 134 before giving your answer.

SOURCE C

A London slum in the nineteenth century. The rapid growth of cities during the industrial revolution caused social problems and the spread of disease.

KEY WORDS

Endemic – *regularly found and common among a particular group or in a particular place.*

Epidemic – *a sudden appearance of an illness, affecting many people.*

SOURCE E

Dwellings are occupied by from five to fifteen families huddled together in dirty rooms. There are slaughter houses in Butcher Row with putrid heaps of offal. Pigs are kept in large numbers. Poultry are kept in cellars and outhouses. There are dung-heaps everywhere.

From *The History of the Cholera in Exeter in 1832*, written by Dr Thomas Shapter in 1841

SOURCE D

Exeter 1832. A Cholera victim's bedclothes are washed in the Mill Stream.

11.3 The development of public health systems (1)

LEARNING OBJECTIVES

In this lesson you will:

- discover what individuals and groups did to help develop public health systems by 1848
- investigate the role in history of the individual Edwin Chadwick.

GETTING STARTED

Give three reasons why you think most 19th-century MPs might have believed in 'laissez-faire' in relation to public health.

Edwin Chadwick and public health.

The crisis brought about by the cholera epidemic of 1832 prompted the government to act. Edwin Chadwick published the *Report on the Sanitary Condition of the Labouring Population of Great Britain* in 1842. It contained evidence from doctors involved in the workings of the **Poor Law** all over the country. The information it contained about the squalor in which many working people lived and worked shocked and horrified the wealthy classes. The picture painted by the report, together with statistics about birth and death compiled by William Farr, from 1839, made people realise that something had to be done about public health in Britain.

Chadwick was convinced that sickness was the cause of poverty. He was supported by the findings of Dr Southwood Smith who, in 1838, found 14,000 cases of fever among the poor of Whitechapel, London.

KEY WORDS

Poor Law – *laws in the past, setting out how the poor should be supported. Under the Poor Law in the 19th century, those needing support were sent to workhouses.*

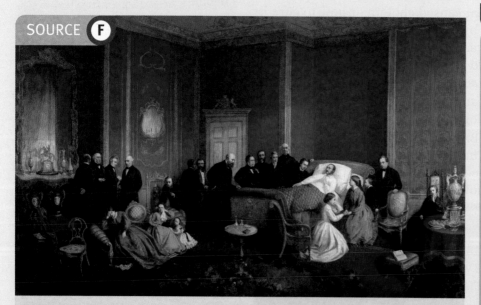

SOURCE **F**

Not even the most privileged could escape disease. This painting from 1862 shows the last moments of Prince Albert, Queen Victoria's husband. He died of typhoid fever in 1861, caught from the drains of Windsor Castle.

ACTIVITIES

1 What public health problems resulted from the Industrial Revolution?

2 How do you think the death of Prince Albert would have affected people's views about the cause of disease?

3 What were the effects of the cholera epidemic of 1831–32?

4 What motives did Edwin Chadwick have for trying to improve public health?

5 Study the profile of Edwin Chadwick. What were his good and bad qualities? How important was the part that he played in the development of public health?

SOURCE G

Epidemic disease amongst the labouring classes is caused by atmospheric impurities produced by decomposing animal and vegetable substances, by damp and filth, and overcrowded dwellings. The annual loss of life is greater than the loss from death or wounds in any wars in modern times. The most important and practical measures are drainage, refuse removal and the improvement of water supplies. This expense would be a financial gain by lessening the cost of sickness and death. To prevent disease it would be efficient to appoint a district medical officer.

Chadwick's main conclusions from the *Report* of 1842

The sanitary reform movement

Public health reform was slow to happen. However, Chadwick's 1842 report did spark off a fierce debate about cleaning up the towns. Supporters of reform became known as the 'Clean Party'. In 1844 the Health of Towns Association was founded to campaign for healthier living conditions. Local branches of the association were set up across the country. Each produced evidence of filthy streets, lack of sewage facilities and inadequate supplies of fresh water. The association called for an Act of Parliament.

In 1847 a Public Health Bill was finally introduced to Parliament. It was strongly opposed by a group of MPs who were nicknamed the 'Dirty Party'. They believed in *laissez-faire* and argued that it was not the government's responsibility to clean up the towns. Furthermore, cleaning up the towns would cost too much and make the government too powerful. The poor were often looked down on and it was thought that they should try to help themselves. The poor did not have votes, so why should the wealthy try to help? Although Chadwick's report clearly showed that there was a connection between dirty living conditions and disease, no one knew exactly what caused these diseases.

Then, in 1848, cholera struck again and MPs voted in favour of the Bill, which became the first Public Health Act.

KEY PEOPLE

Edwin Chadwick 1800–90

Chadwick believed that all laws should be useful and efficient. He first worked as a lawyer.

1832 Became a civil servant when he helped to investigate the Poor Laws.

1838 Was given permission to enquire into the living conditions of the poor in the East End of London.

1840 Began a national investigation into living conditions, which led to his *Report on the Sanitary Condition of the Labouring Population of Great Britain* in 1842. The report revealed terrible conditions in the towns and shocked the nation. Chadwick argued that if the towns were cleaner, there would be less disease and people would not need to take time off work. As a result, fewer people would need poor relief and this would save the ratepayers money. His work inspired the sanitary reform movement.

Chadwick said that Parliament should pass legislation to improve sewage disposal and water supplies. Although he was hard-working and intelligent, Chadwick could often be argumentative and tactless. He was 'pensioned off' by the government in 1854.

SOURCE H

THE FIRST PUBLIC HEALTH ACT 1848

A Central Board of Health in London is to sit for five years.

Local Boards of Health can be set up in towns if 10 per cent of the ratepayers agree. These boards have the power to improve the water supply and the disposal of sewage. They will take over from private companies and individuals.

The act is not compulsory.

The terms of the first Public Health Act 1848

ACTIVITIES

6 Study Sources G and H. How far would the 1848 Act have satisfied Chadwick? Use details from the sources and your own knowledge to support your answer.

7 Why was there opposition to reform in the 1840s?

8 Why was the first Public Health Act eventually passed in 1848?

11.4 The development of public health systems (2)

LEARNING OBJECTIVES

In this lesson you will:

- investigate how public health systems were developed between 1848 and 1900
- explain the relative importance of different individuals in the development of public health systems.

GETTING STARTED

In 1854, an editorial in *The Times* said, 'We prefer to take our chance of cholera and the rest than be bullied into health.' What do you think the writer meant, and why would the writer hold such views at that time?

KEY WORDS

Privy Council – *a body of persons who advise the king or queen in matters of state. The majority of members are selected by the prime minister.*

The impact of the 1848 Public Health Act

The 1848 Act brought only limited improvements. Local health boards, as described in the Act, were set up in only 182 towns. As a result, sewage disposal and water supplies were improved in some of these places.

In 1854, opponents of the Central Board of Health in London were able to bring it to an end. Many water companies, landlords and builders had hated its existence. Others held firm to the belief that it was wrong for the government to interfere in people's private lives. There was also bad feeling between Edwin Chadwick and the medical profession. Chadwick thought that preventing the environment from becoming filthy was the key to a healthy nation, and so he emphasised the need for clean water supplies and good sanitation. He did not appreciate that curative measures, such as good doctors and hospitals, also had a part to play. Meanwhile, in September 1854, Dr John Snow had deduced that water was responsible for the spread of cholera.

In 1858 public health came under the control of the **Privy Council** and Sir John Simon, a surgeon, was made the Medical Officer of Health. He believed that public health involved both preventative and curative measures.

Further government measures

By the mid-1860s the government realised that it would have to become more consistently involved in providing public health. A number of factors brought about this change of attitude, as the diagram shows.

Factors leading to state intervention in public health

Further cholera outbreaks in 1854 and 1866 frighten the authorities once more.

In 1854 Dr John Snow showed that cholera was spread by contaminated water.

In 1864 Louis Pasteur demonstrated the germ theory of disease. Need for cleanliness became clear.

By the 1870s statistics showed that poor living conditions and disease were connected.

Need for state intervention

1875 Second Public Health Act

- Brought together all previous laws under one act.
- Councils compelled to provide street lighting, clean water, drainage and sewage disposal.
- Councils had to employ medical inspectors.

1875 Artisans' Dwellings Act

- Councils given power to buy up areas of slum housing, knock them down and build new houses.
- Few councils took advantage.

In 1869 Sir John Simon persuaded the government to set up the Royal Sanitary Commission. It found that the provision of clean water was still very patchy and recommended that 'uniform, universal and imperative' laws should be made. The government responded by forming the Local Government Board (1871) to oversee the administration of public health. The 1872 Public Health Act divided the country into 'sanitary areas', each with a medical officer of health. In 1875, Benjamin Disraeli's Conservative government passed a second Public Health Act and the Artisans' Dwellings Act. Together these formed the most wide-reaching legislation to date.

KEY PEOPLE

John Snow 1813–58

Born in York. At the aged of 14, he was apprenticed to a surgeon in Newcastle-upon-Tyne.

1833 Saw his first cases of cholera when working at Killingworth Colliery.

1838 Travelled to London and qualified as a member of the Royal College of Surgeons. He then set up a medical practice in Soho. One of his most famous acts was to administer chloroform to Queen Victoria to ease the pain of childbirth.

1848 During the outbreak of cholera in London he spent a great deal of time investigating the causes of the disease. He discovered that, in one area, the people who caught cholera drank water that came from the Thames. In the same area, some people took their water from a pump using fresh spring water and they did not catch cholera. He set out his ideas that the disease was transmitted through water, not through the air, but not everyone accepted his view.

1854 In September he found that victims of cholera in Broad Street, London, all used water from the same local pump. He removed the handle of the pump and the disease disappeared. This was further proof that water was responsible for the spread of cholera.

KEY PEOPLE

Octavia Hill 1838–1912

Born in 1838. Her parents and grandparents were involved in charity work, so she naturally joined in.

1853 Started to work with a group of women called the Ladies' Guild. She taught in a **ragged school**, the first instance of her working with the poor. By 1858 she and her sister had set up their own school. Working in poor areas, she saw the appalling housing conditions of the poor and began to plan how they could be improved.

1865 Raised enough money to buy the leases of three houses. She repaired them, collected the rent regularly and got to know the tenants. She made sure that tenants did not take in lodgers, which could lead to overcrowding and the spread of infection. She got rid of the bad tenants and improved the homes for the remaining tenants, who then looked after the houses. Octavia's scheme was a success. Her tenants cared for their homes and paid the rent on time. This quickly paid off the costs of improvements. Everyone was better-off.

Soon, many people were paying Octavia to manage their properties for them. With the money she made from this, she bought more houses for the poor. People began to think that she talked a lot of sense about how to help the poor. She campaigned for better conditions for the poor right up to her death in 1912.

Explanation

Look at the following question and the examiner's tip.

1 Who was more important in the development of public health?

Edwin Chadwick

Octavia Hill

John Snow

Explain your answer fully.

Now consider this question that looks at both Roman and 19th century Britain.

2 Were the advances in public health made by the Romans more important than those made in nineteenth century Britain? Explain your answer.

Examiner's tip

This is an example of the type of question you will find in parts of Unit A951. In your answer you need to explain how all the people listed played their own part in the development of public health. Then you must try to reach an overall judgement about which person was most important. For this, you need to think about the effects of each person's work on changing provision for public health for the population at that time. For each person, you might consider:

- how many people were affected by their work
- whether their work led the government to make changes or introduce new laws
- whether their work changed attitudes to public health at that time

In the end, if you still cannot decide which person is most important, you might conclude that they were all equally important in their own different ways. Have a go at the question for yourself!

SOURCE I

FATHER THAMES INTRODUCING HIS OFFSPRING TO THE FAIR CITY OF LONDON.
(A Design for a Fresco in the New Houses of Parliament.)

A *Punch* cartoon of 1858, showing Father Thames introducing his children (diphtheria, scrofula and cholera) to London.

SOURCE J

In hot, dry weather the Thames becomes like a huge lake. The water level falls so that little of the river reaches the sea. Instead it receives the filth of more than 2 million inhabitants which collects there until there is enough rain to swell the water. In times of cholera the evacuations of patients join the impurities in the river.

A description of the River Thames from the 1850s

It is a black, dilapidated street, avoided by all decent people...these tumbling tenements contain, by night a swarm of misery. As, on the ruined human wretch, vermin parasites appear, so these ruined shelters have bred a crowd of foul existence that crawls in and out of gaps in walls and boards; and coils itself to sleep, in maggot numbers, where the rain drips in; and comes and goes, fetching and carrying fever, and sowing more evil in its every footprint...

Dickens's description in *Bleak House* of Tom-All-Alone's, a street in St Giles, east London.

ACTIVITIES

Look at Sources I, J and K. Then try to answer the following question.

These three sources prove that there was no progress in providing better public health in London between 1850 and 1912.

1 Do you agree or disagree with this view? Use information from the sources and your own knowledge to support your answer.

2 Which of the four sources on pages 146–47 is the most useful for finding out about the state of London in the 19th century? Explain your answer using details in the sources and your own knowledge.

3 'Source K is from a novel by Charles Dickens. Therefore it is unreliable as evidence about 19th-century London.' Explain whether you agree or disagree with this view.

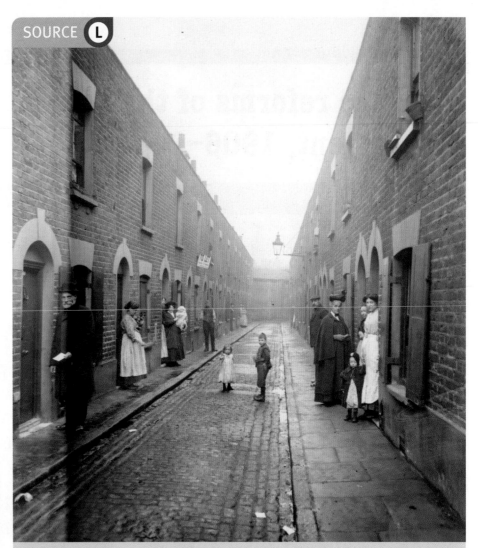

Slum housing in the East End of London in 1912.

Fact file

The General Atmosphere of Victorian London

- With the combination of sewage, coal fires and unwashed bodies, the odour of London was horrendous. Both the rich and the poor had to contend with the evil air around the city.
- Even the Royal Family was not immune to the smells and at one time was forced to cancel a water excursion due to raw sewage being dumped into the Thames.
- Joseph Bazalgette built miles of piping to direct sewage away from Victorian London. However, London streets were still filled with manure from horses.
- Every surface was coated with soot from the use of coal. New buildings being constructed didn't stay fresh and clean for long. The air people breathed was often foggy with the smoke from coal fires.
- Adding to the confusion, until the mid-1800s, cattle were driven through the streets of Victorian London, to and from the slaughter-houses that could be found in Smithfield.

11.5 The reforms of the Liberal government, 1906–14

LEARNING OBJECTIVES

In this lesson you will:

- discover what laws were passed by the Liberals to tackle public health issues
- analyse the usefulness of cartoons as evidence for investigating the Liberal reforms.

GETTING STARTED

Look at this picture. It shows a poor family at home in the 1890s. They only have this one room in which to live. List the problems that the family might experience. If you were an MP in the 1890s, what would you do about these problems?

Between 1886 and 1903 Charles Booth, a ship owner and social investigator, carried out a survey into living conditions in the East End of London. He published his findings in *Life and Labour of the People in London*. Booth concluded that about one-third of the people lived on incomes lower than 21 shillings (£1.05) per week. In his opinion, this was below the poverty line. The people lived in sub-standard housing and had a poor diet. If they fell ill, they could not afford to pay a doctor. In 1899, Seebohm Rowntree, a member of the chocolate-manufacturing family, conducted his own inquiry into living conditions in York, and his findings were very similar to Booth's.

Booth said that poverty was caused by sickness, old age, low wages and lack of employment – not laziness and drunkenness, as many believed. There were no old age pensions. Old people who could not support themselves had only the **workhouse** to turn to. Many skilled workers could afford to pay into **friendly societies** and insure themselves against unemployment and illness. Unskilled workers, however, could not afford the subscriptions.

Time for action

In 1902 the nation was shocked when 40 per cent of the British men who volunteered to fight in the Boer War were found to be suffering from malnutrition and diseases such as rickets, caused by poor diet. It was clear that ill-health was linked to poverty and that government action was needed to raise living standards. Some Liberal MPs were also concerned that, if they did not help the poor now, people would vote for the newly formed Labour Party.

The Liberals went on to pass a wide range of reforms. Winston Churchill said, 'Our cause is the cause of the left-out millions. We are all agreed that the state must concern itself with the care of the sick, the aged and, above all, children.'

KEY WORDS

Friendly society – *in Britain, an organisation to which members pay small amounts of money over a long period so that, when they are ill or old, they can receive money back.*

Workhouse – *in Britain in the past, a building where poor people were put to work, in exchange for food and shelter.*

Social reforms of the Liberal government 1906–14

Date	Legislation
1906	Provision of school meals – local authorities are given the power to provide free school meals.
1907	School medical inspections.
1909	Old Age Pension Act – people over 70 receive 5 shillings [25p] per week state pension, as long as their income from other sources is not more than 12 shillings [60p] per week.
1909	Labour exchanges are set up to help the unemployed find work.
1911	National Insurance Act – two parts: Part I: Workers in manual trades earning less than £160 per year are to pay 4d [2p] per week. The employer will add 3d [1.5p] and the government 2d [1p]. Workers are then entitled to receive 10 shillings [50p] per week if they are off work sick, for up to 26 weeks. Free medical treatment is available from a panel doctor. Part 2: Workers earning less than £160 per year in certain trades, together with the government and their employers, are to pay in 2 1/2d [1p] per week. These workers can claim 7 shillings [35p] unemployment pay for up to 15 weeks.

How did people react to the reforms?

For the first time the state had made a co-ordinated attack on poverty. However, much of the legislation was not very far-reaching and the Chancellor of the Exchequer, David Lloyd George, admitted that the government had only made a start. Nevertheless there was fierce resistance to some of the measures.

To pay for old age pensions, Lloyd George introduced the 'People's Budget', which aimed to tax the rich to provide for the poor. The House of Lords, largely made up of wealthy landowners, refused to pass the budget. This issue forced two general elections in 1910. The Liberals were narrowly returned. The budget was then allowed through but, in 1911, the power of the House of Lords to throw out finance bills was abolished by the Parliament Act. The Labour Party said that pensions should have been made payable at age 65, whereas many Conservatives were of the opinion that pensions 'would profoundly weaken the moral fibre of the nation' (report in *The Times*, 17 December 1909). People who qualified for a pension, however, were thankful to 'Lord' George.

The National Insurance Act was also widely condemned. Friendly societies and private insurance companies said that they would lose business. To overcome this, Lloyd George agreed to drop proposals for pensions to be paid to orphans and widows. He also allowed the Act to be administered by private insurance companies, acting as 'approved societies' on behalf of the government. The Labour Party said that workers should not have to pay any money at all into the scheme, arguing that benefits should be paid entirely from taxes. Many doctors opposed the Act. They now had to register with a panel (a local list) and would receive 6 shillings (30p) for each patient under their care. Doctors argued that this meant a loss of independence and would cause medical standards to drop. In the face of such opposition, Lloyd George had to be strong and prepared to negotiate.

ACTIVITIES

Study the source below and then answer the questions that follow.

1 Explain who 'Domestic Servants' were.
2 What do you think the writer of the letter meant by what is written in the second paragraph?
3 Since the National Insurance Act was designed to make life better for poor workers, why do you think the National Association of Domestic Servants was opposed to it?
4 How do you think David Lloyd George might have reacted to this letter?

SOURCE Ⓜ

Dear Sir,
INSURANCE BILL
Referring to the above measures on behalf of our Members I shall be glad to know, if you can see your way clear, to have the clauses relating to the Domestic Servants deleted...
I am quite willing to believe, that when drafting the bill you were prompted by the most humane consideration for the lot of the poor worker, and such consideration will always stand to your credit in the years to come.
In the case of the Domestic Servants, however, I, and numbers of our Members really think your bill will do us serious injury, just in the same way that it will injure Commercial Clerks, who (as a class) are well looked after by their employers.
The benefits offered by the bill are of small use, and the regulations are likely to destroy the friendly relationship that I am glad to say still prevails between Mistress and Maid in the majority of cases.
I trust therefore, you will give the plea of our members your serious consideration, and amend the bill as we respectfully suggest.
I am, Dear Sir,
Yours very truly,
E Balfour SECRETARY
The National Association of Domestic Servants

From a letter to David Lloyd George in 1911.

Look at Source N and then answer the question that follows.

Do you think the cartoonist is in favour of Lloyd George's Old Age Pension Act or against it? Explain your answer, using details from the source and your own knowledge.

Source N

PUNCH, OR THE LONDON CHARIVARI.—August 5, 1908.

THE PHILANTHROPIC HIGHWAYMAN.

Mr. Lloyd-George. "I'LL MAKE 'EM PITY THE AGED POOR!"

A cartoonist's view of Lloyd George's Old Age Pensions Act of 1908.

Examiner's tip

Cartoons can be difficult to use. They often contain subtle and partly hidden messages. It is important to look at all the details in the scene, even those that might at first look only decorative . Every detail in a cartoon is there for a purpose, intended to get the cartoonist's opinion across. Consider the following.

- What is Lloyd George doing in this cartoon? The clues are in what he is holding in his right and left hands.
- Where is he standing?
- Which people might come past him in this scene?
- What type of famous 18th-century character does he remind you of?
- What point is the cartoonist trying to make about funding Lloyd George's pension reforms? Where does the cartoonist think Lloyd George is going to get the money from? How does this compare with what you have read about other people's reactions to the reforms?

Thinking along these lines will help you to unravel the message in the cartoon and allow you to answer the question.

Government and social welfare, 1919–39

In 1919 the Ministry of Health was set up to administer all matters to do with health. During the First World War, house-building had been neglected and so, in 1919, the new Minister for Health, Christopher Addison, passed the Housing and Town Planning Act. Under this Act the government gave local authorities a grant to help them build council houses. In 1920 the Unemployment Insurance Act extended insurance cover to all workers (except farm labourers and domestic servants) who earned less than £250 per year.

The main problem in this period was the muddled way in which the welfare services were administered. Some services were provided by the government and some by private organisations. Health care, in particular, was a 'chaotic mixture', as the diagram on page 151 shows. The opinion was growing that the health care system needed to be reformed. The Socialist Medical Association and the trade unions said that health services should be organised by the state. Other people, however, still believed that voluntary organisations and self-help had a part to play. Many thought that social welfare should be provided only for the poor. It was argued that people who had the money should pay for their own medical treatment and schooling. The Second World War (1939–45) was to change many people's attitudes to welfare provision.

An uncoordinated system

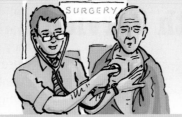

Hospitals

- About 3000 in Britain, 1000 were run by voluntary funds. Hospitals unevenly spread.
- Poor people were treated in workhouse infirmaries.

Doctors

- Wealthy received best treatment as they could afford the fees.
- Some workers, covered by National Insurance, had panel doctors (dependants not covered).

Other services

Local authorities provided:

- school medical inspectors
- antenatal clinics
- infant-welfare centres.

SOURCE O

RICH FARE.

THE GIANT LLOYD-GORGIBUSTER: "FEE, FI, FO, FAT,
I SMELL THE BLOOD OF A PLUTOCRAT;
BE HE ALIVE OR BE HE DEAD,
I'LL GRIND HIS BONES TO MAKE MY BREAD."

A cartoon from *Punch* in 1909. The caption beneath it reads: 'RICH FARE. FEE FI FO FAT, I SMELL THE BLOOD OF A PLUTOCRAT. BE HE ALIVE OR BE HE DEAD, I WILL GRIND HIS BONES TO MAKE MY BREAD.'

ACTIVITIES

1 Why did the Liberals pass a wide range of social reforms?

2 Summarise the main acts passed by the Liberals under these headings:

- Acts dealing with children
- Acts dealing with the unemployed
- Acts dealing with health and sickness
- Acts dealing with the elderly

3 Study Source O. Look back at the question and examiner's tip on page 150. Do you think the cartoonist supports or opposes Lloyd George's reforms? Explain your answer.

4 Study the chart of 'Liberal Social Reforms' on page 149 and decide which of the following two views best describes the reforms.

- *View 1:* The Liberal reforms of 1906–14 were wide-ranging and would play a huge part in sweeping away the public health problems of the past.
- *View 2:* The Liberal reforms of 1906–14 merely scratched the surface of the public health problems in Britain and did little to change people's lives.

11.6 The introduction of the National Health Service

LEARNING OBJECTIVES

In this lesson you will:

- explore the reasons why a National Health Service was set up in 1945
- evaluate the relative importance of the factors that led to the setting up of the welfare state.

GETTING STARTED

During the Second World War, the government evacuated children from towns and cities that they feared would be bombed. The children were sent to live with families in the countryside. The government received 1700 complaints from the host families, for example about children who arrived with head lice and skin disease and who were prone to bed-wetting.

How do you think this would have affected the attitudes of middle-class families towards public health?

Slow change

During the early years of the 20th century the Liberals had brought in a series of reforms to improve the living and working conditions of the people of Britain. In the 1920s and 1930s there were further improvements in housing, unemployment benefit and pensions (see page 150). But these were only the first steps towards the government accepting responsibility for providing help for everyone in need. During the 1930s, as the impact of the Wall Street Crash was felt across the world, the British economy experienced great difficulties. There was no money to spend on extending government welfare services. Instead, the government was struggling to raise money to finance its existing commitments.

The war years

In 1939 the Second World War broke out in Europe. The measures that the government took to help win the war also proved important in bringing about increases in social support in Britain.

- During the war there were shortages of food. The government was determined that children should be fed properly, and so it ordered local education authorities to extend their provision of free school meals. Free school milk was also provided.

- Britain suffered heavy bombing during the war, particularly during the Blitz of 1940–41. To cope with the casualties, the government set up the Emergency Medical Service. Hospitals were placed under the Ministry of Health and free treatment was provided. This arrangement proved very successful and people accepted that the government should be more involved in running the 'health service'.

- The government ordered that children from the inner cities should be evacuated to rural areas, in order to escape the air raids. The people with whom they went to stay were often shocked at the filthy, deprived and badly-clothed state of the evacuee children. Lord Chandos, who took in 31 evacuees, complained that they regarded 'the floors and carpets as suitable places on which to relieve themselves'.

SOURCE P

They were filthy; we have never seen so many children with lice and nits and lacking any knowledge of clean and hygienic habits. It seemed as if they hadn't bathed for months. Some children had dirty, septic sores all over their bodies. Many of the children were bed-wetters and were not in the habit of doing anything else.

From a report of the Women's Institute in 1940

YOUR VICTORY GARDEN
counts more than ever!

SOURCE Q

A poster published during the Second World War. Posters like this were used to encourage the public to grow their own food.

ACTIVITIES

1 Look at Sources P and Q. How do they suggest that war helped to change people's attitudes to public health?

2 Look back at some of your earlier work. Explain how war affected the work of the following:
   a Paré   **b** Nightingale and Seacole
   c Fleming, Florey and Chain.

   In which of these three areas did war play the biggest part? Explain your answer fully.

The Beveridge Report

In 1941 the government asked Sir William Beveridge, a well-known economist, to suggest what it could do to help the sick, the unemployed, low-paid workers and retired people. In 1942 the *Beveridge Report* was published. He recommended that the government should provide a welfare state, 'taking charge of social security from the cradle to the grave'. In other words, it was the duty of the government to look after all members of society, not just the poor. Beveridge argued that all cities had a right to be free from five 'giants' that could ruin people's lives. These were:

- want (need)   - ignorance   - squalor
- disease   - idleness.

The *Beveridge Report* became a best-seller, with over 100,000 copies sold in the first month. Members of all political parties welcomed the report, but the Prime Minister, Winston Churchill, feared that the country might not be able to afford to introduce all the measures it suggested. In a cabinet meeting in 1943, Churchill asked whether 'we are committing our 45 million people to burdens beyond their capacity to bear'.

The National Health Service

In July 1945 the Labour Party came to power, and it fell to them to introduce a Beveridge-style welfare state. **Family Allowances** and compulsory **National Insurance** for everyone were introduced in 1948. At the centre of Labour's reform programme was the National Health Service (NHS), masterminded by the Minister of Health, Aneurin Bevan. The NHS was to provide free medical treatment for everyone. It came into operation on 5 July 1948. Hospitals came under the control of the state, and local authorities were to provide free services, including ambulances, vaccination programmes, environmental health, maternity clinics and health visitors. Doctors, opticians and dentists provided a free service.

In 1951 the government increased taxes to pay for the NHS and the Korean War. These measures included the introduction of charges for prescriptions given by doctors and dentists. Bevan was so angry about this that he resigned from the government.

KEY WORDS

Family allowance – *an amount of money given weekly by the state for the support of children.*

National Insurance – *a system of compulsory insurance, paid for by weekly contributions by employers and employees, and used to pay for benefits for the sick, retired and unemployed.*

SOURCE **R**

A cartoon by Leslie Illingworth, published on 23 November 1942.

KEY PEOPLE

Sir William Beveridge 1879–1963

Beveridge was educated at Oxford University.

1919 Was knighted after the First World War. He also became Director of the London School of Economics.

1937 Became Master of University College, Oxford.

1942 Produced the *Beveridge Report*.

1944 Entered Parliament as a Liberal MP.

1946 Was created the 1st Baron Beveridge of Tuggal, in recognition of his part in helping to bring about the welfare state.

ACTIVITIES

3 What part did the following factors play in the introduction of a welfare state after 1945?
   - the work of the Liberal government, 1906–14
   - changing social attitudes
   - the 1942 *Beveridge Report*
   - Labour's election victory in 1945

   Which of these factors do you think was the most important? Explain your answer.

11.7 The impact of the NHS

LEARNING OBJECTIVES

In this lesson you will:

- study reactions to the establishment of the NHS
- analyse how far the NHS changed health services for people after 1948.

GETTING STARTED

Look at Source T. Do you think that the cartoonist approved or disapproved of the NHS? Explain your answer by using details from the source.

Reactions to the NHS

Mostly, the NHS was received with great enthusiasm. Immediately people took advantage of the free medical service. Yet there were also many people who were opposed to the new system. In early 1948 the British Medical Association (BMA), which represented the medical profession, carried out a survey to see what doctors thought. The results were as follows:

In favour of the NHS	4,734
Opposed to the NHS	40,814

Doctors feared that the new system would give the government too much control. They would now be employed by the government and might be told where they had to practise. They could no longer charge for their services, and would be on a fixed salary. This might lead to a reduction in their income.

Aneurin Bevan, the Minister of Health responsible for introducing the NHS, was not a man to back down in the face of opposition. He had many angry discussions with the leader of the British Medical Association, Charles Hill, before agreement was reached. In the end Bevan won over the doctors by stating that they would receive a fee for each patient they registered, and that they would still be able to treat private, fee-paying patients if they wished. By June 1948, 92 per cent of doctors and the vast majority of hospitals had agreed to work under the NHS.

SOURCE T

DOTHEBOYS HALL
"It still tastes awful."

A cartoon from 1948, showing Aneurin Bevan dishing out 'NHS medicine' to the doctors.

SOURCE S

Medical treatment should be made available to rich and poor alike in accordance with medical need and no other criteria. Worry about money in a time of sickness is a serious hindrance to recovery, apart from its unnecessary cruelty. The records show that it is the mother in the average family who suffers most from the absence of a full health service. In trying to balance her budget she puts her own needs last... The essence of a satisfactory health service is that the rich and the poor are treated alike, that poverty is not a disability, and wealth is not advantaged.

From a speech by Aneurin Bevan in 1946

SOURCE U

I am unable to accept the proposal to set up a national health service based on the family doctor. The pernicious habit of getting something for nothing will be encouraged. If the bill is passed, no patient or doctor will feel safe from interference by some ministerial edict or regulation. The minister's spies will be everywhere.

The views of a doctor in 1948

Look at Sources V and W and read the examiner's tip before attempting the question that follows.

Source V

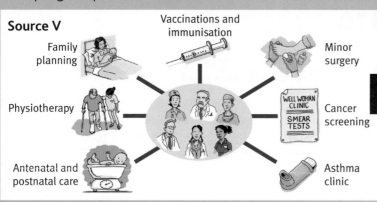

Family planning

Vaccinations and immunisation

Minor surgery

Physiotherapy

WELL WOMAN CLINIC
SMEAR TESTS

Cancer screening

Antenatal and postnatal care

Asthma clinic

Services provided by GP practice

Source W

Budget facts and figures
The NHS continues to grow. 2008 saw the biggest spending increase in the history of the NHS.
40 billion [pounds sterling] of extra resources has been invested, compared with 2002–03.
The annual average growth will be 7.3% above inflation over the next five years.
Over seven years, there will be an additional 15,000 GPs and consultants, 30,000 more therapists and scientists, and 35,000 more nurses, midwives and health visitors in the NHS.
By 2008, an additional 42 major hospital schemes will be operational, with 13 more under construction. The extra investment will allow an increase in treatment capacity equivalent to more than 10,000 beds.

From the Annual Report of the Department of Health, 2008

Exam Question:

'Sources V and W prove that the NHS has been a huge success.' Do you agree with this statement? **[8 marks]**

Examiner's tip

When answering a question like this, it is tempting to use lots of detail from either or both of the sources to back up the statement. If you use both sources in this way, you will reach Level 2 and probably score about 4 marks. You will reach Level 3 and score 5–6 marks if you also show how the sources do not provide enough information to prove the statement. For example, you might explain that some important details are missing from the sources, such as how many patients are being treated compared to earlier years. To reach Level 4 and head towards full marks, you will need to look at who produced the sources and assess whether the evidence they give is unbiased and reliable.

The impact of the NHS

The NHS has had an enormous impact on women. It has prioritised women's health and women are now four times more likely to consult doctors than men. Life expectancy for women has risen from 66 years in 1948 to 81 years today. The mortality rate of mothers in childbirth has dropped dramatically. The NHS has enabled women to retain their role as the main carers in families, but without the worry that lack of money might get in the way of family health.

The NHS has also transformed the role of the family doctor. GPs now work as part of teams that offer a whole range of health services.

VOICE YOUR OPINION!

Work with a partner. One of you should take the role of Aneurin Bevan and the other should take the role of a doctor opposed to the National Health Service. Using all the information you have studied, set down the main arguments that you will use when you come to take part in a discussion of your opposing views, and then role-play the discussion, trying to persuade your partner that you are right. Afterwards, find out from others in the class how their discussions went. Which arguments were more popular, those of Aneurin Bevan or those of the doctors?

ACTIVITY

Review all of your work in this chapter and re-read pages 148–151. Compare health services before the introduction of the NHS with health services since 1948.
Did the NHS significantly change health services after 1948? Explain your answer fully.

11.8 The continuing debate about the provision of healthcare

LEARNING OBJECTIVES

In this lesson you will:
- understand why the NHS is facing problems
- give your opinions about the role of the state in providing for the nation's health today.

GETTING STARTED

Look at Source X. How useful is this source in helping us to understand the problems that the NHS faces? What other sources would you like to see, to get a more complete picture?

Problems faced by the NHS

When the NHS was set up, its aim was to provide the best possible care for everyone. This was to be paid for out of people's taxes and National Insurance contributions. However, two significant factors have made it increasingly difficult to provide the NHS with all the funds it needs. Firstly, the death rate has declined and people are living longer. So there are more people to treat. Secondly, new cures have been found and new illnesses have developed and need treatment. Some new cures and treatments are very costly – for instance, transplant operations and many of the new drugs produced for illnesses such as AIDS which had not been heard of in 1948. These two factors have led to an enormous increase in government spending on the NHS.

There has been heated debate about how to pay for the increased spending on the NHS. One way has been to increase prescription charges. Another has been to encourage people to take out private medical insurance, to take the pressure off the NHS. Both of these measures have been controversial. Opponents of prescription charges say that such charges are contrary to the idea of a free NHS. Some people argue that extending private medicine would lead to a two-tier system, in which the wealthy would receive the better treatment.

Shortage of money has led to doctors and hospitals having to make some difficult choices. Treatment is sometimes refused because of lack of money, or because a patient's illness is 'self-inflicted' (for example, an illness caused by smoking). In the 1990s it was reported that patients sometimes had to wait so long for important operations that they died before the operation could be carried out. The

SOURCE

YEAR	UK £ billion
1950	9.5
1960	11.5
1970	17.0
1980	26.0
1990	34.5
2000	50.0
2008	105.6 (estimate)

Spending on the NHS 1950–2008

Labour government elected in 1997 took measures to try to improve the NHS. Some patients were transferred to other countries, such as France, to have operations, rather than suffer a long wait in Britain. In March 2002 the Chancellor of the Exchequer, Gordon Brown, introduced a budget that increased National Insurance contributions. He said that he wanted to use the income to increase spending on the NHS by 7.4 per cent per year. The reforms set out under the government's 'NHS Plan' have had an impact on waiting lists. More money has been invested in the recruitment and retention of staff, and increasing their skills has enabled them to extend their roles. Measures like these have contributed significantly to shorter waits for patients. The total number of people waiting for treatment has fallen below one million since 2003, and 88 per cent of patients nationally are offered a GP appointment within two working days.

Vaccination programmes

The drive to improve the population's personal health was stepped up after 1948. Vaccination programmes, funded by the state, were put in place for all children. In 1954 Jonas Salk produced an effective vaccine against polio, a terrifying disease which, at its worst, could cause paralysis; it struck particularly at young people. In 1960 Albert Sabin produced an improved polio vaccine which could be taken orally on a sugar lump. Today eight out of every ten children have been vaccinated against the major killer-diseases.

At times, there have been doubts about the safety of certain vaccines. In 1998, a study published in the medical journal *The Lancet* suggested that the 'three-in-one' MMR vaccination, given to young children to protect them against mumps, measles and rubella, might be linked to autism and bowel disease. A media furore followed, and prompted many parents to decide against the vaccination for their children. Some chose instead to have their children vaccinated with single injections for each of the three diseases. Others did nothing at all. Many doctors have become concerned that the drop in MMR vaccination levels could leave many children at risk from mumps, measles and rubella, which are serious diseases. The number of confirmed measles cases in England and Wales rose from 56 in 1998 to just under 1000 in 2007, according to provisional data.

Meanwhile, the author of the original study, suggesting the problem with the MMR vaccine, has been discredited. His research was based on very few cases, and he had been funded by a group of parents who were fundamentally opposed to the vaccine. An authoritative report published by the Department of Health in 2008 concludes that there is no link between MMR and autism or bowel disease.

HISTORY DETECTIVE

You may like to carry out some further research into the alternative therapies mentioned on this page, or into other examples of alternative medicine, such as chiropractice, osteopathy, reflexology and aromatherapy.

Alternative medicine

Developments in drugs have meant that a pill or potion can often be given to rapidly cure an illness or disease. Although this seems a sign of success, in recent times some people have begun to question the wisdom of such an approach. They argue that continually bombarding the body with strong drugs cannot be beneficial in the long term. Our bodies develop immunity to drugs, and so we need even stronger ones to cure the problem. Strong drugs can have unpleasant side effects or lead to addiction. Critics talk of a 'Valium society' where problems with lifestyle are solved by regularly taking anti-depressants.

In the 21st century there is a growing interest in maintaining both physical and mental health. This has led some people to focus on the general health of the patient as a whole, rather than thinking only about individual symptoms. A number of different approaches to medicine have become increasingly popular. Since they are alternatives to modern 'scientific' medicine, they have been labelled 'alternative medicine'. These are the main types:

- **Herbal medicine**. This uses natural cures, made from plants.
- **Hypnotherapy.** This aims to treat problems of the mind rather than the body. (Spiritual or faith healing, which often involves 'the laying on of hands', is also used. Sceptics dismiss this as unscientific or even 'bogus', yet in a recent survey 90 per cent of people using faith healing were satisfied with its effects.)
- **Acupuncture.** Developed 4000 years ago in China, this involves inserting needles into pressure points in the body. The needles are said to release 'blocked energy'. Acupuncture has proved effective for migraines and as an anaesthetic during surgery.
- **Homeopathy.** This is based on the theory that 'like cures like'. A diluted substance similar to the original illness is taken and this provokes the body into providing its own natural cure.

VOICE YOUR OPINION!

Can the NHS survive?
Should the state continue to provide a central system of care 'from the cradle to the grave'?

1 Almost everyone in Britain has access to fresh water

but is that water clean – and is there enough of it?

2 Sewage is disposed of so that it doesn't spread in towns and cities

but it sometimes pollutes beaches and kills wildlife.

3 There are laws to control waste disposal and rubbish dumping

but toxic waste can still leak into our water supply and some things cannot be disposed of safely.

4 Clean Air Action has stopped factories and coal fires polluting

but car exhaust fumes create polluted air which can spread from one country to another. Some environmental problems need international solutions.

5 Houses are better built and they have healthier features than they did in 1900

but there are still some people who have no home at all.

6 There are laws to enforce safe working conditions

but new dangers to health are always emerging.

7 Food must be carefully labelled and hygenically stored

but some people may still have an unhealthy diet.

8 Public health may have improved in developed countries

but they are only a small proportion of the world's population. The majority of people are still facing the problems which developed countries faced in the nineteenth century.

Pros and cons of modern Public Health

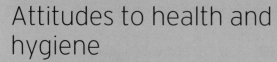 GradeStudio

Attitudes to health and hygiene

 Explanation

Review your work in this lesson and think back to your earlier work on health and hygiene. Now study the following quotation and consider the Examiner's tip before you answer the question.

The outcry against the MMR vaccine in the late twentieth century was similar in scale to the outcry against Jenner's work on vaccination in the early nineteenth century. This proves that there has been more continuity than change in attitudes to health and hygiene since those times.

Do you agree or disagree with this statement? Explain your answer fully.

Mark scheme

Level 1: General assertions.
Valid, but general answers. No specific contextual knowledge. [1 mark]

Level 2: Identifies or describes examples of continuity and/or change.
Specific contextual knowledge demonstrated but no explanation.
2–3 marks for 1–2 examples of continuity or change.
4 marks for examples of both continuity and change.
[2–4 marks]

Level 3: Explains example(s) of continuity or of change.
7 marks for explanation of long-term impact of one of the examples given. [5–7 marks]

Level 4: Comes to a supported conclusion.
To get into this level reasons must be given to support the conclusion. [8 marks]

Examiner's tip

In this question you will need to compare ideas over a long period of time. It is not necessary to explain attitudes to health and hygiene throughout the period. You will not be rewarded for simply writing down everything you know about health and hygiene between 1800 and 1998. It is vital that you find examples of continuity in attitudes to health and hygiene and add your own explanation of the significance of these examples. For instance, the outcry against MMR became very irrational at times. There were public protests about the perceived harmful effects of the triple vaccine. Protestors were prepared to be arrested for bringing attention to their views; there were examples of public order disturbances. This is similar to the way in which the anti-vaccination league made fun of Jenner's ideas in order to try to discredit his work. Even so, most of the medical profession supported the development of MMR, whereas Jenner did not get the same level of support because he could not prove how vaccination worked. You will also need to consider the impact of developments like the germ theory, or the effect of the Second World War on public attitudes to health and hygiene. Look at the mark scheme before you attempt to answer this question.

It is revision time again! Here are some suggestions for how you might revise this topic.

Use a timeline

Why not make use of the timeline on pages 138–139? You could make your own larger version of it and add on other facts and information that you have learnt whilst studying this chapter. When you have added the details to the timeline, try to answer the following questions.

- Which year represented the biggest turning-point in the development of public health after 1800? Why was it the most significant turning-point?

- Out of all the Acts of Parliament dealing with health that have been passed since 1800, which one made the greatest change to public health in Britain? Why?

Play fact games

To help you learn key dates and facts, write out a series of facts on one set of cards and the dates of these facts on a separate set of cards. Then try matching them up.

Another way to revise basic facts is to write down a sequence of facts, names or dates, and then try to argue which is the odd one out. This is a good activity to do with a revision partner, because the more you argue and debate, the more you will remember! For example, try these:

1831   1848   1908   1948

What do you think? 1831 might be the odd one out, because the other three dates are when the government passed important legislation to improve public health. 1831 was when the cholera epidemic first struck. But watch out – there was also a cholera epidemic in 1848! This proves you can extend your knowledge by debating the odd one out.

Here are some more 'odd one out' lists for you to look at:

Octavia Hill
John Snow

Edwin Chadwick
Aneurin Bevan

Hypnotherapy
Homeopathy

Acupuncture
Vaccination

Charles Booth
Second World War

Boer War
Louis Pasteur

Use a chart

You could support your ability to write explanations (AO1) in the exam by copying and completing a chart like this.

Factor	How it contributed to the development of public health
Government action	The government passed Public Health Acts in 1848 and 1875. This meant that town councils had to take more responsibility for cleaning up towns and improving sanitation and water supply. In 1906–14, the Liberal government…
Role of the individual	Edwin Chadwick Octavia Hill John Snow Aneurin Bevan
War	Boer War Second World War
Epidemic disease	Cholera

Enquiry

The 1831 cholera epidemic

Look at the following background information and study Sources A to F. The examination question shown here is typical of the final question on Unit A952, which is normally worth a significant proportion of the total marks – so it is important to know how to answer such questions!

> Study all the sources.
>
> *In 1831 people had very little understanding of the causes of cholera.*
>
> How far do Sources A to F support this view? Explain your answer. Remember to identify the sources you use. [10]

Background information

In 1831 a new disease arrived in Britain. This was cholera. One of the first places affected was Sunderland, on the north-east coast of England. On 26 October 1831 Sunderland experienced its first death from the disease. By the end of 1832, 21,000 people in Britain had been killed by cholera. Does this mean that people had very little understanding of the causes of cholera?

Source A

The following are the symptoms of the disease: giddiness, sick stomach, slow or weak pulse, cramp at the top of the fingers and toes. This is followed by vomiting and diarrhoea. The face becomes sharp and shrunken, the eyes sink and look wild, the lips, face, neck, hands and feet and the whole surface of the body turns blue, purple and black. The skin is deadly cold and damp.

All methods to restore the warmth of the body should be tried without delay, including poultices of mustard to the stomach and in very severe cases 20 to 30 drops of laudanum [opium] may be given.

However, in the treatment of this disease, it is necessary to state that no specific remedy has yet been discovered, nor has any cure been sufficiently successful to recommend its use. But the greatest confidence may be expressed in the intelligence and enthusiasm of the doctors of this country who will surely find a cure.

A report in the Sunderland Herald, *a local newspaper, in early October 1831*

Source B

Victims of cholera

Case One: William Sproat, aged sixty, a local dock worker.

Sproat had been affected with diarrhoea for a week or ten days, but had not been too ill to go to work. On 19 October 1831, he became worse and was unable to continue his work. On the evening of 20 October, I was called to him and found him vomiting, but with no signs of collapse. On the morning of 26 October he was much weaker; the pulse was barely beating and his face was shrunken with dark blue lips. At twelve noon, he died.

Case Four: Eliza Turnbull, a young nurse at Sunderland Infirmary.

Eliza was a strong, healthy woman, who was taken ill at about one o'clock on 31 October 1831. We opened a vein in each arm, from which flowed only a few drops of blood, like treacle. Our treatment failed to stop her death.

It is necessary to state that she had no communication with any person suffering from cholera, other than helping to carry the body of William Sproat from the fever house to the mortuary.

Extracts from the casebook of Dr R. Clanney, a senior physician at Sunderland Infirmary and a member of the Sunderland Board of Health

Four days after the death of William Sproat, the government ordered that, until further notice, no ship should be allowed to enter or leave the port of Sunderland.

Source C

A drawing from the mid-19th century, showing the body of a cholera victim being taken out of his house in the port of Exeter, in 1832. His sheets are being washed in a nearby stream. Local residents took their drinking water from this stream.

GradeStudio

Source D

It is the strong opinion of this meeting that the town is now in a healthier state than is usual for this time of year. We have made extensive enquiries about the disorder which has caused panic throughout the kingdom and we have come to the conclusion that it is not cholera. The few deaths of sickness in the last six weeks have been caused through common bowel complaints, hunger and uncleanliness. The measures taken by His Majesty's government forcing Sunderland ships into quarantine and guarding them by a warship are totally uncalled for.

Part of a resolution passed at a well-attended public meeting of ship owners, merchants and other inhabitants of Sunderland on 11 November 1831

Source E

I intend to put the public's mind at rest about cholera in Sunderland. I live within five miles of the town and have taken great trouble to be informed on the subject. I feel quite satisfied that the reports and statements on this fatal disease have been greatly exaggerated. I am so convinced that I shall not remove my family or myself from the area. I enclose with this letter a letter from Doctor Brown, an old army medical officer who served with me and is now in constant attendance on my family.

An extract from a letter written by Sunderland mine owner, Lord Londonderry

Lord Londonderry sent this letter, together with one from Dr Brown (Source F), to a London newspaper on 13 November 1831. Both letters were also published in the *Sunderland Herald* on 19 November 1831.

Source F

My Lord Londonderry

After much observation, I have come to the following conclusions:

1 That the disease has certainly not been imported.
2 That it has attacked the lower classes, living in the worst conditions, who have been made weak by previous diseases and too much alcohol.
3 That the disease is on the decline.
4 That the restrictions based on trade are unnecessary as the disease is not infectious.

Your Lordship's Obedient Servant

Dr. J Brown

A letter written by Dr J. Brown to the Sunderland mine owner, Lord Londonderry, in November 1831

Examiner's tip

Here are some important things to remember when you answer questions like this in the examination.
- Before writing your answer, review all the sources and read the captions carefully. Try to decide which sources support the statement and which sources do not.
- Remember to read the background information and use it in your answer if it is relevant.
- Decide whether you can use any of your own knowledge in your answer – but remember: this question requires you to use your skills in analysing sources; it is not an opportunity to write everything you know about public health.
- Be sure to leave enough time to answer this question well. It is worth more marks than any other on the paper.
- In your answer, try not to simply run through the sources like a list. Examiners call this 'source trotting'. Use the sources in order to support your arguments. Don't just paraphrase the content of the sources; try to make good inferences from the sources to support your overall argument.
- Make sure you try to consider whether the sources are reliable and whether there are enough sources to reach a definite conclusion.
- Always refer to the sources directly, either by their number or letter, or by quoting from them.
- As a general rule, the more sources you use, the higher the mark you will obtain – provided that what you say about the sources is valid.
- Always try to reach a well-supported conclusion.

Now let's have a look at the mark scheme and study some candidates' answers to see if they have applied the tips above.

Mark scheme

Level 1: Answers which do not use the sources [1–2 marks]
Level 2: Answers which are non-specific in source use [3 marks]
Level 3: Uses sources to support or oppose the interpretation [4–7 marks]
Level 4: Uses sources to support and oppose the interpretation [7–9 marks]

Bonus marks will be given for considering the reliability and sufficiency of sources, but the overall mark will not exceed 10.

Answer 1

Some sources show that people didn't understand what caused the cholera. I mean, who in their right mind would wash cholera-infected clothes in the river?

This wasn't such a bad start. It is obvious that the candidate has studied Source C, but there is no direct reference to it in the answer. If only the candidate had stated that 'Source C proves they did not understand the causes of cholera…'! If the rest of the answer had said what it does above, this would probably have reached Level 3. As it is, it is only a Level 2 answer – not a disaster, but not good enough if you're looking for a higher grade.

Answer 2

I think this is definitely true. In Source A it actually says that no specific remedy has been found, which suggests that if they didn't know how to treat it, they probably didn't know what caused it. In Source F, Brown seems to think it is something to do with alcohol.

This is better than Answer 1. You can clearly see which sources the candidate has used, and a couple of valid points have been made. Usually, the examiner awards 1 mark for every source validly used at this level. Since this answer uses two sources, it would gain two of the marks within the range available. So this answer reaches Level 3. To get better marks than this, one thing you need to do is use more of the sources to support the statement. Another way to get higher marks is to talk about the sources which support the statement and the sources which don't.

Answer 3

I think this is definitely true. In Source A it actually says that no specific remedy has been found, which suggests that if they didn't know how to treat it, they probably didn't know what caused it. In Source F, Brown seems to think it is something to do with alcohol. In Source B, Clanney obviously doesn't realise that cholera is not contagious because the doctor feels the need to talk about how Eliza Turnbull had no contact with other people suffering from cholera. They also don't realise that the disease is water-borne and seem to think that bloodletting will cure it. At least the government has put restrictions on movement of ships, as it says in the caption to Source B, so they know it can somehow be spread by people.

This is good. The candidate has used three sources to support the statement and one to oppose it. This would be a Level 4 answer. The candidate has not said anything about the reliability or the sufficiency of the sources, so no bonus marks can be awarded. In addition, the candidate could have used more than four sources in the answer. So whilst this is a good answer, it is not perfect, and it shows that there is always room for improvement!

Now have a go yourself and go for 10 marks!

Exam Café

Tools and Tips

Right, now you are ready for the exam. Or are you?

What do you need to do to prepare?

Exam Café will help you focus on the skills that you will need to display in order to do well in the exam. There is also a CD-ROM with specific advice for each of the units you will have studied. If you have used Grade Studio and Brain Boost throughout the course, you will already have practised some of the key skills that are vital in revision and the final exam. There will be specific content on the CD-ROM wherever you see this logo.

Getting started

Remember, the purpose of revision is to help you understand content and be able to present it in the right way in the exam.

Revision may seem like a daunting task, but if you follow these hints and tips it will seem much more simple.

- Organise your notes before you start, make sure you have everything you need.
- Know what you will be tested on in each exam. There are check lists on the CD-ROM which will help you work out what you need for each paper.
- Plan a realistic revision timetable. Remember that history is not the only subject you will need to revise and you are still allowed to have a social life as well! On the CD-ROM there are examples of how to organise a revision timetable.
- When revising make sure you are in a calm and organised environment. If your desk is messy you won't be as focused!
- Set yourself realistic targets and divide your time into small sections of about half an hour at a time with lots of breaks and rewards.
- Some people find it helps to revise with a friend and test each other.
- Try not to cram too much in. Pick out key points and summarise the main ideas and events. See your CD-ROM for useful hints on how to summarise.
- Find a revision style that suits you. Everyone is different, so don't worry if your friends are revising in a different way from you. If your way works then stick to it.
- Don't leave everything until the last minute!

There are lots of ways to revise and it is important that you find one that suits you. On the next page there are some examples of techniques that you might find useful.

Revision

Revision techniques

Mind maps

A mind map is a diagram used to represent key topic ideas branching from a central key word.

Try to use colour, images and short snappy phrases (rather than lots of writing) on your mind map. If you make it look good you are more likely to remember what's on it.

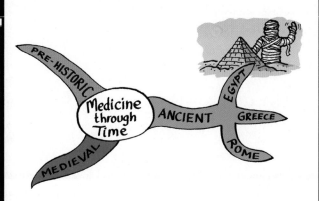

Flash Cards

Flash cards are good for helping you remember key facts and figures.

Have a question or a clue on one side and all the information you need to remember on the other.

Try to use images, bullet points and mnemonics on your flash cards as these will help you remember things.

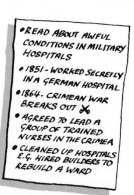

Mnemonics

A mnemonic is where you take the first letter of each word you are trying to remember and turn it into a different phrase.

For example:
Pirate
Valery
Hates
Jelly

helps you remember some of the key individuals you will need to know about.

Paré, Vesalius, Harvey, Jenner.

You could also add images to help visualise ideas in the exam.

Timelines

A timeline will help you see the 'big picture' in history. By putting all your ideas together chronologically you will be able to see how events link to each other.

The Second World War		War ends, soldiers return injured, Labour win the election	
1939	1942	1945	1948
	Bevin suggests a free NHS		First day of the NHS

On timelines you can mark turning points and measure progress or change.

You could also colour code topics and key ideas and add images to help you memorise the content.

Exam**Café**

Revision

1.1 Themes in Medicine through time (A951)

LEARNING OBJECTIVES

In this lesson you will:
- examine the themes that you could be assessed on in Unit A951
- think of examples for each era that you have studied.

GETTING STARTED

Can you list the eras that you have studied in chronological order?
Over the next four pages you will revise the topics you need to know
for your Unit A951 exam. The aim is to put together all the topics you
will have learnt about chronologically, by studying the themes that link
them all together.
Ask your teacher for a check list of the topics you will need to know.
Use this list to make sure that you have notes on everything you need to know about.

Themes in Medicine Through Time

Throughout the course you have studied the changes, developments and individuals that helped
medicine progress (and sometimes regress) over time. The main aspects of medicine that you
will have studied are:
- what people believed caused illness
- what people believed cured illness
- understanding of human anatomy (how the body works)
- understanding of surgical procedures
- provision for public health.

Activities

On a copy of the table below (if you ask your teacher nicely they might give you a copy!)
complete each box to make summary notes for era:

Era	Cause	Cure	Anatomy	Surgery	Public health
Prehistoric					
Ancient Egypt					
Ancient Greece					
Ancient Rome					
The Middle Ages					
Renaissance					
19th century					
20th century					

Use the boxes below to help you complete your table, but don't forget to add your own ideas from the notes you have made throughout the course.

The Romans brought clean water to their settlements using aqueducts.	It was believed that trephining released evil spirits.	The Christian Church taught that praying to God could cure illnesses.
Jenner discovered vaccination to help prevent illness.	Galen dissected pigs to understand how the body worked.	Pasteur developed 'Germ theory'.
In Ancient Egypt dead bodies were mummified.	The four humours and use of opposites.	Simpson discovered anaesthetics.

Exam preparation Exam Café

In Unit A951 you may be asked about one of these themes and how it progressed over an era.

Use the mark scheme at the bottom of this page in order to have a go at the following Unit A951-style question:

'Between the time of the Ancient Greeks and the end of the 19th century there has been more continuity than change in ideas about the causes of disease.' Explain how far you agree with this statement.

[8 marks]

Level	Description	Mark
1	General assertions, no specific contextual knowledge.	1
2	Identifies or describes examples of continuity and/or change. 2/3 marks for 1/2 examples of continuity **or** change, 4 marks for examples of continuity **and** change.	2–4
3	Explains examples of continuity **or** change.	5–6
4	Explains examples of continuity **and** change.	7
5	As level four, but also comes to a supported conclusion.	8

Revision

1.2 Factors that influenced medical change

LEARNING OBJECTIVES

In this lesson you will:
- examine the factors that influenced change
- support your ideas with specific contextual knowledge.

GETTING STARTED

Answer the following Unit A951-style question:

Briefly describe the impact of religion on Ancient Greek medicine.

[5 marks]

Examiners often ask how different factors helped medicine to progress or made it regress. In your Unit A951 exam you might be asked about the various factors that effected medical change during a specific era or you might be asked to compare a factor over different eras.

- chance (luck)

- war

- individuals

- the media/communications

- government

- scientific and technological breakthroughs.

- religion

The most common factors that influenced medical change are:

While you may feel more comfortable revising each topic chronologically, remember that you may be asked thematic questions about the factors that influenced change.

Examiner's tip
You will notice that there are symbols next to each factor. When you revise each era you could draw the relevant symbol(s) to help you recognise the themes that you have studied. This will help you to organise your notes and prepare in case you are asked a thematic question in Unit A951.

Activities

Make a copy of the following table:

Chance	Individuals	Government	Religion	War	Media and communications	Science and technology

Now read through the following statements.

Write the letter of each statement into your table in the correct column(s).

A In Ancient Egypt mummification was practised.

B Pare ran out of oil and tried egg yolks, rose oil and turpentine instead.

C When the printing press was invented ideas could be shared easily.

D The French and German governments funded Pasteur and Koch.

E Nightingale cleaned up hospitals during the Crimean War.

F Hippocrates believed in clinical observation.

G During the Middle Ages monks living in monasteries cared for the ill.

H Organs that are going to be transplanted have to be transported quickly.

I The Roman Senate built aqueducts to keep the army healthy.

J Trephining was used by to get evil spirits out of the body.

K During the Black Death people went on pilgrimages.

L Anaesthetics became popular when Queen Victoria used them.

Can you think of any more examples to illustrate how each of the factors influenced medical change? Create a mind map that shows your ideas.

Exam preparation

1.3 Unit A951. Turning descriptions into explanations

LEARNING OBJECTIVES

In this lesson you will:
- practise answering Unit A951-style structured questions
- learn the difference between a description and an explanation.

GETTING STARTED

Many students find it difficult to develop a description into an explanation. Use this example to help you:

Activities

1 **Describe** what the policeman is wearing.
2 Now **explain** why the policeman has to wear this type of hat.

Structured Questions

In the second section of Unit A951 you will chose between three structured questions. Each question is divided into three parts and you have to answer all of these. Make sure you read all the questions carefully before choosing which one you want to do.

Examiner's tip
Don't forget that there are more examples of Unit A951 style questions on the CD-ROM. The more practice you get the better prepared you will be for the final exam!

Exam Café

Activities

Look at the example structured question below. Read through the examiner's tip and then have a go at answering the question yourself by improving the example.

Question
Explain ways in which chance has had an impact on the development of medicine.   **[7 marks]**

Examiner's comment

Candidate's answer

Chance helped the development of medicine because Fleming noticed some fungi growing in one of his dishes of bacteria. This was penicillin. Fleming realised that where the penicillin was growing the bacteria had died so he knew that penicillin could be used to cure illnesses.

This answer describes how Fleming discovered penicillin, rather than explaining how chance helped his discovery. To develop this answer the candidate needs to link their ideas more closely to the question and explain how chance helped Fleming's discovery.
To improve the answer further still, the candidate would need to explain another situation in which chance had an impact on the development of medicine.

Task:
Use the examiner's comments to have a go at improving this answer.

Extension Task:
Next have a go at answering a similar question on your own.

Choose from one of the following questions:

Explain ways in which individual genius has had an impact on the development of medicine.	
Explain ways in which government has had an impact on the development of medicine.	
Explain ways in which religion has had an impact on the development of medicine.	7 marks
Explain ways in which war has had an impact on the development of medicine.	
Explain ways in which the media and communications have had an impact on the development of medicine.	
Explain ways in which scientific and technological developments have had an impact on the development of medicine.	

Don't forget that there are more examples of Unit A951 style questions on the CD-ROM. The more practice you get the better prepared you will be for the final exam!

ExamCafé

Exam preparation ![Exam Café]

1.4 Unit A952: Understanding question types

LEARNING OBJECTIVES

In this lesson you will:
- examine the topics that you could be assessed on in Unit A952
- understand the types of questions you might be asked about sources.

GETTING STARTED

Study Source A.
What impression does this source give of Lister?

In Unit A952 it is important that you are able to place the sources you are given into historical context, so you need to know the topic that you have studied.

The precise topic in the exam will be chosen from one of the following case studies:
- public health in the Middle Ages
- the Black Death in England
- quack doctors
- Jenner and the development of vaccination; opposition to it during the 19th century
- developments in anaesthetics and antiseptics, including the work of Simpson and Lister
- the development of hospitals and caring for the ill, including the contributions of Florence Nightingale and Mary Seacole
- the impact of industrialisation on living conditions and health and hygiene and the development of public health systems in the 19th century
- the development of penicillin; the work of Fleming, Florey and Chain and the debate around the importance of their contributions.

Your teacher will know which one of these case studies will form the focus for the Unit A952 investigation in the year of your exam, so you will only have to revise **one** of these.

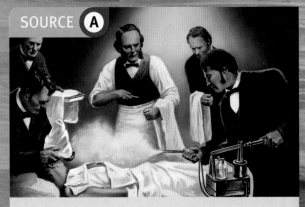

SOURCE A

A painting showing Joseph Lister directing use of carbolic acid spray in one of his earliest antiseptic surgical operations, from around 1865

Examiner's tip

You might want to begin by going back to the relevant sections of your notes and your text book and read those sections again. Revising for Unit A952 does not mean endless hours of trying to learn mountains of facts! It is much more important to practise your source-handling skills.

Your teacher will give you a copy of a source from the assessment topic that will be assessed on Unit A952 this year.
- What is the purpose of this source?
- What type of questions will you be asked?

The exam will include some background information and a range of sources on a particular topic.

You will be asked 6 questions about these sources and what they tell you about the topic you are studying. The exam will mainly test your understanding of the uses and limitations of sources as evidence.

You will often be asked the following types of questions about the sources:

1 What **impression** do they give of a person or event.
2 Whether (and how far) a source is **useful** for an enquiry.
3 Whether a source is **reliable** for an enquiry.
4 Why different sources can say different things about a person or event.
5 What the **purpose** of a source is.
6 How far the sources **support** a particular viewpoint or opinion.

Activities

1 Copy out the types of questions listed above.
2 In the boxes below there is advice on how to answer each of the types of source-based questions. Can you match them to the types of questions?

You will need to say what you can and cannot learn from the source. Use your own knowledge to explain what the source does not show.	You will need to say whether you can trust that the source gives an accurate or truthful representation of events and explain why you think this.	You will need to use all the sources and say whether they support or do not support the view. Remember to use evidence from the sources to support your ideas and make your own judgement regarding whether or not you agree with the statement in your last paragraph.
You will need to say why a source was made at that particular time. What is it trying to achieve?	You will need to **compare** what the sources say and explain why you think the authors of the source say these things.	You will need to make inferences about the content in the source, which you must support with evidence.

Exam**Café**

Exam preparation  Exam Café

1.5 Using sources in Unit A952

LEARNING OBJECTIVES

In this lesson you will:
- examine the skills that the examiner is looking for in Unit A952
- use mark schemes to help improve your grade.

GETTING STARTED

Use the mark scheme to answer the following question:

Study Source B
What impression does this give of Jenner?
[6 marks]

In this type of question, you need to use the source to make judgements about Jenner and support these judgements from the content of the source. Look at the mark scheme:

Level	Description	Mark
1	Uses surface details only.	1
2	Unsupported inferences.	2–3
3	Supported inferences.	3–6

Here are some Unit A952 sources for you to practise with. The case study here is Jenner and the development of vaccination.

EDWARD JENNER AND THE DEVELOPMENT OF VACCINATION

Study Source B and Source C
'Source C is clearly more useful to the historian studying Edward Jenner.' Explain whether you agree or disagree with this view. **[8 marks]**

In this type of question you need to show how both sources can be useful. There are things that you can find out in Source B that you cannot find out in Source C. Equally, there are things that you can find out in Source C that are not shown in Source B.

SOURCE B

I selected a healthy boy, (James Phipps) about eight years old. The cowpox matter was inserted into the arm of the boy on 14 May 1796. On the seventh day he complained of uneasiness, on the ninth day he became a little chilly, lost his appetite and had a slight headache but next day he was perfectly well. Then he was inoculated with smallpox, but no disease followed.

Edward Jenner, writing about his vaccination experiment in 1798

SOURCE C

An illustration of Edward Jenner vaccinating James Phipps in 1796. This painting was produced in the nineteenth century.

Level	Description	Mark
1	Agrees or disagrees using surface details only.	1–2
2	Agrees or disagrees by explaining what the historian can discover in one source but not in the other.	3–4
3	Explains that both sources can be useful because both contain important information and only by using both sources can a rounded picture be obtained.	5–6
4	Answer focuses on the reliability of one or both sources.	7–8

SOURCE D

This day is published, price one shilling [5p], a letter from John Birch, Esquire. In this publication it is noticed that there was a Parliamentary grant of £30,000 to Dr Jenner for an unsuccessful experiment. There is also a letter proving the production of a new and fatal disease called the 'vaccine ulcer' described by Astley Cooper, Esquire, surgeon of Guy's Hospital. There is a letter from Mr Westcott of Ringwood proving the failures of the experiment there. A list of those who died of cowpox there… There is also a list of other failures under the treatment of the Jennerian Institution.

Opposition to Jenner and the smallpox vaccination shown in a contemporary letter

SOURCE E

Medicine has never before produced any single improvement of such usefulness. You have erased from the list of human afflictions one of the greatest. Future generations will only know through history that the loathsome smallpox has existed and has been wiped out by you.

A letter to Edward Jenner from Thomas Jefferson, President of the USA, 1802

Study sources D and E
How do you explain the differences in these two accounts of Jenner's impact on vaccination? **[6 marks]**

In this type of question, it is important to explain *why* the sources give different opinions of Jenner, using the source detail and your own knowledge.

Level	Description	Mark
1	Describes how the sources differ, and not why they differ.	1–2
2	Explains why they differ, using details in the sources and captions to explain the different motives or perspectives of the authors of the sources.	3–5
3	As level 2, but also uses own knowledge to explain that Jenner's work provoked different reactions, and these sources represent opposite sides of the debate.	6

Agar – a jelly prepared from seaweed for bacteria to grow on for use in experiments.

AIDS – Acquired Immune Deficiency Syndrome. It is caused by HIV, a virus that attacks the immune system, leaving the sufferer exposed to infection.

Amputation – cutting off (all or part of a limb or digit of the body) through surgery.

Anaesthetic – something used by doctors to reduce pain. It can be a general anaesthetic, which affects the whole body, or a local anaesthetic, which just affects part of the body.

Analogy – a comparison of one thing to another, which helps people to understand the first thing. Analogies have been important in the history of medicine. The ancient Egyptians made an analogy between the vessels that carry liquid around the human body and the irrigation channels from the River Nile. They knew that good, working irrigation channels carried water to the fields so that healthy crops would grow. This helped them to understand, by analogy, that vessels carried liquid around the body, keeping it healthy.

Antibiotic – a medicine that can destroy harmful bacteria in the body, or limit their growth.

Antibodies – proteins produced in the blood which fight diseases by attacking and killing harmful bacteria.

Anticoagulant – a substance that prevents clotting.

Arsenic – a chemical element which, though poisonous, is sometimes used in small quantities in medicines.

Asepsis – sterilising the air, the clothing and tools of doctors in the operating room to remove the risk of germs.

Attenuation – thinning something out or weakening. In medicine, attenuation refers to the idea of weakening a germ, so it loses its effectiveness.

Back-to-back houses – a form of terrace, in which the houses are joined by their side and rear walls. The houses were built for working-class people and were usually of low quality, sometimes with only two rooms, one on each floor. They were dark and poorly ventilated because three of their four walls were shared with other buildings and contained no doors or windows.

Bacteriology – the scientific study of bacteria and other microscopic living things, especially those that cause disease.

Change – a break with the past, when something is completely new.

Clone – to make an exact copy (a genetically identical copy) of cells or an organism. In recent years, scientists have been able to clone animals such as sheep.

Culture – a growth of micro-organisms in the laboratory. They may be grown in either a solid or a liquid.

Development – something that has developed from a previous idea. It is based on what went before. For example, when iPods were first introduced, they represented a change in portable music machines – they don't use tapes or CDs. However, if you think about an iPod in the context of computers, it is a development – it is a new use for a smaller hard disc.

Diphtheria – a serious infectious disease which causes fever and difficulty in breathing and swallowing.

Empathy – the skill of looking at something from another person's point of view. It is important in history because we need to understand why people did things, and to properly understand we need to know what their beliefs and values were.

Empirical – based on observation not theory. For example, you can have empirical knowledge that cars need petrol to go, but not have the theoretical understanding of how petrol is used in the engine to make the car go.

Endemic – regularly found and common among a particular group or in a particular place.

Epidemic – a sudden appearance of an illness, affecting many people.

Family allowance – an amount of money given weekly by the state for the support of children.

Freeze-dried plasma – the yellow liquid part of the blood which has been separated and freeze-dried so that it can be stored and used later.

Friendly society – in Britain, an organisation to which members pay small amounts of money over a long period so that, when they are ill or old, they can receive money back.

General anaesthetics – these are usually inhaled and make the patient unconscious.

Germ – a very small organism that causes disease. Some other terms for 'germ' include 'microbe', 'bacterium' and 'bacillus'.

Grafting – transplanting or implanting (living tissue, for example) surgically into a bodily part, to replace a damaged part or to compensate for a defect.

Immunity – protection against disease through the body's own defences.

Inference – a conclusion reached by studying and judging evidence.

Keyhole surgery – operating through a very small incision, perhaps only a few centimetres in size.

Laissez-faire – an economic theory from the 18th century, which was strongly opposed to any government intervention in business affairs. 'Laissez faire' is French for 'leave alone'.

Local anaesthetics – these are usually injected and have the effect of numbing the feeling in one particular part of the body, such as a tooth. They do not make the patient unconscious.

MRSA – a 'superbug' which is resistant to many antibiotics. It stands for Methicillin-Resistant Staphylococcus Aureus.

National Insurance – a system of compulsory insurance, paid for by weekly contributions by employers and employees, and used to pay for benefits for the sick, retired and unemployed.

Philosophy – the name the Greeks gave to the study of wisdom and knowledge. Philosophers tried to find out the causes for things and to explain the world.

Pituitary gland – a small organ at the base of the brain which controls the growth and activity of the body by producing hormones.

Poor Law – laws in the past, setting out how the poor should be supported. Under the Poor Law in the 19th century, those needing support were sent to workhouses.

Privy Council – a body of persons who advise the king or queen in matters of state. The majority of members are selected by the prime minister.

Progress – to move forwards. In the context of the story of medicine, to improve, get better.

Public health – health measures that affect the whole community, not just a few people. In Roman times this meant clean water, sewers and toilets. Today, as well as these three, public health includes things like vaccination against diseases.

Ragged school – a name given to 19th-century charity schools in the United Kingdom, which provided education and, in most cases, food, clothing and lodging for destitute children. The schools received no government support.

Regress – to move backwards. In the story of medicine, to get worse.

Serum – watery, colourless part of the blood, sometimes taken from an animal and injected into humans to fight infection.

Sutures – surgeons' stitches.

Tissue rejection – when a transplant recipient's immune system attacks a transplanted organ or tissue.

Trend – a gradual change, happening over a long time, and made up of a series of events.

Tuberculosis – a serious infectious disease which can attack many parts of a person's body, especially the lungs.

Turning point – a change that happens quickly and may be just one event. Afterwards, things are different in at least one important way.

Vaccine – killed or weakened forms of bacteria which are injected into the body to give it resistance against disease.

Workhouse – in Britain in the past, a building where poor people were put to work, in exchange for food and shelter.

Index

Single User Licence Agreement: OCR GCSE History A Schools History Project Medicine Through Time ActiveBook CD-ROM

Warning:

This is a legally binding agreement between You (the user or purchasing institution) and Pearson Education Limited of Edinburgh Gate, Harlow, Essex, CM20 2JE, United Kingdom ('PEL').

By retaining this Licence, any software media or accompanying written materials or carrying out any of the permitted activities You are agreeing to be bound by the terms and conditions of this Licence. If You do not agree to the terms and conditions of this Licence, do not continue to use the OCR GCSE History A Schools History Project Medicine Through Time ActiveBook CD-ROM and promptly return the entire publication (this Licence and all software, written materials, packaging and any other component received with it) with Your sales receipt to Your supplier for a full refund.

Intellectual Property Rights:

This OCR GCSE History A Schools History Project Medicine Through Time ActiveBook CD-ROM consists of copyright software and data. All intellectual property rights, including the copyright is owned by PEL or its licensors and shall remain vested in them at all times. You only own the disk on which the software is supplied. If You do not continue to do only what You are allowed to do as contained in this Licence you will be in breach of the Licence and PEL shall have the right to terminate this Licence by written notice and take action to recover from you any damages suffered by PEL as a result of your breach.

The PEL name, PEL logo, and all other trademarks appearing on the software and OCR GCSE History A Schools History Project Medicine Through Time ActiveBook CD-ROM are trademarks of PEL. You shall not utilise any such trademarks for any purpose whatsoever other than as they appear on the software and OCR GCSE History A Schools History Project Medicine Through Time ActiveBook CD-ROM.

Yes, You can:

1 use this OCR GCSE History A Schools History Project Medicine Through Time ActiveBook CD-ROM on Your own personal computer as a single individual user. You may make a copy of the OCR GCSE History A Schools History Project Medicine Through Time ActiveBook CD-ROM in machine readable form for backup purposes only. The backup copy must include all copyright information contained in the original.

No, You cannot:

1 copy this OCR GCSE History A Schools History Project Medicine Through Time ActiveBook CD-ROM (other than making one copy for back-up purposes as set out in the Yes, You can table above);

2 alter, disassemble, or modify this OCR GCSE History A Schools History Project Medicine Through Time ActiveBook CD-ROM, or in any way reverse engineer, decompile or create a derivative product from the contents of the database or any software included in it;

3 include any materials or software data from the OCR GCSE History A Schools History Project Medicine Through Time ActiveBook CD-ROM in any other product or software materials;

4 rent, hire, lend, sub-licence or sell the OCR GCSE History A Schools History Project Medicine Through Time ActiveBook CD-ROM;

5 copy any part of the documentation except where specifically indicated otherwise;

6 use the software in any way not specified above without the prior written consent of PEL;

7 subject the software, OCR GCSE History A Schools History Project Medicine Through Time ActiveBook CD-ROM or any PEL content to any derogatory treatment or use them in such a way that would bring PEL into disrepute or cause PEL to incur liability to any third party.

Grant of Licence:

PEL grants You, provided You only do what is allowed under the 'Yes, You can' table above, and do nothing under the 'No, You cannot' table above, a non-exclusive, non-transferable Licence to use this OCR GCSE History A Schools History Project Medicine Through Time ActiveBook CD-ROM.

The terms and conditions of this Licence become operative when using this OCR GCSE History A Schools History Project Medicine Through Time ActiveBook CD-ROM.

Limited Warranty:

PEL warrants that the disk or CD-ROM on which the software is supplied is free from defects in material and workmanship in normal use for ninety (90) days from the date You receive it. This warranty is limited to You and is not transferable.

This limited warranty is void if any damage has resulted from accident, abuse, misapplication, service or modification by someone other than PEL. In no event shall PEL be liable for any damages whatsoever arising out of installation of the software, even if advised of the possibility of such damages. PEL will not be liable for any loss or damage of any nature suffered by any party as a result of reliance upon or reproduction of any errors in the content of the publication.

PEL does not warrant that the functions of the software meet Your requirements or that the media is compatible with any computer system on which it is used or that the operation of the software will be unlimited or error free. You assume responsibility for selecting the software to achieve Your intended results and for the installation of, the use of and the results obtained from the software.

PEL shall not be liable for any loss or damage of any kind (except for personal injury or death) arising from the use of this OCR GCSE History A Schools History Project Medicine Through Time ActiveBook CD-ROM or from errors, deficiencies or faults therein, whether such loss or damage is caused by negligence or otherwise.

The entire liability of PEL and your only remedy shall be replacement free of charge of the components that do not meet this warranty.

No information or advice (oral, written or otherwise) given by PEL or PEL's agents shall create a warranty or in any way increase the scope of this warranty.

To the extent the law permits, PEL disclaims all other warranties, either express or implied, including by way of example and not limitation, warranties of merchantability and fitness for a particular purpose in respect of this OCR GCSE History A Schools History Project Medicine Through Time ActiveBook CD-ROM.

Termination:

This Licence shall automatically terminate without notice from PEL if You fail to comply with any of its provisions or the purchasing institution becomes insolvent or subject to receivership, liquidation or similar external administration. PEL may also terminate this Licence by notice in writing. Upon termination for whatever reason You agree to destroy the OCR GCSE History A Schools History Project Medicine Through Time ActiveBook CD-ROM and any back-up copies and delete any part of the OCR GCSE History A Schools History Project Medicine Through Time ActiveBook CD-ROM stored on your computer.

Governing Law:

This Licence will be governed by and construed in accordance with English law.